Cath

Seasons
OF CONTENT

To Ned and Bess with love and gratitude, and to all the other inhabitants, human and otherwise, of the valley

Seasons
OF CONTENT

JACKIE FRENCH

ILLUSTRATIONS BY GWEN HARRISON

Angus&Robertson
An imprint of HarperCollins*Publishers*

Angus&Robertson
An imprint of HarperCollins*Publishers*, Australia

First published in Australia in 1998
by HarperCollins*Publishers* Pty Limited
ACN 009 913 517
A member of the HarperCollins*Publishers* (Australia) Pty Limited Group
http://www.harpercollins.com.au

HarperCollins*Publishers*
25 Ryde Road, Pymble, Sydney NSW 2073, Australia
31 View Road, Glenfield, Auckland 10, New Zealand
77–85 Fulham Palace Road, London W6 8JB, United Kingdom
Hazelton Lanes, 55 Avenue Road, Suite 2900, Toronto, Ontario M5R 3L2
and 1995 Markham Road, Scarborough, Ontario M1B 5M8, Canada
10 East 53rd Street, New York NY 10032, USA

National Library of Australia Cataloguing-in-Publication data:

French, Jackie.
Seasons of content.
Includes index.
ISBN 0 207 19645 1.
1. French, Jackie – Homes and haunts – New South Wales – Araluen Region. 2.
Araluen Region (N.S.W.) – Description and travel. I. Title.
994.47

Cover and internal illustrations by Gwen Harrison
Printed in Australia by Griffin Press Pty Ltd on 79gsm Bulky Paperback

9 8 7 6 5 4 3 2 1   98 99 00 01

CONTENTS

SPRING

❋ September 2

It rained last night – soft rain, thick as silk. The grass on the hills was lichen green this morning as I drove Edward through the orchards down to the school bus.

'Mum, Mum, look at the spider webs!' he yelled, sticking his head out through the open window into air so fresh it seemed to vacuum out your nasal passages.

The spider webs were silver; they hung from old barbed wire and dripped between the bare peach branches. You could almost see the gum trees photosynthesising. Mornings after rain have their own strange light; it's as though the leaves have edges of quartz catching the sun.

I came back into a kitchen that smelled of toasted bun and boiled eggs; good smells, but rain-fresh air is a novelty at the moment, so even though it's chilly I propped the kitchen door open.

Bryan looked up from his toast. He has the same toast every morning: a bun from the bakery, with sesame seeds *not* poppy seeds, sliced into three, and grilled to just pale brown, then spread with plum or apricot jam or blackberry jelly (he doesn't like the pips in blackberry jam) or lime butter, depending on the season, or marmalade if someone has given us some in exchange for fruit. (We give away so much fruit that we're always getting marmalade in exchange; it's been years since I made any.)

'How much rain did we get?' I asked.

'Eight millimetres. I haven't emptied the gauge yet.'

I wish there had been more. Eight millimetres is enough to dampen the first inch of soil and send up green shoots, but not enough for water to seep into the creek or springs.

But it's hard to worry about drought when the air smells damp.

This is the exciting time in the valley – not the peach picking (which is hot and furry and exhausting), not the first blossom (which always looks slightly out of place among the frost-scarred hills) but now – when the flowers are falling, petals like pink rain gusting across the road as you drive down the valley, fluttering down into our vegetable garden and into crevices in the bark, petal drifts so thick you could put your tongue out and catch a petal – but it'd feel clammy probably, a sort of pungent slice of Wettex, nothing like the magic in the air. And under the petals the peaches are swelling, furry nuts that grow bigger every day.

Maybe this is why I've sat down at my computer (having got Edward down to the school bus, with both shoes *and* homework *and* signed permission note, had breakfast and a mooch up the hill with Bryan to watch the light pour down into the valley – the sun still comes late into the valley this time of year) ...

So now, ignoring the lyrebirds scratching up the last of the primulas outside my window and shredding the going-to-seed broccoli down the garden (I could go and yell at them but they just ignore me – they know I haven't got the soul of a predator) ...

So now I have decided to write about the weather and the people and the wombats in the valley ... and peaches and all the things that go into growing peaches ... but most of all about food and how it rules our year – because after all, what is life apart from food, and friends, and family and shelter, and daydreams and how to create them ...

But food is the basis of it all, which is a fact that many people forget nowadays. Your way of life is dependent on what you eat and the choices you make about your food. If you choose to work in an office from 9 a.m. till who knows when, you'll live on food cooked by other people, or on what you can scavenge – after it's been washed and then packaged under plastic – in a supermarket, under artificial light.

For most people food is something they buy, then cook. Or, more and more commonly, they buy and defrost or heat (cooking implies some level of transformation of raw, separate ingredients). Or they eat food prepared by a stranger's hands among other strangers. The food most people eat is becoming more and more isolated – away from the hands that prepare it, the hands that grow it, the fingers that harvest it (but it's usually machines that harvest now).

Here in the valley, food is part of our lives: we watch the trees bud and flower then fruit; we listen to the wombats snipping off the grass at 2 a.m. and leaving fat green droppings that feed the soil; we watch the wallabies sipping young wonga-vine like spaghetti and pruning the apple trees into 'interesting' shapes.

Food here is a matter of feeding scraps to the soil so it's rich in organic matter and the beetles and worms and nematodes that live in the soil can eat from it too.

When I eat a peach here I remember the smell of the soil as I planted the tree (good soil really does taste chocolaty – it's not just the fantasy of a chocaholic). I remember the February glare turning the leaf tops silver, the smell of peach across the orchard, the larder's almost sickly scent after months of stored apples, the middle ones gone bad and their stickiness dripping across the floor as I race them out to the chooks' bucket ...

I could buy a peach in the supermarket and it would probably taste good – but not quite as good, as it's been picked green and firm enough to travel, not sticky ripe from the tree (and sunlight does have a taste, it's just that most of us have forgotten it) – but it wouldn't have the memories. No matter how good the taste, it wouldn't be as rich.

So that is why I'm writing this. A celebration, if you like, of the lives outside my window as I type: the lyrebirds and the broccoli, the peaches and the wombats ... our lives here in the valley and the seasons of our food.

DRIED PEACH AND PINE NUT CAKES

You can pretend these cakes are muffins and eat them for breakfast; in my youth we called today's muffins 'fairy cakes' and ate them for afternoon tea. You can eat these for afternoon tea, too. Or for dessert – arrange them nicely with cream or icecream and a scatter of fresh orange zest.

They keep well in a sealed tin, but are much more fragrant if eaten the same day.

(By the way, pine nuts are extraordinarily easy to grow. Just plant a Mexican or Swiss stone pine and wait five to ten years. Be warned, both grow *very* big. In a decade or two you will have an enormous harvest *and* an enormous tree to cope with.)

HALF A CUP BUTTER *or* A MIXTURE
OF BUTTER AND CANOLA OIL

HALF A CUP BROWN SUGAR

2 EGGS

1 CUP PINE NUTS, CHOPPED AND
BROWNED ON A TRAY IN THE OVEN

Optional

1 CUP CURRANTS

1 CUP GROUND ALMONDS

HALF A CUP CHOPPED DRIED
PEACHES, SOAKED IN HALF A CUP
BOILING WATER TILL COOL

1 CUP SELF-RAISING FLOUR

1 TEASPOON GRAND MARNIER *or*
2 TEASPOONS ORANGE ZEST *or*
BOTH (WHY BE HALF-HEARTED?)

1 DESSERTSPOON MARMALADE

Preheat the oven to 200°C while you are preparing the
cake mixture.

Beat sugar and butter. Add eggs one by one. Fold in
everything including the Grand Marnier and Zest but
not the marmalade.

The mixture should flop down from the spoon just
like a semi-liquid cowpat. If the mixture is too dry, add
a little water or (better still) orange juice.

Place spoonfuls in paper patty cases or in a greased
muffin pan. Bake for 20 to 25 minutes or till each cake
is browned on top and springs back when you press it
lightly in the middle.

Remove from oven.

While the cakes are still hot, quickly heat the marmalade
to almost boiling and brush it over the tops of the cakes.

※ *September 3*

'Eight-forty,' said Bryan this morning, checking his watch as the sun brushed over the ridge.

The sun doesn't touch us till 9.22 a.m. in midwinter. (Yes, exactly. Two minutes matters in the dead frost of winter.) Then as spring advances the sun creeps over the ridge earlier and earlier, and the air is sun gold instead of shadow green.

You can almost rub the air between your fingers in spring. It's thicker. The sun seems brighter now, except when you turn your back on it. In Spring the world turns colder as soon as your face is away from the light, a phenomenon you don't get when the sun is more directly overhead.

Spring jumps out at you. You're out walking and the air tastes cold and suddenly there's a warm breeze above your head smelling of blossom and you look again and the leaf buds are swelling. Edward ran his finger over one this morning: 'Will this be a peach?'

'No, a leaf.'

'How can you tell?'

So I showed him. He looked at the fruit buds with satisfaction; I think he was tempted to count them, but we were late for school and had to run to get down to the bus.

Yawning at breakfast. Might be all the pollen in the air (a slight allergic reaction that makes me sleepy) but more likely it's just the noises of spring. The rats were dancing in the ceiling again last night. They always dance in spring.

The rats in the ceiling are mostly introduced black rats

who practise their traditional ethnic European choreography at two o'clock in the morning with gumboots on.

The rats at ground level are native bush rats – softer and fluffier, and fewer in number. I think the black rats must drive them out. The bush rats don't dance. They drop things – trying to break open apricot stones by dropping them from the bench. This doesn't work and hasn't in the dozen years they've been trying it, so perhaps they're not after the apricot kernels inside after all but are merely playing soccer.

At 6.30 a.m. the shrike-thrush arrives. He comes every morning at dawn till well into blowfly season. (Blowflies also wake you early, but less pleasantly than thrushes.)

The shrike-thrush perches on the edge of the pergola and pecks the bedroom window, carolling at the top of his voice. By the time you've given up sleep and headed for the bathroom the sun angle has changed and he pops round there too, for a change of window, then round to the kitchen window for an hour or so's pecking till the sun is higher and he retires.

Spring is the macho time. The lyrebirds are having one last deep throated burst before they're silent in the heat of summer (except on misty mornings when their song echoes up from the creek). The wonga pigeons are having booming competitions, half a dozen of them at different points across the valley, wonga-ing away as loudly as possible, not quite in synch so that you long to stand on the tallest casuarina and call out: 'Okay boys, all together now at the stroke of the baton ...'

Spring is also mating season. If the birds are blatant in spring (and the bees for that matter, spring cleaning out the annual slaughter of the drones; anyone who complains about industry 'downsizing' has never watched the ruthlessness of bees), echidnas are even worse.

'Mum,' said Edward yesterday. 'There's an echidna on the flat. Hey, Mum! There's two echidnas on the flat.' And then in a tone that meant he wanted this explained: 'Mum, there's *three* echidnas on the flat …'

'Are they playing chase?' he asked.

'Not quite,' I said.

A randy male echidna will trot for miles after a female. Sometimes you see four males in a row behind a sexy female, sniffing short-sightedly at her rear.

Snakes are discreet. A few amorous twinings and that's that. You hardly know it happens with snakes, though there were a couple of browns down here who stayed coiled up together most of summer. I called them Troilus and Cressida, till Cressida (I think it was Cressida) tried to bite me in the chook house.

That was the end of Cressida.

Troilus still sunbakes at the scene of their passion. He likes eggs too but is less greedy than his mate, and too fat to bother about attacking anyone.

Goering the-gander-down-on-the-flat's idea of romance is to hold Elizabeth's head under the water till she submits. Male bowerbirds wait till their beloved is neck deep in an orange or kiwi fruit and strike while she's too absorbed to notice.

Male bowerbirds can be romantic though. I planted 500 anemones this year and the bowerbirds picked every one of them – the flowers were borne off in the beaks of banditing Lotharios to decorate their bowers, while I'm left with the stalks.

Actually, I suspect that no matter how romantic a bowerbird looks flying across the garden with a daffodil in his beak, he's really doing it to impress the other males. (A visiting martian might assume that human males drive low fast cars to impress their potential mates, but they don't.) And come to think of it, bowerbirds *eat* flowers. A jonquil to a bowerbird may be the human equivalent of roast lamb or a box of chocolates – an edible display rather than an aesthetic one.

Lyrebirds sing about it for months before and after, but the actual event scarcely interrupts the melody.

Kangaroos box about it – you can catch them up on the hill above the apricots, every afternoon, sometimes sparring for so long the participants snooze between each stroke. Then the matter is over in seconds while the female scarcely breaks her chewing, unless the bastard bites her neck to get her in position. She just looks round with the kangaroo equivalent of 'Get on with it, George.'

Wisbey's bull broods about it for days then trots off three seconds later.

The most sexually preoccupied animal I ever met was Willy the Wanker.

Willy was a red-necked wallaby. Red-necks are a friendly sort of wallaby. They graze in groups about the hills – unlike the black-tails, who mostly feed alone, ducking under the thorn bushes if they're startled and leaving their tails to poke out like black snakes taking the sun.

Willy's pleasures, however, were solitary.

I remember one formal tea party with an elderly friend under the apricot tree. Tablecloth, Earl Grey and china cups – 'More tea? More cake?' – and Willy just behind her, absentmindedly masturbating while he sniffed the ripening apricots.

My friend must have noticed something in my face. Finally she turned. Just as Willy finished.

'Why it's a wallaby! How sweet! How long has he been there?'

'Long enough,' I said.

'The darling. Here boy! Here boy! Have some cake? Nice wallaby.'

The nice wallaby wiped a paw on his stomach, bounded over and ate the cake. I was afraid for weeks he might see it as a Pavlovian reward, and perform whenever he felt the urge for cake. But he didn't.

Wallabies use their paws not just for sex – Willy's the only one I've ever seen who did – but for peeling mandarins and picking bread out of the chooks' bucket and pulling wonga-vine from bushes. Kangaroos can use their tongues, the rare ones who use some finesse. Echidnas use their noses.

And as for humans – well, it's spring and a joy to feel the air on bare skin again, the sun pouring through the bedroom doors soaking down into your bones after a winter huddling beneath the blankets. (I've packed my hot-water bottle back into the larder, and my long johns are on the washing line.)

✳ *September 4*

Bryan opened the bedroom doors last night, the first time they've stayed open all night since the start of winter.

Suddenly the bedroom was full of the sound of frogs, the washing of the creek across the rocks (even as low as the creek is, the sound of water still laps through all other valley sounds), casuarina branches brushing their backs against the wind, Chocolate the wombat grunting on the grass, the squeak of the climbing rose against the roof. (One day I really will prune it, yes Bryan, I promise.)

The room was full of spring air, and we woke up this morning grinning at each other.

✳ *September 5*

I realised last night you can smell moonlight – or maybe moonlight just lures you out of doors so you sniff: jasmine, jonquils, clematis, wonga-vine, elderflowers, wisteria, lime-blossom, violets, alyssum … spring …

I don't think I have ever heard so many birds – not since last spring anyway. The shrike-thrush still yelling *SUGareee!* as it pecks at its reflection, the Lewin honeyeater's deep chortle, the lyrebirds and the *cheep* of a hundred red-browed finches.

Even the kookaburras are calling. 'You don't realise they've been silent till you hear them again,' said Bryan, out on the balcony yawning at the early morning. What with birds and sudden sunlight, we're getting up half an hour earlier than last month.

Chocolate wombat re-established his territory last night. There were wombat droppings at regular intervals when we came out this morning.

'Why are they green?' asked Edward, prodding the droppings with his gumboot.

'Green grass,' I said. 'The grass was tough and brown before and that's why his droppings were different – darker and drier.'

Edward nodded. He's at the age to be interested in droppings – the wallaby droppings on the flat and the possum droppings on the rocks by the creek.

'Why are they on the rocks?' he asked.

I pointed upwards. 'They dropped down from the tree.'

'Oh,' said Edward and bent down to poke them apart with a stick to see what they'd been eating.

I wish we'd get more rain. The droppings will be brown again before we know it.

❋ *September 6*

Picked the first asparagus today – pale purple ludicrously phallic heads pushing through the dirt. At first you think there's hardly any, then after ten minutes' kneeling you realise you have both hands full, and after half an hour your jumper is full as well. (Bryan complains my jumpers are always out of shape and stained as well; but if you have a full-sized bosom, things naturally dribble onto your bust.)

I steamed today's asparagus for lunch, except for three bits I nibbled in the garden and the stalk Bryan pinched from the bench and the three stems I saved for Edward after school. Later we'll cover the asparagus with mustardy vinaigrette or bearnaise sauce or simmer it in soup. But not today.

Afterthought: why don't people grow more asparagus? It grows itself, despite its finicky reputation – just toss it a handful of food in summer and you can pick it all through spring – in fact we haven't bothered feeding ours for years;

though I will this summer, I promise. (As I've promised for the last two years.) It's pretty too, in a suburban ferny sort of way, and the birds love the berries.

I always wonder why the wombats don't eat asparagus; surely the tips are tempting for a wombat? But they don't. The odd stalk is trodden on; and the black-tailed wallabies have a munch, but they don't like it and spit it back onto the ground (which is odd when you think about it, as black-tails like everything else, from marguerite daisies to orange leaves and pansies).

The bowerbirds are eating the cumquats outside my study window as I write, four fluffy green females or youngsters and one dark velvet male, and a lyrebird is perched up in the loquat tree.

Lyrebirds are ludicrous birds. I don't know why everyone thinks they're beautiful. Probably because so few Australians ever see a lyrebird — just pretty pictures of their tails extended (which they very rarely are) so you can't see the ungainly body at all. And of course they look a bit like peacocks, and peacocks have grandeur so lyrebirds must too.

Lyrebird necks are too long, their heads too small, their beaks too wide, their bodies scrawny, their legs like wrinkled chopsticks and their feet the most fearsome weapon a vegetable garden has to face. (I thought we had wild pigs the first time I saw an orchard churned up by lyrebird feet.)

Of course, their song is glorious, though some are much better singers than others. (The present lot around here are pretty feeble, but I remember one ten years ago — whole symphonies echoing through late winter mist.)

Edward gazed with satisfaction at the steadily leafing peach trees in Wisbey's orchard this morning on the way down to the school bus. 'Soon,' he said happily.

FRAGRANT WINDOW CLEANER

I washed the windows today (well, some of them). We're knee-deep in clear gold light. You don't realise how filthy windows are till the sun is higher in the sky and suddenly all winter's dust and rain spots are shining clear.

PEEL OF 2 LEMONS

1 CUP LAVENDER FLOWERS

2 DROPS EUCALYPTUS OIL

1 CUP METHO

Mix. Place in a jar and leave overnight. Strain. Add 1 tablespoon to half a bucket of water. Wipe on windows and wipe off with newspaper.

❋ September 7

Gabby arrived today, in a cardboard box with her special blanket and a sack of Womba-roo – a special milk formula for marsupials, and a heck of a lot easier than the brews I had to concoct a decade or so ago (of soy milk and egg yolk and Farax and vitamins and cod liver oil and I can't remember what else …).

Gabby is small and round and brown; almost a toy wombat.

We get orphaned wombats regularly from the Wildlife Information & Rescue Service (WIRES). Our job is to reaccustom them to the bush. Any wombat or roo brought up by humans has almost no chance of survival if it's put straight back into the wild. Its education has to be gradual.

So we feed them and pet them but let them know (firmly – you must be firm with wombats, as they are possibly the world's most dogmatic species and need no-nonsense convincing) that they are creatures of the outdoors, not the kitchen. And sooner or later they leave …

Sometimes it takes two months for them to realise they are wombats and turn their backs on us; sometimes it takes two years, but eventually their absences in the bush get longer and longer … and I miss them desperately, even with all the other wombats here. I suppose that's what a parent feels like when one child is gone – all the others combined never quite fill the empty place.

Gabby was shut-eyed and hairless when she was given to WIRES – she'd be the youngest wombat ever to be reared successfully by humans, I think. Now she is brown-eyed and hairy. She has a slight touch of mange or eczema, perhaps brought on by stress; the two wombats she was raised with 'went bush' a month ago and she's still upset by their loss. I'll inject her tonight, and then again in ten days' time; mange can be agony for a wombat, and often fatal.

Gabby seems a bit dullwitted; I don't think it's just that she's sleepy or upset by the change.

Wombats are normally intelligent creatures about anything that interests them, which is basically food and dirt. I put a carrot in front of Gabby and she had to think about it for perhaps a minute before she ate it.

'Do you think she's brain damaged?' asked Bryan, but I don't know. Perhaps there *was* brain damage before she was rescued from the corpse of her mother – a roadkill left bloated at the side of the bitumen till someone passing finally looked inside the pouch.

Gabby is definitely not as bright as the other wombats we've taught to be wombats – or at least kept an eye on while wombathood reclaimed them. We start by introducing them to the wombat hole behind the bathroom. They stop, sniff, push into the darkness cautiously but firmly; then return half an hour later covered in mud with toothy wombat grins that say: 'Ah dirt! So this is what being a wombat is all about.'

Gabby sniffed, paused, sniffed again. And then looked at us as though to say: 'Don't you realise it's dirty in there?' and trotted back inside and onto the sofa.

But she is not a cat; she's a wombat. And she has to learn that dirt is her destiny.

* *September 8*

Chocolate has accepted Gabby; I thought he probably would, as she's female. He gave the last baby wombat here a hard time. That was Ricki, who now lives down on the flat and only visits here occasionally. Ricki learnt early to acknowledge Chocolate as head wombat, and still does.

Maybe Chocolate doesn't think Gabby is a real wombat (she still hasn't taken to the hole and probably smells more of kitchens than soil); or maybe she's too small to bother

with. He did covet her carrot tonight. He tried to grab it
out of her mouth, but she wouldn't let go; so he ate half
and she ate half till they met in the middle of the carrot,
nose to nose – which looked ridiculous as Gabby is tiny
and Chocolate is the largest wombat I've ever seen, a
massive body, square nose and the lushest whiskers ever
seen down a wombat hole.

I give Gabby her bottle by the wombat hole, to let her
get used to the hole's smell. I've stuffed her blanket in
there too, so she has something familiar. Chocolate doesn't
like that hole (I think it's too narrow for him anyway). He
has his own palatial complex up the hill. All the baby
wombats we've had have lived in the bathroom hole for a
few months, then moved out to better quarters as they've
grown more confident.

Still no rain; and it's getting warmer. The creek is still chortling to itself, but come the first day of real heat it'll shrink between the rocks.

❋ *September 10*

At 2 a.m. Gabby scratched at the back door.

'If we let her in she'll think we'll come down and play with her every night,' muttered Bryan. He went back to sleep. I didn't.

Gabby kept scratching. The scratches are millimetres deep this morning. When scratches didn't work, she chewed. (Three nights gnawing is enough to demolish a wooden door, which is why our doors are reinforced with steel sheeting. Luckily the rest of the house is made of granite, which defeats even wombats – so far.) By 3 a.m. she was shoving with the full force of wombat shoulders.

At 4 a.m. I fell asleep.

I woke at seven and fumbled down the stairs. The bottom step was occupied by a small boy and a wombat.

'I think you're cruel,' said Edward reproachfully. 'She's been outside all night.'

'She's supposed to be outside,' I said. 'She's a wombat.'

'I still love you, Gabby,' said Edward, ignoring me and cuddling the wombat closer, covering his pyjamas with mud.

When I was young I used to dream of being captured by aliens from Alpha Centauri who'd offer me the universe (this was mostly in my maths class). I've never lived with aliens, but I've lived with wombats. Wombats are as close as

I'm likely to get to aliens from Alpha Centauri. Most animals humans know are domesticated. They've become humanised over the years. Not wombats.

You can't teach a wombat to be ashamed, as a dog will be ashamed if it's disappointed you. You can make a wombat afraid but you can't teach it right or wrong. Wombats are eternal arbiters of their own morality. You can never domesticate a wombat, though a wombat will often successfully tame you.

The first wombat I lived with was Smudge. The shed I lived in was on Smudge's territory. Every night he'd inspect it – inside the cupboards and under the bed – and if I didn't leave the door open he'd push it in.

We'd eat breakfast together as the sun slid above the ridge. I followed him about the bush, first from loneliness, and then for a deeper reason, as I learnt for a time how not to be human, to look at the world in different ways. (Those nights formed the basis for my gardening theories, and my fiction … which is another story.)

Smudge liked company at breakfast. He liked company at night, sitting on the hill watching the moonshadows deepen round the trees. He loved music – preferred Mozart, hated the Rolling Stones (marched down to the creek till I turned off the tape deck), sat for hours in the doorway as I played Bach. Smudge is the only animal, human or marsupial, who's enjoyed my violin playing. He'd sit until I stopped, then wander off.

Smudge died in the last year of the drought. In the last months he'd grown thin, even though I watered the grass around the shed with the dishwater. He panted for three days, then lay down in the shade of the young corn.

Smudge was a friend, not a pet. He's buried at the end of the vegetable garden. A wallaby grazes there now.

Meanwhile Gabby has padded out the back door, over the doormat she chewed up last night (I don't know why I buy doormats). She's waiting for her carrots. Then she'll go to bed – in the wombat hole if we can coax her in, otherwise spread out on the remnants of the doormat.

It's not like living with a wild wombat. I'll probably never live so close to a genuinely wild animal again. Those were the days before commitments, the cries of 'Mum where're my socks?', electric light and column deadlines. To live with a wild animal you have to bend to its timetables. I can't, any more. I'm too preoccupied for rambles in the dusk.

But … it was about a year ago. I looked out the window. Edward was under the persimmon with a wombat. I thought it was Fudge – the WIRES wombat we were caring for then. (When I last saw Fudge she was big and bold and hairy, living on the far side of the creek.) I looked again.

It was a wild wombat – Chocolate. Edward was feeding him a carrot and Chocolate was eating it, with a puzzled look as though to say: 'I'm not sure what's happening but it's nice …'

Chocolate is Edward's friend, not mine, though he accepts my nightly handout of carrots and the occasional rolled-oats or wombat biscuit (made of extruded lucerne and who knows what else – a factory in South Australia makes them). Sometimes boy and beast wander together in the twilight, while I chop onions in the kitchen.

If the aliens landed tomorrow and offered me the

universe I'd have to check my diary first. But now I think they'd make their invitation to the next generation.

LIME JUICE CARROTS

One more month and the carrots will have gone to seed – tough centres and great white umbrella tops fuzzy with hoverflies. I'm inspecting them every day for signs of incipient seediness, and using them as fast as I can. (No, I'm not feeding them to Gabby. Home-grown carrots are wasted on wombats. We buy hers at the supermarket.)

1 TABLESPOON OLIVE OIL

1 DESSERTSPOON MIXED CHOPPED
PARSLEY, GARLIC CHIVES, SHALLOTS
(*or* WHATEVER GREEN STUFF YOU
CAN GET HOLD OF)

1 CUP WATER

4 LARGE CARROTS, PEELED AND
THICKLY SLICED (THE SHAPE IS UP
TO YOU)

1 TEASPOON VERY THINLY SLICED
LIME ZEST, WITH NO WHITE

1 DESSERTSPOON LIME JUICE

2 TEASPOONS BROWN SUGAR (YOU
MAY NEED MORE IF YOUR CARROTS
ARE SHOP BOUGHT, *or* LESS IF THEY
ARE HOME GROWN AND SWEET)

Sauté green stuff in the oil till wilted. Add everything else and simmer till the water has evaporated.
Serve hot as an accompaniment, or cold as a salad.

✳ *September 11*

The air is utterly still, blanket grey, cold clouds trapping yesterday's smoke. Suddenly everyone is burning off before the start of the fire season on October 1, but despite the rain a few weeks ago everything is dry again, so that the flames guzzle the dead bark and leaves and leap up into the trees, red spires laughing at the people who thought they could control them.

Yesterday morning the sky was blue, that special deep spring blue that says there's a wind too high to touch; and then the smoke dusted the valley, so yesterday's lunch party was interrupted by calls to man the tankers or the radio shack – two major bushfires from so-called 'burning off'. (They were warned it was too hot, too dry, too windy, too late to burn safely.)

The fires are under control today. We climbed the mountain behind the house early this morning to look for smoke spires, but the air is so thick with smoke it's hard to see where any is rising; but homogenous air usually means some degree of safety. And besides, there's no updraught today to feed the fire. Yesterday was howling – only maniacs would light fires yesterday. As we head into a hot dry summer it's frightening to realise how many maniacs are around.

Russell the goat man lit the hill above Major's Creek last weekend in gale-force winds – the trees are brown or black and there's no undergrowth any more in the wet gullies. But at least the surrounding houses were saved.

The very early peaches down the valley are in leaf now, looking quite uninteresting. It's too early to see the peaches from the road yet, as they are nestled against the twigs. The main orchards aren't pink yet just that slightly furry bud swelling you can only see close up.

It's a waiting time now: a touch of plum blossom out here, and the first of the apricot flowers, and every morning I inspect the crab-apples and try not to think how fast all this could be killed if fire sweeps up the valley or flares across the ridges.

I found Gabby asleep in the middle of the road this morning – half an hour more and she might have died of heat exhaustion or been run over. I carried her up to the wood shed and laid her in the shade. (I couldn't manage stuffing her down the hole.) She's a small wombat, but feels like a sack of flour after you've carried her for ten minutes.

All my clothes smell of wombat now. Luckily I like the smell.

✳ *September something ...*

I haven't yet looked at the calendar today.

The sky is still clear blue, with smoke seeping across the horizon. Everyone is still burning off – blackened scars across the paddocks and along the roads where, come Christmas time, some idiot (always) will throw out a still-smouldering cigarette butt.

Suddenly everything is flowering – or almost – the white plum flowers and the darker late peach flowers and the pale pink apricot blooms. Every day I measure the crab-apple buds. We got the first flower yesterday – maybe another week to total blooming. There's an urgency in waiting for the blooms this year. It's been a worse winter than most – dry and sort of savage cold; more things cut by frost than I've ever known, in spite of the mild beginning.

Most gardens look like blasted heaths – and summer will probably be worse. (Everyone's asking if anyone's heard a long-range forecast – just in case a new oracle has predicted rain in the coming two to three or six months – and they all say the same thing, that it will be dry, dry, dry.)

The river down by the school bus stop ceased flowing yesterday, leaving a white trail of flaking slime, and every day the creek level drops. The lizards are fattening on sunlight and on the million tiny black things that infest dead algae.

It is frightening to be so powerless – something we're not used to as humans – knowing that weather is irrevocable and has no malice, hears no appeal.

✴ *September 13*

Sue is back, her hair a bit wild. She walked down the mountain to visit us – about four kilometres – but she likes the walk. We sat in the kitchen, drinking tea. She propped her feet up on a kitchen chair so I could see the silver ankle-bracelet she bought in Singapore, and told me about last month's adventures as a shearers' cook in Nyngan.

'There was this one shearer. "Cookie . . ." he said to me, sounding really worried. Shearers can never remember your name when you're the cook, they see so many of them. I looked up from the gravy and said: "What's up, Gary?"

'He said: "Cookie, how would you feel if a bloke was undressing you and he fell asleep halfway through?"

'So I said: "Well, tell me more, Gary, give me details."'

Sue held out her mug for more tea.

'What happened then?' I ask.

'Well, it turns out they'd all gone into town, the whole mob of them after the shed was finished for the day, and they were all drunk as skunks. Turns out he'd found two girls, was trying the old "two birds in the hand" trick, but then he got so drunk one of them gave up on him, so he took the other one up to the hotel bedroom and it was three o'clock in the morning by then, and he'd been shearing since 7.30 the morning before …

'"And I was in the middle of undressing her and I reckon I must just have fallen asleep. I mean, Cookie, how would you feel if a bloke did that to you?"

'I just looked at him, and said: "At three o'clock in the morning? Gary, it'd be a blessed release." And he laughed, and it was all right after that.'

This was Nyngan, 45 degrees Celsius in the shade as long as you don't have the stove on. It's a flat, orange world according to Sue, where the main topic of conversation is how far up the walls the flood marks have gone, and there are emus instead of trees.

Sue, Richard and the boys came from Manchester to Australia eighteen months ago. Their house in Major's Creek burnt down – it was underinsured, and now they're building their own out of stone, very slowly.

It'll be a palace when they're done – not at all like the wood and fibro one that burnt down (they'd lit a halloween pumpkin and thought the candle was out but it wasn't and it burnt through the floor), but even a house that you build yourself out of stone from local paddocks and quarries costs money.

So Sue has gone cooking for shearers so she and Richard can finish the place, while he looks after the boys at home. Her boss rang her on the Thursday night and said she had to be in Nyngan to give the men dinner on Sunday. She'd only just got her P plates, and the only driving she'd done in Australia had been into Canberra a couple of times for a modelling job. It's more than 1,000 kilometres to Nyngan.

'That first Sunday was the worst. I stayed in town the night before, and all the men on the street looked at me as though I was from another planet ... there's no way a woman could go into a pub by herself without having a few blokes join her. I went into a Chinese restaurant, and the bloke at the next table started talking to me, and I thought, well, he's another human being, so I said hello back. He wanted to know where I was from and what I was doing. He didn't have a good word for shearers, he'd have you believe it was going to be gang rape and the overseer looking on. I didn't believe it, though. I mean I was necessary to them if they wanted to eat. I didn't think it could be that bad.

'He asked me how much I was getting, then he offered me $100 a day to go with him instead. I said no thanks. At least I only had to *cook* for the shearers.

'I drove out to the shed next day wondering what I'd got myself into. I wondered even more when I got there. They promised me the stores'd be there by 8 a.m., and they weren't there by 4 p.m., and I was panicking, thinking: "There are seventeen men going to rush in here at 6.30 and they'll all want to be fed and what am I going to give them?"

'They'd promised someone would have two carcasses ready for me, that they'd have killed them the day before, but they hadn't, and all I could lay my hands on were two great frozen legs of mutton. So I chopped them with a cleaver and we all had chops and mashed potatoes and frozen peas for dinner. It was eleven o'clock by the time I'd cleaned up, and the sweat was still running down my back and the flies were still into everything. Then, when I opened my bedroom door, eight swallows flew out, and I remembered I'd forgotten my torch – there wasn't any light of course – and by the time I'd gone back and got it the swallows were in again, and every time I'd push a couple out, three more would fly back in. So there I was, trying to sleep with eight swallows hanging over my face, and it was too hot to sleep much anyway, even though I was exhausted, and I knew I had to start cooking again at 4.30.'

'What did you give them?'

Sue takes another biscuit. 'I hardly ate up there,' she explains. 'Too hot. Well, at 5.30 I'd start breakfast – chops and more chops and bacon and eggs and sliced tomato and sausages and gravy. Lots of gravy if they wanted it. There was toast too, and cereal. Then I'd start work on the food for lunch – any left over sausages and bacon and the cake I'd made that morning.

'By then it was 45 degrees and there were no fly screens, no fans, and no way you could store the cooked food. At least the cookhouse had a wooden floor you could sweep.

'The men left at seven o'clock, so I'd spend the rest of the day making cakes for smoko, and peeling buckets of vegetables, and boning meat so I could give them pies, because you couldn't give them roasts every night. A normal night they'd eat two legs and two shoulders and a bucket full of potatoes and half a bucket of carrots and a quarter of a bucket of frozen peas, which was all I had for greens, then gravy in a big, big pan. I always gave them a proper gravy, I hate the powdered stuff.

'Puddings were almost impossible to make because of the heat – the butter'd melt before I could stir it in – and the puddings were stale almost as soon as they came out of the oven, because there wasn't anywhere you could cool them down. I made some Chelsea buns the first day and they were like rocks even before they'd cooled down.

'I tried to make them bread and butter pudding once. I think you make it differently in Australia anyway. In England we make it with buttered bread, then another layer and another, with the custard poured on top, so it comes out solid like a cake.

'Well, I tried it up at Nyngan, and they were hysterical, they couldn't believe such a thing ever came out of a kitchen. I put it on the bench after I took it out of the oven, and it went as hard as concrete, and one of the men said: "What've you got there, Cookie?" Well, I wouldn't show it to him, I was so ashamed of it. He tried to grab it, so I picked it up and ran out into the yard with it, and they all followed me, and there I was running round the yard with this great lumpen pudding clasped to my bosom and they were chasing after me, till finally I started gouging out handfuls and hurled it at them.'

I must have been looking a Sue in horror, because she grinned.

'It was great,' she said. 'I loved it. Can't wait till the next job. Are there any more of these biscuits?'

❋ *September 14*

I traipsed down to the chooks with the scrap bucket this morning. Bryan usually takes it down when he goes down to the shed, but he had to go to town on fire business.

Bryan is Captain, Radio Communications, Tallaganda Shire – at least, a title something along those lines. An impressive title – the new reorganisation of NSW Bush Fire Brigades is rich in titles and bureaucracy. Unfortunately they are also alienating many of the stalwarts who have fought fires for forty years and don't take kindly to newcomers telling them to fill in forms in triplicate, and reallocating 'resources' – often equipment the locals have spent years raising money to buy.

They expect a bad fire season this year – but then I've never known a year when someone didn't say: 'I reckon it'll be a bad fire season this year alright.'

In the absence of Bryan I scraped the last of the porridge into the bucket and had a brief hunt through the fridge for leftovers, and wandered down towards the chooks. (Gabby butting my ankles all the way, at least till we got to the chook shed; I think the noise of the chooks confuses her, so she hung about under the elderberry tree till I returned.)

It's peaceful watching chooks. I can see why Bryan's positioned his workbench so he can watch them every day. There's the sheer stereotypicality (is there such a word? there should be) of their social life – the randy roosters,

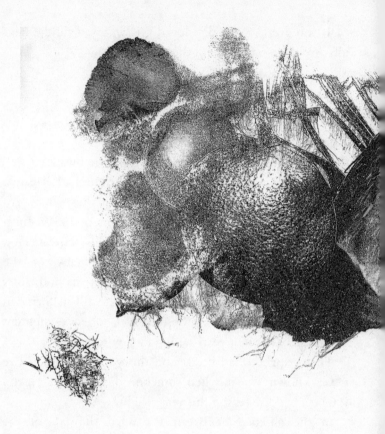

submissive hens, the odd furtive one dashing off to lay an egg in forbidden ground (i.e. my lavender garden). There's the cartoon humour when Rodney Rooster tries to mount one of Arnold Schwarzenfeather's hens, and Arnie chases Rodney around the garden; but mostly they're just peaceful.

They enjoy the chook bucket. Scraps to us are fillet steak and bearnaise sauce to them. I realise too how much the chook bucket says about our lives.

There were never any scraps in my father's kitchen, no drifts of spilt flour either. Most houses seem to have much tidier kitchens than ours. Ours is crammed with food and too much furniture. (I'm tempted to say with more living too.)

I'm always amazed in other people's houses – foraging for bread or Vegemite or cereal in the morning – how little actual food they have on hand; how many houses keep no flour (plain, corn, arrowroot, wholemeal and self raising), and no rice (brown and white, long and short grain for risotto or puddings) on hand. Not to mention no dried fruit, breadcrumbs, olive oil, strings of garlic, sesame seeds, poppy seeds, vanilla extract, rosewater, cans of emergency tomatoes and tomato paste, asparagus, stock, smoked oysters, tinned salmon, at least six assorted varieties of pasta, four sorts of sugar, and the other essentials of our larder. Fewer and fewer people actually seem to cook nowadays …

But to get back to the bucket. The gluggy porridge, in horrid greyish lumps. The chooks loved that. Yesterday's stale bread. The scrapings of last night's asparagus soufflé, last week's roast chicken bones (chooks are quite happy to be cannibals either unwittingly or knowingly – they're savage brutes under those sweet feathers – anyone who thinks chooks are vegetarians hasn't seen them with a nest of baby rats or a young snake, beetle larvae and the rest), Bryan's boiled egg shell, three greenish cheese rinds, a mass of silverbeet stalks, outside lettuce (still with slugs attached), beetroot and dandelion leaves, an onion skin, quite a lot of that paper stuff that garlic is naturally wrapped in, a trout head (yesterday's lunch), Bryan's potato skins (I eat mine) and a hunk of pumpkin rind, a scrape of hollandaise sauce that I couldn't bear to throw away till this morning and Edward's soggy Vita Brits – he really didn't want the second bowlful.

Today's a normal sort of chook-bucket day. Fridge-cleaning-out days are much more lavish; and once a year or so the cupboards get cleaned out too, usually before we go away for a week and lock up the chooks (for fear of foxes), so I toss out the stale stuff in partial compensation.

The veg garden gets weeded then too: barrow loads of old turnips and parsnips gone to seed and chickweed and spent bean plants, about a metre deep in the chook run to keep them going till we get home, with the stale Vita Brits (Edward changes his cereal allegiance with the season, so there's always packets of stale stuff on hand), breadcrumbs left open too long, soggy Milk Arrowroots, forgotten Saos, the quarter of slightly furry Christmas cake that I've finally accepted we'll never eat, the tin of biscuits a relative gave us as a Christmas present (our friends know we never eat tinned biscuits; I don't know what even the best taste of, but it isn't butter, sugar and flour) ...

Sometimes I wonder what households who don't have chooks do with their scraps. Can they really bear to throw them away?

But maybe our eating and throwing away habits are just conditioned by having chooks. Nothing is ever really wasted. Perhaps most households don't have scraps at all.

※ *September 16*

Spent the morning chasing round, black cattle back down the valley. I discovered the fattest munching my daffodils when I went out to feed the wombats. Water's getting scarce down the creek, and there's not much grass either. Not that there's much water or grass up here, but at least there are a few pickings – and the daffodils.

Got back to find that Chocolate wombat has dug a large hole under the roses – parsnip hunting. Parsnips go down about twenty centimetres. This hole is about a metre deep – maybe he thought there might be more buried underneath. Or maybe he just had fun digging.

Gabby has yet to dig anything and still doesn't graze much either. She mostly sleeps, or follows Bryan's ankles.

The bowerbirds are circling the chook run like vultures trying to find a way in to the wheat in the hopper; and the lyrebirds are scratching up any place we put the hose, and not even scampering when you run after them till they've got the particular worm they're after; and I have the feeling there are ten thousand wallabies sniffing the air and saying: 'There's greenery that way, mate – let's go.'

At least there's cloud today – high, grey cloud that might have three drops of moisture if you squeezed it. You can almost smell the drought coming, a pervasive horror that's spread though the whole community. It's dry now but there's much worse to come.

As Edward said yesterday: 'Why are the gum trees dropping their leaves so early? It's not that dry yet.' Then a pause, 'I suppose they know,' he said.

HOT DRIED-PEACH SALAD

This salad goes well with any rich, fairly plain meat dish, or with potatoes baked in their skins.

10 DRIED PEACHES HALVES

4 CUPS BOILING WATER

JUICE OF 2 LEMONS

2 CLOVES GARLIC, CRUSHED

1 FIRM APPLE, LIKE GRANNY SMITH, CHOPPED

1 TEASPOON CHOPPED PARSLEY

1 TEASPOON CHOPPED WALNUTS *or*
MACADAMIAS

4 TABLESPOONS OLIVE OIL

Soak the peach halves in the boiling water overnight. Drain well, pat off excess moisture and leave on a tray in a warm place to dry for at least 2 hours.

Mix the other ingredients, add the peaches, place in an ovenproof dish and place in a hot over for 10 minutes, or till warm. Don't leave any longer or the peaches will lose their shape and the apple and nuts will cook. The essence of this dish is the hot soft peaches and the hot crisp nuts and apple.

Serve hot.

.... 🥀 ....

❋ *September something ...*

I planted the first tomatoes today – much too early, but the wind was warm on my face and the valley was yelling 'Plant me, plant me'. So I did.

I know the old English saying, don't plant tomatoes till you can sit on the soil with a bare bum, which makes sense, as the soil is where the roots are, and even if the air is warm the soil is still cold, much too cold for me to try the bare-bum trick. But I planted them anyway, and lettuce and rocket and a stretch of lawn thyme that hopefully by next autumn I'll be rolling on (I've always wanted a thyme lawn to gambol on).

Gabby decided to help plant the tomatoes; which basically meant butting me from every possible angle while treading on the seedlings. She doesn't like to be more than a whisker length away from my feet, which makes working outside difficult. What she really wants to do is curl up in my shadow and go to sleep, preferably with me stroking her tummy; somehow I have to convince her that wombats sleep in holes, away from the sunlight that can be deadly for a wombat.

Picked the largest head of broccoli ever today – the stem thicker than my wrist. Also cauliflower (which we're sick of – boiled, with cheese sauce, stir-fried with almonds, made into soup, cauliflower quiche with hollandaise sauce or garlic and lemon juice or mustardy vinaigrette, or stewed with cumin and tomatoes, or curried).

I'll turn this one into potato and cauliflower soup, then give the rest of the crop away. Caulies don't do well at Giles and Victoria's up the mountain, for some reason, so they'll like them … and what they don't eat the chooks can have.

POTATO AND CAULIFLOWER SOUP

1 CUP CAULIFLOWER

2 POTATOES

4 CUPS CHICKEN STOCK (USE A
STOCK CUBE IF YOU LIKE –
CAULIFLOWER IS SO PUNGENT, THE
SUBTLETY OF GOOD CHICKEN
STOCK IS LOST)

2 TEASPOONS DILL LEAVES

1 GLOP OF CREAM

Chop the cauliflower and potatoes, simmer in the chicken stock with the dill leaves. Mash well with a potato

masher (the slight chunkiness is nice). Add more dill if
the cauli was stale and tasteless, then a drop of cream.
Serve hot and pretend it isn't cauliflower.

❋ *September something …*

Just enough rain to sting your face in bitter wind.
Everyone in town is making jokes about it:

'Hey, Les, what's that stuff out there?'

'Dunno, Steve, it's been so long I can't remember. What
d'yer reckon, snow?'

The drops were flat, like they really might have been
melted snowflakes, and stopped before they'd properly wet
the ground. The windscreen was opaque as the last six
weeks of dust oozed down the glass. But at least the cool
weather is keeping everything from wilting.

Collected three days' worth of mail in town, then sat in the cafe and opened it. The menu looked disgustingly familiar – cauliflower quiche and broccoli soup and silverbeet lasagne and chicken and cauliflower curry – all based on local produce that is the same as the stuff we're eating from our garden. All very well in theory but not if you eat fresh and local all the time. I had good unhealthy scones instead.

You get the best scones in the world at the cafe. Jenny and Natalie and Angela spent six weeks testing every scone recipe they could find: I think this one dates from 1910. They also tested the best biscuit recipes too, for months before the cafe opened – which was great fun for all their friends.

As usual, there were more staff in the kitchen than customers out the front, though most of the 'staff' are probably just visiting – it's called 'sink therapy'. Jen and Natalie and Angela stick all their world-weary city friends at the washing-up, and after a week of talk and laughter the *weltzschmerz* has disappeared.

Angela's laughter gurgles out through the studio, to the footpath. (Her ex-headmistress from three decades ago heard it last Christmas, and wandered in muttering: 'I thought it was you Marshall, I recognised the laughter, what *are* you doing now?', and Angela wilted as she must have done at thirteen.)

Everyone sat watching the windows in the cafe, as though counting the raindrops … one two three four …

The nights are full of wombat screams. Chocolate is defending his territory. Not from Gabby. Gabby is still no threat to anyone. There was a strange mother and baby here last week – the baby was small and round and brown and climbing between its mother's legs and under her and over her, while she concentrated on munching grass.

'Let's call it Caramel,' said Edward, but they were gone next day. Chocolate had hunted them off. I don't think Gabby even noticed, and Chocolate only seems to register Gabby when he pinches her carrots. Gabby is still entirely human orientated; if a visitor drives up she's padding out immediately, but doesn't even sniff at wombat dung.

Another almost Chocolate-sized wombat is lurking round the edges of the garden, staying downwind of Chocolate, just far enough away not to make it worth his while to charge him, though I think there must be collisions later at night, judging by all the noise. There was a massive roo at the bottom of the garden this afternoon too; great shoulder muscles like he's been lifting weights or odd jobbing as a fencing contractor – the first roo I've seen in the garden since the last drought (normally all we get are wallabies).

I've never seen so many roadkills either. The roadside verges are the only greenery that's left.

LIME-JUICE SYRUP

The lime trees are laden now; one good wind and there'll be fruit all over the ground. This stuff is wonderful – better than any so called lime cordial you'll buy in the shops.

1 EGG WHITE

1 KILOGRAM SUGAR

2 CUPS WATER

2 CUPS LIME JUICE

Optional

1 DESSERTSPOON CITRIC ACID

1 DESSERTSPOON TARTARIC ACID

Beat the egg white till stiff. Combine the egg white, sugar and water and stir till the sugar is dissolved. Bring it to the boil, take off the heat till it stops bubbling, then bring it to the boil again. Skim off any scum – rigorously, or the juice may later ferment. Add the lime juice once the liquid is cool. You can add citric acid and tartaric acid at the end, if you like. It makes it more cordial-like. I usually don't bother.

Keep it in the fridge in sealed bottles. It should keep for a year; but may not.

....🍃..

✳ *October 4*

Too much asparagus and dandelion leaves last night: both diuretics. Actually it was only one dandelion leaf – I'm not really fond of them, but it's good to blame something other than my asparagus gluttony. Do other people eat kilos of asparagus at a time? But how can you resist it when it's there, poking inquiringly out of the soil as though to say: 'Here I am, come eat me!', and you've been eating boring Brussels sprouts, cabbages and broccoli for months …

Which is why I wandered onto the balcony sometime in the early morning, to relieve my bladder in the bucket that serves as a chamber pot – an en suite would be boring after years of moonlight, and anyway the roses like the urine; we choose a different rose to throw it onto every morning. You'd think the smell would stop the wallabies munching the rose leaves – but it doesn't. Obviously they don't find the scent of Bryan or me at all threatening.

The sky always seems higher at 4 a.m., as though someone is standing above it and stretching it as high as it will go. Stars like moth holes in the fabric of space–time and last night a lattice of cloud: a high wind above the ridges blowing from the east and an even higher one perhaps blowing from the west, so the sky was crisscrossed with the thinnest webs of mist.

Back to bed, which always seems more comfortable when you've been out of it; but of course by then sleep was impossible, and so I thought about death instead. 4 a.m. is the perfect time to consider death, especially if it's towards the end of my monthly cycle and there's a whisper of depression in my mind.

Not that I'm depressed about death. Angry sometimes: I think this was my first reaction when I really accepted for the first time that I would die (I was about twenty-one, sitting in front of a fire watching the flames snicker back into the coals and suddenly I knew ...). It seemed the most outrageous trick of fate to give you consciousness then take it away. And worse – to leave you knowing all through your life that consciousness was temporary, borrowed from the universe.

The rage subsided somewhat over the next few years. I reasoned that as an instinctive animal *of course* I wanted more than anything to escape death; it was programmed into me. That if it wasn't, my ancestors would have cast themselves into tar pits or the jaws of tigers long before they'd had a chance to breed, that there was nothing intrinsically malicious about death.

By now my feelings about death wander with the years, and probably with my monthly cycle too. But last night, lying in a comfortable bed in a room I love, with a wombat scratching itself on the garden table outside and Bryan snuffling beside me and Edward down below − things that I hold very dear, and would feel extraordinary sadness to let go − I also realised that I have never heard a tale of afterlife that wasn't human based, an extrapolation of our existence here.

Everything I've heard or read about an afterlife is an extension somehow of existing consciousness; and much as I love the world around me now, I think I would feel cheated if I woke up after death and found it even a little bit the same.

Of course one can say that the only way we limited humans can think of death or its aftermath is in terms of what we know; it is impossible to describe the totally unexperienced. But I don't want *any* of the afterlives I've read about. I don't want non-existence either. Not that I reckon I'll have much choice.

Sometime after the first rooster hiccup I fell asleep (probably conditioned by now, as I expect to go to sleep as soon as the rooster crows).

The insomnia's genetic: my mother always wakes between four and dawn. I don't think Grandma did. She preferred to get up at rooster crow, or whatever the city equivalent was, in her middle and old age, and sit with a cup of tea and one or two Sao biscuits with butter and sliced tomato, facing a blank wall – a practice I wondered at as a child (why not a book or at least a window with a view) till lately I've found myself also facing blank walls, though not with a cup of tea, for the sort of peaceful thought that doesn't want distractions.

I wonder what my grandmother thought about death? I asked her once, but she was noncommittal.

✳ *October 6*

The pittosporums are flowering. Pittosporum blossom is supposed to send bees mad and, according to (male) Aboriginal lore, send women mad with passion too. Male hope springs eternal, no matter what the culture, especially in spring – no woman who has stood under a flowering pittosporum here has been driven mad with lust, and the bees mostly ignore the flowers too.

Gabby had a pittosporum flower in her fur this morning. At least with the anti-mange injections she doesn't have ticks yet; I used to spend hours deticking Ricki – not that I think he noticed if the ticks were there or not.

HOT DRIED-FRUIT SALAD FOR BREAKFAST

1 CUP DRIED PEACHES

1 CUP DRIED APRICOTS

1 CUP DRIED PRUNES

1 CUP DRIED APPLE

1 CUP DRIED APRICOTS

2 WHOLE CLOVES

A SLIVER OF CINNAMON BARK
(*not* THE DRIED STUFF ... IT LOOKS
LIKE THE REMNANTS DRIED IN
YOUR HANKY AFTER A COLD)

Simmer in 3 cups of water for 10 minutes. Cool in the syrup. Store in the fridge for up to two weeks.

Scoop out what you want for breakfast and reheat. A little grated lemon peel or a squeeze of lime juice before reheating helps bring the flavours out.

.... 🍂 ....

❋ October 9

It's snowing – except the flakes are crab-apple petals. Every time the breeze gusts, the garden is filled with them, fluttering across the lawn and slipping down to almost pink drifts along the windows.

'Mum!' yelled Edward this morning, 'Gabby's asleep on the doormat and I can't get out!'

So I lifted her – minus the doormat – and carried her into the shade. She didn't wake up. Sometimes I'm terrified for her – it only takes a few hours for a wombat to die in full sunlight, and Gabby doesn't seem to notice if it's night or day.

❋ October 10

Inspected our peach trees this morning. We only have half a dozen now. There used to be hundreds when I first came here, mostly half dead from old age, starvation and cattle damage. Now we're down to two new ones, and four old ones that still produce that lovely white, totally squashable fruit that never reaches the markets (it would be one large bruise if it did) and tastes like heaven might if you could squeeze the juice from it.

Hundreds of peaches, nut sized and just as hard, on the early season white (they'll all be small but sweet), and nearly as many on the Golden Queen – a late variety that really is the queen of peaches. I'm salivating at the memory but it'll be six months before I taste another Golden Queen.

DRIED-PEACH FOOL WITH MACADAMIAS

1 CUP DRIED PEACHES

1 CUP WATER

1 CUP CREAM

1 TEASPOON COINTREAU

1 TEASPOON FINELY GRATED ZEST
AND JUICE OF 1 ORANGE

2 TABLESPOONS CASTER SUGAR

1–2 TABLESPOONS FINELY CHOPPED
MACADAMIAS

Simmer 1 cup dried peaches in 1 cup water till soft (about 20 minutes) and mash well so it becomes a purée.

In a separate bowl, whip the cream with the Cointreau, zest, juice and caster sugar. Sprinkle the macadamias onto the peaches, then swirl the peach purée carefully through the cream – it should stay in discrete stripes, not amalgamate.

Spoon into glasses. Serve within an hour or it may separate.

❋ *October 12*

Hauled back a jumper full of avocados this morning (they take a week or two to soften after picking – unlike the oranges, lemons, limes and so on, we can't just wander out and pick them when we want them). Also a couple of Seville oranges (lovely bitter things – I'll grill them dotted with brown sugar), six navel oranges, two limes, one very small custard apple (they don't grow big here, which doesn't matter as none of us really like them, I just bung them in fruit salad) and more asparagus, a whole plastic bag full for lunch, the purple spears peering out the top. Edward and I will pick more asparagus for dinner. He's the best asparagus spotter I know: has a real eye for the odd spear lurking under the bracken or behind a comfrey leaf.

I suppose we've earned a bit of the fat of the land since I planted my first tree here, twenty years ago. The soil was pale yellow powder then. Not even grass would grow – there were blackberries instead. Now the trees *are* trees, not just sticks nibbled by wallabies and shrivelled by drought; and the larder's full of honey and the garden's full of veg and the soil is full of worms. This is truly harvest time.

And the herb garden, which changes with the years as our needs change (it's no longer filled with aloe vera plants for Edward's baby bum, or parsley to chop into everything as a way of getting a three-year-old to eat his greens without being aware of them), is filled now with tarragon and Good King Henry and lettuce-leafed basil, because somehow during the past couple of years I seem to have found time to cook again, which I never seemed to have time to do when Edward was a toddler.

Bryan counted 127 different sorts of birds last year – the garden's filled with the descendants of birds who moved in five, eight, ten years ago and stayed and bred …

There are hoverflies on the alyssum and hanging space for the clothes …

This is both harvest time and blossom time …

❋ *October 16*

When we drove down to the school bus Rod and 'the boys' were up the ladders among the orchards, thinning the peaches.

Too many peaches on each branch means tiny peaches and customers only want great fat ones. I find large peaches too much of a good thing – I'd rather eat four small ones than one big one, but the big ones do look beautifully pulchritudinous, as though if you poked your finger at them they'd spurt out juice.

Still can't get over the light and the colours. The sun here hovers on the edges of the ridges all winter so you never get direct light at all; and now it's climbing the sky and you realise you've forgotten quite what depth green can have, or how brilliant red can be …

❋ *October 19*

Gabby's eczema is getting worse, despite the injections. I'm pretty sure now it is eczema, not mange. I rang WIRES again. They recommended a mix of sorbolene and sulphur. I applied it liberally. Gabby didn't object. I think it took her five minutes to work out what was happening. By that time I'd got it done. She looks ridiculous – brown with yellow streaks and spiky fur. Punk wombat.

I stink of sulphur, like I've been bathing in a volcano.

The cream seems to soothe her, but not enough to stop her scratching …

The jets were sparkling under the peach trees as we drove back through the orchards after school – the scent of cold water on hot soil, with the faintest almond tang of peach leaves.

'When will the peaches be ready?' demands Edward, squinting to see how they've swollen among the leaves.

'By your birthday. Maybe,' I say.

❋ *October 20*

The chemist is out of sulphur and so am I. It does seem to soothe the eczema a bit; or maybe I'm just grasping at straws. They ordered it in but apparently the distributor is out of sulphur too. Maybe every wombat on the Eastern seaboard is being treated for the itch. Meanwhile Gabby keeps scratching.

The avocado leaves are all drooping as the trees begin to flower – incredibly huge bunches of cream blossom poking up towards the sky.

The avocados are at their most luscious now – so smooth you feel like stroking them. There hardly seem to be any when the blossom falls – only one flower in about twenty sets fruit and then they begin to swell and swell, and the branches droop with the weight of them.

Theoretically, most should be picked now, but we leave a lot on the tree, to get bigger and lighter and even more delicious – overripe avocados, though they aren't really. Avocados don't ripen till you pick them or till a currawong pecks a hole in the side and they ripen and fall off. (To be finished off by the wallabies below – happy wallabies – they love ripe avocado.)

❋ *October 24*

The woman from the chemist hailed me triumphantly at the post office when I was picking up the mail. She's tracked down four jars of sulphur.

I mixed a good batch of yellow goo and applied it to Gabby's bald patches but she wasn't grateful. It's not so much that she's strong – for a wombat she's small and very gentle and even when she bites you it doesn't break the skin (Ricki could chomp a steel girder in half and probably munched granite boulders for breakfast) – she's just so compact there's really nothing to get a grip on.

Maybe I should add some comfrey juice and calendula to the mixture, and heart's-ease flowers too ... just accept that it's eczema not mange and needs soothing, not killing. I've got some already mixed in the larder, left over from a batch I made last year for Noel. I'll try it tomorrow.

❋ *October 25*

By now we've been picking asparagus for about a month – a few fat spears at first, not enough each time to cook, so we nibble them raw as we inspect the beds. They have a slightly bitter greenish taste, still with the tang of winter soil.

Today's harvest was about three kilos. Most days we pick about half a kilo, but yesterday we went bushwalking and the day before we went to town to get the groceries and the day before … Anyway, it's been four days since we picked over the beds. The biggest spears were up to my knees, fat as my big toe, with thin shoots from last year's seedlings even taller with a ferny brush on top.

The asparagus bed doesn't get weeded, fed or watered – just picked. It grows on top of an old blackberry bed.

About twenty years ago I covered it in carpet then in mulch – two months of truck loads of stable tailings from the bedding of (Melbourne Cup winner) Whiskey Road, whose progeny were later to win race after race, and he imbues the asparagus with the same spirit.

The asparagus has grown steadily ever since, sprinting away in spring and settling down to a good steady lope for the rest of the year, till the red berries burst in later summer and it dies down in winter. Then we mow what's left of it – and the comfrey that spread from an accidental tilling and the blackberries that have crept back – and the weeds feed and mulch the asparagus, and sometime (maybe this year) I may get round to spreading on some hen manure, so the little shoots can keep on growing fatter.

Today's pick had tough white stalks at the soil end, and some of the green stalk was tough as well. But the tips were wonderful.

Bryan has his usual spring lunch of asparagus omelette, while Edward and I just had big bowls of boiled asparagus – the giant spears broken up into a pot with water halfway up, and boiled till they turn a deeper green (a minute or two only), then thrown out of the saucepan into the sink to cool down under the tank water from the cold tap. Then a dribble of salad dressing.

Our taste in salad dressing changes from week to week, sometimes thick with garlic chives, or fragrant with seedy mustard, or lemony or tart with lime juice. But the asparagus never changes, always the same big bowlful till the end of the season – and I do mean *big* bowlful – I put on weight in asparagus season, never mind that it's supposed to be low calorie (but not in the quantities that I eat it). The same goes for the first few weeks of Jonathan and Golden Delicious apples too.

Bryan's asparagus omelette is more discreet – a lovely bright yellow thing with dots of green oozing juice out onto the plate. You only get that colour of course with your own eggs.

The chooks eyed us thoughtfully from their dust baths under the casuarinas as we brought the asparagus over in a plastic bag, hoping that we'd brought stale bread, which usually gets delivered to them in plastic bags, but we hadn't, so they wriggled down again, into the gritty sand and decomposing casuarina needles – one of the most fragrant dust baths around.

Tried the new cream mix on Gabby. She seems more comfortable with it. I wish she'd take to the wombat hole though – wombats need the perfect moist humidity of wombat holes. I wish she'd graze more too. I tried cutting down her food but she just got thinner and unhappy.

The kiwi fruit are leafing out the window – their pale leaves are almost silver in the sunlight. They'll darken soon. The pergola will be shaded again and we will breakfast there in the green light and the leaves will shade the kitchen and in the morning the bedroom light will be dappled, leaf prints on white walls.

ASPARAGUS OMELETTE

3 EGGS

1 GENEROUS TABLESPOON BUTTER

1–6 ASPARAGUS TIPS, VERY FINELY
CHOPPED (ONLY PRECOOK IF THE
ASPARAGUS IS BOUGHT, NOT IF IT'S
FRESH)

Optional

COLD CHOPPED POTATO (MAKE
SURE IT IS VERY DRY AND COLD *or*
IT WILL STICK)

A SCATTER OF GARLIC CHIVES *or*
SALAD BURNET *or* TARRAGON

A SCATTER OF SOFT RED CAPSICUM
SLICED SO FINE IT'S ALMOST
TRANSPARENT (IF YOU'VE BEEN
TEMPTED TO BUY ONE – THERE
WON'T BE ONE READY YET IN YOUR
GARDEN IN OCTOBER)

GRATED CHEESE (FOR A REALLY
SOLID MEAL)

Heat your pan before you do anything else. If it isn't hot the omelette will stick and you'll get scrambled eggs, alternatively raw and singed, not a lovely thing firm on the bottom and creamy on the top. I use an old cast-iron pan – smooth from a thousand oilings – my hand knows the weight of it now, I can flip it and wriggle it without thinking, know just how long a bit of meat will take to brown. You need to form a good relationship with your frying pan – the sort of friendship that matures and seasons with the years.

So – heat the pan (this is part of the process of friendship). While it's heating, beat the eggs in a bowl with a fork – not too much or they'll get tough. Omelettes are gentle things.

The asparagus tips should be chopped as finely as you can. If they are very fresh – just picked – they'll crumble in your fingers. Otherwise you'll need to use a knife – asparagus, like most veg, soon go rubbery. (I distrust any veg that I can bend.)

The pan should now be hot. Throw in the butter and the asparagus tips. The asparagus will seethe and splutter in the hot butter. (If you want a more substantial meal, tip in some chopped spuds.) Stir the whole lot round a couple of times – this all takes about 20 seconds – then pour in the eggs.

Now shake the pan like mad, back and forth, till the eggs start to set and become fluffy. Then leave the pan alone for 10 seconds or so to form a firm bottom.

At this stage you can add a scatter of herbs or sliced capsicum, or even cheese for a really solid meal.

As soon as the omelette is nearly set, fold it in half with a spatula, then in half again, and lift out the quartered omelette – which will start it oozing straight away – and place it on a plate, which you'll have warmed if you're organised. (I rarely am, and Bryan eats his lunchtime omelettes on cold plates.)

Don't overcook it. It'll turn into leather if you leave it in the pan till it's set on top. It will keep cooking anyway for about five minutes after you've taken it from the pan

— but by that time it should have amalgamated with its consumer, who'll be reaching for the lime and poppy-seed cake or lemon curd tart to have with his or her Ecco.

.... ✬ ....

❉ *October sometime …*

Who cares what the date is when the air is thick with scent? Jasmine and the last of the daphne and late jonquils and the honey scent from the final burst of tree-lucerne flowers.

Down to dinner with Noel and Bev Wisbey last night. The Wisbeys are one of the valley's major peach growers — Noel and Bev at one end of the valley and Rod and Sandra Wisbey at the other, presided over by Ned and Bess Wisbey.

It was Ned and his father who planted the first peaches in the valley during the Depression, up on the hills where they'd be safe from frost.

In those days Ned had just one shirt, which he washed on Fridays so it was fresh for the dance on Friday night (if they held the dance on Saturday night they had to stop for the Sabbath, which was no good because they wanted to dance till dawn). He didn't have any shoes either. Bess says she first saw him when she was driving down the valley with her brother. 'That's Ned Wisbey,' her brother had said. 'Don't you worry about him, he's never had a pair of shoes in his life.'

He has shoes now — and a million-dollar business — but he doesn't wear them most of summer, sitting in his shorts and nothing else in a chair outside Noel's shed or Rod's, yarning about the valley and the peaches and the flood back in '42 …

We talked about the peach crop. Noel seemed cautiously optimistic – as optimistic as any peach grower can be without tempting hail, flood and six weeks of fog that'll rot the blossom. No late frosts, enough rain (just – they're watering already, which means for the last two weeks there's been no water in what was once the river), sufficient chilling – a whole season so far without hazards – and only another month to go till the first picking, though the main crop will come from December onwards.

It's a watching time in the valley now. Winter's work is over – the pruning, which everyone seems to dread from year to year (cold tired fingers and endless trees like skeletons waiting for surgery), fertilising, spraying, planting new trees and fencing new orchards – what hasn't been done by now has to wait for next year. The pickers are lined up (most come every year, others apply till about the end of August when the books are filled), males in the orchards mostly and women in the shed packing, though a stroppy female will insist on outdoor work and if she does insist, she'll get it. Most however are happy for the shade, and the (relative) freedom from the peach fluff that gets in every crevice and has the pickers itching till the season's over.

This is the time you watch the peaches swelling, from the first slight curve as the blossom drops, to the first faint white of fuzz – hard and fuzzy white at first – then bigger, greening through the white and finally yellowing, blushing with the edge of red that customers expect nowadays.

The best varieties (according to me and various old-fashioned peach growers) are still the firm dull-skinned varieties – Golden Queen with its greenish yellow coat or that mottled white fleshed early peach that looks like a teenager fed on junk food, and you can't eat it without dribbling juice.

Hardly anyone grows that early peach nowadays. It's too delicate, bruises with any bump and doesn't last, and is not a freestone either – the peach flesh still clings to the stone no matter how long you suck at it – but that's half the joy of a peach, sucking at the stone, trying to get the last of the membranes from between the crevices and down into your gullet.

Gabby is getting thinner – which she shouldn't be, as there's plenty of grass. But she doesn't eat grass like other wombats; just a taste here and a nibble over there, while she waits for the real food – her bottle and oats and wombat nuts and carrots. I stopped giving her a bottle last week, hoping that she'd eat more grass, and I feed her in the morning now, so that she'll fill up on grass at night … but she doesn't.

❋ October 26

Picked the first artichokes today – tiny bud-like things not the tennis-ball flowers you get in the shops. You can eat most of the artichoke when it's small. Even the stalk is delicious.

Artichokes are a peasant crop that for some reason has been elevated to a luxury. I don't know why. They grow like weeds. (Try a hedge along your front fence – the prickles keep out dogs and rollerblading kids.) Basically that's what they are – weeds. Artichokes are cultivated thistles.

Nothing kills artichokes: they will survive drought, salt winds, plagues of locusts, rampaging wallabies, hordes of twelve-year-olds with basketballs. Even if you starve an artichoke plant it will still bear 'chokes' – tiny ones, fit for a gnome's dinner party. We feed ours muck from the chook house and they're enormous: great globular things, about six to ten on every bush.

Gradually commercial growers are also realising that artichokes grow like weeds: you can sometimes buy great bags incredibly cheaply.

This is good. Artichokes should not be treated as a delicacy. The languid dipping of artichokes, leaf by leaf into sauce is one of the odder French customs, a sort of harking back to the days of the aristocracy when the Comte de Such and Such had time to take his calories individually.

Spring's a time to guzzle. (Just watch the wombats if you don't believe me.) Artichokes should be eaten *en masse*.

ARTICHOKES ARALUEN, PEASANT STYLE

Find a pair of scissors (in our house this takes some time). Snip all the leaves back to the succulent soft bits at the bottom (see note). You'll now have a 'heart' or base – about a third to a tenth of what you started with. Peel the stalk. It's good too.

Boil the artichoke heart and peeled stalk until tender (around 5 to 20 minutes, depending on the size of the heart).

Serve with a good vinaigrette, heavy on the French mustard and garlic and chives. I make mine with lime or lemon juice instead of vinegar. Good hot or cold.

*Note: The outside leaves needn't be wasted — simmer
1 cup of leaves for 20 minutes in one of those convenient
boxes of chicken stock with a squeeze of lemon or lime
juice and half a cup of water. Strain into bowls, and
you've got Artichoke Soup.*

I met my first artichokes in tins, after years of reading
about them in English novels — a very exotic thing mostly
served by the French or under glass at The Savoy with
hollandaise sauce and junior members of the aristocracy à
la Dorothy Sayers.

In the 1970s artichokes were fashionable in salads —
watery canned lumps that soaked up the salad dressing and
dribbled it down your front. (One of the hazards of being
large bosomed — if you're smaller you get the drips on your
lap, where the napkin absorbs them — it's a sign of our lack
of gusto in eating that we don't use bibs.)

The best artichokes I ever ate were at Val Plumwood's. Val cooks well. This should be a common accomplishment, but it isn't. Val can take any recipe and produce delicious food, just as my elderly neighbour Mrs Hobbins could make superb tea out of an aluminium teapot and tank water and Bushells Green Label – she had the knack, the affinity with tea just as Val has an affinity with food.

Val and I always intend to see each other more often – we only live a few valleys away as the crow flies. But neither of us is a crow, and to get to Val's from our place we have to drive up to Braidwood, then as far again along another road, then along her track.

We bumped up her track for half an hour (Val does it in fifteen minutes) – thin orange soil through dry thin forest, regrowth of a hundred years of clearing and cattle – then skidded through the mud along the rest of the track, deep, rich, red brown mud with tree ferns wiping at the windscreen and lyrebirds tails disappearing up the hill.

Val's house is built of stone, like ours; and she built her own, like we did. But whereas ours is built of granite from the creek, hers is a crazy quilt of conglomerate sandstone, each lugged up the mountain in a pack on her back and jigsawed into shape, so the result is an almost immaculate hexagon in a clearing of vegie garden and waratahs among the rainforest.

It was artichokes for lunch, she informed us, because she hadn't been into town to shop for a fortnight – she was trying to finish a paper (on the death of gender I think) and had been living from the garden.

'You can have an omelette too if you like,' she offered. 'But it'll have to be from goose eggs – a grey goshawk's frightening the chooks and they're only giving three or four a day. I eat those for breakfast.'

We declined the omelette (not because we don't like goose eggs – they make a good if slightly tough and fragrant omelette, but because Val obviously hoped we wouldn't – perhaps the goose egg was destined for her dinner). But there were plenty of artichokes.

We went down to help her pick them, inspecting our feet for leeches every few minutes (which soon turns into a sort of dance, flicking your heels up and twisting), keeping an eye on the gander who was feeling springlike and longing to dart at our backsides; and the artichokes were rising tall and green among the red mignonette lettuce and patches of yarrow.

We picked perhaps twenty and came inside.

Back in the house the artichokes were snipped so that the tough outer leaves were trimmed back closer to the tender inner core. The new potatoes were roughly washed, and the whole lot thrown into a deep heavy iron pot, black from about twenty years of fires (Val doesn't have an oven – cooking is on the top of a gas ring, or in the fireplace when it's cold), with the most generous splash of olive oil I'd ever seen. She put the lid on, turned the gas down low, plunked on the pot, and left the artichokes to sweat.

We waited, discussing wombats, rabbit control (roasting them with a touch of honey and soy sauce is a much more humane method of control than myxo), the outrageously male-dominated world of Australian philosophy, and a new companion in Val's life – very nice she said, though a little uneducated about feminism, but she'd given him a pile of books last weekend to study and she thought he'd soon be much improved.

The pot steamed gently for about two hours. We were starving. Val finally wandered down to the garden again, pulling up rocket leaves and garlic tops and red chicory leaves and a few very tiny Japanese turnips – we just brushed the dirt off and crunched them in the garden and they were sweeter than apples – and a few asparagus tops and a rabbit-nibbled mignonette lettuce.

These were all washed, tossed into a wooden bowl, drizzled with olive oil and a bit of the juice of one of the limes we'd brought her (we'd brought avocados too but they weren't ripe yet); then she finally pulled the pot off the stove.

The scent was incredible – not just potato and artichoke and oil but something more. We ate the lot with a drizzle of more lime juice and some of the fresh bread we'd brought from Braidwood – good brown bread with bits of wheat in it baked by the Dutch baker, sodden now with artichoke juice and olive oil and lime, fragrant with potato. (Only fresh spuds taste of anything – with elderly spuds all you get is texture.) And the geese strutted along the terrace hoping we'd throw them some bread.

Ten years ago Val was attacked by a crocodile while canoeing up in Kakadu. She fought it off – one of the few people ever to do so – and escaped, though the croc had chewed part of the way through her upper leg and left other hideous injuries. She dragged her leg for kilometres, then finally crawled, losing blood all the way, till she found a path where someone might find her.

Perhaps it's that single-mindedness that she brings to food and philosophy too.

❋ *October 27*

Suddenly Moon Base 1 has turned into the Garden of Eden. You can almost see the roses opening and the fruit swelling. Everything else is swelling too – wombats (Gabby's stomach is so round it brushes the grass – she's finally decided to start eating herbage) and the wonga pigeons are undoubtedly the fattest in NSW. Also tubby silvereyes, plump shrike-thrushes, rotund eastern spinebills and pinguid possums.

The possums get fatter every year. The present lot (three of them, Nijinsky, Pavlova and the Young One) occupy the pair of apple trees at the top of the garden. They used to roam all round the place but they've got too fat; which means the apple trees look like Belsen victims, all thin and tufty, and the possums sit there burping. They don't even move if you shine the torch at them now; just absentmindedly rub their stomachs as though massaging down the last few hundred apple buds.

Luckily we have forty-six apple trees, so there'll be plenty for all of us; in fact we get too many apples (and no one round here wants apples in a decent apple year), so the possums actually save us a lot of trouble. I might be harder on them if they were on the Golden Delicious or Cox's or Irish peach or Bryan's precious Macintosh (as a Macintosh computer fanatic he's extended his passion to the apples too); but as the possums are just on the Granny Smith and Jonathan, they're excused.

Gabby has lost the hair down one ear. I'm reasonably sure now it isn't mange after all – there's no sign of any beasties and we're giving her the mange dose religiously – and Chocolate's touch of mange has cleared up totally. I have a horrible feeling that she's allergic to grass or air or just to life or has just got into the habit of scratching, so scratch she does – which irritates her skin further, so she keeps scratching.

Went up to Braidwood this afternoon. The hills are still green – a green drought, not a brown one, at least till summer's heat, when the hills turn into skulls, gold grass then brown then even that goes, so they're almost bleached white and eroding. Their clear shadows stretch along the Tableland, reflecting every knob and rock.

The hills are empty now. A year ago they were dotted with cattle, mostly Herefords, brown and white. We're finally officially drought-declared – though many farmers smelled drought coming last year. More than 3,000 cattle were sold last Friday at the Braidwood cattle sale – so many that the cattle trucks were backed up along the road. Last Friday's was only one of many drought sales that are emptying the paddocks and lives and bank accounts.

('It broke my heart to sell them,' said a man in the Bank on Friday. 'But the buggers have been pushing through the fences for the last month … I've had them on the road for the past week to get some pick … I just couldn't hold onto them any longer.')

Last drought, the one that ended in '83, many of the farmers round here took their stock on the 'long paddock' – had them trucked to wetter areas and kept them moving along the roads.

('We lived in a tent,' a farmer's wife reminisced last week. 'The water we washed in went to the dogs next and when they'd finished to the horses. Our biggest luxury was Saos and cheese at morning tea. You just kept moving and looking at the sky.')

No one I've talked to will do it again. In a long drought there's finally nowhere left you can take them. The philosophy this drought seems to be: sell, then wait.

('It seems like I've been watching the sky for sixty years,' said a friend last week. 'It either dries up on you or you've got a flood. It's wearing me down too much this time. I reckon this time I've had enough. I'm selling the whole place this time. I'm going to retire.')

Droughts aren't sudden things. They creep up on you. You're lulled by the still-green grass and don't notice the lowering water table till the clay starts glaring at the edges of the dam or a day's hot spell shrinks the creek and the cooler night doesn't bring the water back.

The ground water seems to have gone much faster this drought than in the last — wells which survived for years last time are mud now. Springs that seeped till '82 last time are dry. Maybe it's because there are more people now depending on the ground water. Maybe as the land is cleared there is just less water stored in the litterless soil. I suspect we use more water now, too — nearly all houses round here have flush toilets, using enough water to keep a sheep every time they're flushed; there are more lawns and gardens … just more people living on the land.

Some people seem to know there's going to be a drought even when it's raining — the pattern of the rain is wrong. I think the roos around here knew first — they came down from the ridges last spring, even though the grass was still soft on the ridges. They haven't done that since the last drought.

Roos stop breeding in a drought. There are quite a lot of roos about a year old, peering out of the bushes or panicking as you walk past – but there aren't any bulging pouches, even though there's still a bit of feed down here. It's too early yet to tell if the wombats have done the same – you usually start to see young ones round here in late spring – but there probably won't be many.

There are wild ducks in the creek again and white-faced herons. This seems to be their drought refuge. It's been ten years since they were last here. I wonder if they have a memory of safe places or if every time it's dry they have to search for water.

Someone's suggested teaching the school kids rain dances just on the off-chance.

It begins to seem eerily like the drought and depression of the 1890s, when after every scattered fall of rain farmers would plant corn and hope to get it through to feed the horses.

My grandmother remembered how her mother bought bottles of lemonade to keep her plants alive (her husband wouldn't spare any water for the garden – so she wangled extra lemonade from the housekeeping) and clothes were stiff from washing in brown water and your bloomers chafed your legs. All you saw or heard was drought in those days.

Now you've got the unreality of TV at night – soap operas where water always comes from the tap and lawns are green and nothing depends on the weather, just the whims of the people next door. (There's much bitterness now about the proposed Welcome Reef Dam which will occupy a lot of this shire – properties and bush lost so Sydney people can keep lawns green – and locals won't get any of the water at all.)

A lot of my grandmother's stories have become funny over the years, like the one about my grandmother warning the gardener at lunch that the tank's tap was dripping, then my uncle (aged three) coming in proudly at afternoon tea, announcing: 'Well, I reckon them taps won't be dripping again' – he'd left the tap on till the tank was empty. Then there was the time he pulled up all her dahlias and dipped them in the sink 'to get their roots wet'. There were games of ping-pong and Scrabble – the winner got first bath – and my grandmother has been unbeatable at ping-pong and Scrabble ever since.

The others dipped themselves in two inches of water that got progressively thicker as the night went on. You wore a handkerchief over your nose on the way to school to block the smell of dead animals round the dam – a friend dyed her hanky blue to match her dress and the dye ran into the sweat on her face and she was stained for days, too embarrassed to go to school …

People don't seem to make jokes about droughts like they do about other human disasters. Maybe it's tempting fate.

You don't realise how used you are to seeing cattle on the hills till they're gone.

('Hell,' said a man looking at the cakes at the Braidwood Show last year. 'It'd make more sense if they had a recipe to make it rain.')

❋ *October 28*

We could see the first blush on the peaches on the way down to the school bus this morning, Edward dragging the comb we keep on the dashboard through his hair and checking his shoes for goosedung, me hoping I didn't have to get out of the car so no-one would see my purple socks. (Not that there's anything wrong with purple socks, but my skirt is red and green and they don't match.) The new paddocks are full of little green dots – capsicums. I had wondered what they were as we drove past last week – they were too small and too late for new peach trees.

Back at the house the scent of magnolia hit me like a wave – evergreen magnolia, the tiny purple flowers hidden in the dark green leaves, but the scent is overwhelming. It's a good time of year for scents: the hot breath of curry bush just starting to waft down from the terraces (on a mid-summer day it's so strong and tempting it's often sent me up to Braidwood for fixings for beef vindaloo); roses of course, fifty different scents (each rose has its own perfume, all different, sweet, citrussy or fruity, not just the whiff of Woolies' perfume-counter bath salts smell); and of course the orange blossom.

Why have we forgotten orange blossom? Middle Eastern countries of course still celebrate it. Even our culture used to strew it in front of brides, scent cakes with orange-flower water, rinse linen in it, mix it in perfumes. It's the most exquisite scent.

I try to remember to keep some of it, just squashing the flowers down in a jar and topping them up with vodka (you can use brandy but then you get the brandy flavour too). One day I might even get my own distillery but till then there's always Orange Blossom Jam.

ORANGE BLOSSOM JAM

You can use this recipe with any fragrant flowers – roses (strong stinky ones), dianthus for a clove scent (good with cold meat and especially with hot turkey), primrose flowers or violets and any of the citrus – but orange blossom is my favourite.

2 KILOGRAMS APPLES (DIFFERENT
APPLES GIVE DIFFERENT FLAVOURS,
BUT ALL ARE GOOD)

2 LITRES WATER

2 KILOGRAMS WHITE SUGAR

8 CUPS ORANGE BLOSSOM (FAIRLY
WELL PACKED DOWN)

Chop the apples. Don't core or peel. Simmer in the water till soft, add the sugar and simmer another 10 minutes, stirring well so the sugar dissolves. Cool, then strain into a pan. For straining, I use a sieve lined with an old clean tea towel. You need to make sure as much of the pulp is strained away as possible.

Add the flowers to the liquid in the pan and simmer for 10 minutes. Cool again, strain again, then simmer till a little just sets in cold water. Bottle and seal.

This jam should be pale green or pale pink – depending on whether you used red or green skinned

apples – with the most gentle fragrance you can
imagine. Too good to bruise the scent with bread – just
spoon it up by itself, or eat it with cream on scones or
pikelets – cream buffers the fragrance from the coarser
smell of flour.

One annoyed wombat on the back doormat –
Chocolate. He hasn't had any carrots or wombat biscuits
for three days, mostly because he hasn't come out till
midnight, by which time we're asleep – or trying to be,
amid the *geek geek geek* and tearing up of cardboard boxes
and other ways wombats have of attracting your attention.
I sprinkled some wombat biscuits under the grape vine
and he almost ran me over to eat them.

Gabby joined him. Chocolate still doesn't object to
Gabby – maybe she doesn't put out the right signals to say
she's a wombat. She shared the biscuits then went to sleep
in the herb bed. I'll have to wake her up when the sun
comes over the ridge. You can't rely on Gabby to wake up
to save her life.

❊ *November 1*

The sky was thick as mushroom soup this afternoon, the
thunder rolling like a helicopter up the gorge. But the clouds
had purple knees, not green – not hail clouds, thank heavens.
The crop's still safe. Hail at this stage would be disaster.

'Look, those peaches are red already. When will the shed
be open?' demanded Edward.

'In a few weeks. Maybe,' I say.

❋ *November 2*

Edward came home distressed about conversations at school – farmers' sons talking about roo hunts.

'But why do you kill them?' asked Edward.

'Because they eat the grass.' As though that explained it all.

'Cattle eat grass too,' said Edward.

'But we're not farming bloody roos!' and the kids laughed, as though it was self evident.

Wildlife is a luxury that farmers decide they can't afford in droughts; why should they bear the cost of city sentimentality? (They do have a point – there need to be land tax rebates to repay farmers for any wildlife sanctuaries they support.)

'Joey's dad's young oats were all eaten by wood ducks,' Edward said. 'They woke up one morning and the whole paddock had been eaten to the soil.'

Not that killing roos or wood ducks will make a difference in the long run – there's not enough grass for stock or wildlife, and if the drought goes on too long both will probably die.

The peaches are in full leaf now; they'll never look this good again – they get tatty after peach picking and droop into autumn.

❋ *November 3*

Chocolate had his nose in my shoes when I came out tonight, as though to say: I can smell her, she must be here somewhere. I put them on and he was most disconcerted – as I would be, if someone somehow came apart and joined themselves together again.

※ *November 4*

'They're out again,' announced Bryan, and they were ... millions of flying termites fluttering through the darkness. I have to keep emptying my underwear – a wingless ant wriggling across your nipple is a feeling that is hard to describe. Once they've flown they drop their wings and wriggle to a hiding place, like in my bra or under the table (wingless termites in the bed aren't so crash-hot either), and next morning the floor is thick with wings, so every breeze gusts them into small grey eddies.

Flying termites usually means rain, but the sky is still clear, stars so near you could almost touch them (maybe I can but am just too lazy to reach up). I've decided that birds and insects can foretell rain; but only about as well as we can.

(Any other year I too would have thought this heat was building up to rain; but I just don't believe in rain any more.)

The grass on the hill looks like dry matches that have been stuck among the rocks. Not a single cloud today or yesterday or the day before.

(And the bastard of a taxi driver last week in Sydney had the hide to say: 'Couldn't be better weather we've been having, could it?')

※ *November 7*

The ants were right. So were the lizards, rolling and tearing at each other as they often do before a change – and the birds and bull ants ...

It's been raining for three days. Two days of gentle moistness, just enough moisture to thicken the air and send green shoots above the brown; then a day and a night of real rain, solid and steady, so the creek is washing through the rocks again and the trees look like they've been washed – which they have. You forget how much dust coats everything till it's gone.

The tree fern at the gate put out seven inches of new frond last night.

It's not a drought breaker but it'll keep us going for a while. At least it might stop the lyrebirds ripping up the garden.

You could almost see the peaches swell this morning.

❋ *November 8*

Today we harvested our cherry crop, all six of them, which is a hundred per cent improvement on last year, when we got three. (I'm not sure how many the birds got.)

Possums like cherries too; perhaps our possums are getting short-sighted – or just too stuffed – to have ignored this lot.

Room-temperature cherries taste quite different from chilled cherries, and sun-warmed cherries taste different too; and of course there are the different cherry varieties, though I have to admit that for me the bigger and blacker and squishier the better.

I can never bear to cook with cherries when they're in season. It's only later, in winter, that I get cravings for cherry jam and cherry strudel and cherry clafouti. I just don't have the strength of will to preserve them in their season – all I get my hands on are eaten. A preserved cherry is only a memory of a cherry, anyway, a reminder of the delights of last year and pleasures to come – unlike apricots and plums, which turn into something quite different when they are preserved.

I offered a pitted cherry to Gabby just to see what she'd do but she ignored it and sat waiting for her carrot, which just adds to my opinion of her intelligence. The mange/eczema is looking better – the new cream did soothe it – in fact there's hair growing on all the bald patches, so she's piebald and looks ridiculous, especially when she's stretched out on the paving eating carrots, toes stretched fore and aft, looking like a doormat someone has shaved by accident. I suppose she likes the warmth on her stomach.

Every other wombat is down its burrow during the day now the weather's hotter but Gabby still comes out at lunchtime, and if she suffers mild heat exhaustion maybe she doesn't notice in the general confusion of her mind.

It's easy to laugh, but I think Gabby may be a real tragedy. She's domesticated, but not really a domestic animal, her life lacking the subtle wombat pleasures, so she really is just the shell of a wombat, no matter how lovable; the joys of soft damp earth and the smell of dusk when the grass is sweetest with the dew, the pleasures of patrolling a territory and leaving your mark, are lost to her. (Gabby leaves her dung in a pile outside the powerhouse door or on the garden steps – somewhere we have to notice it – they're messages left for us, not other wombats.)

'When will the peaches be ready?' asks Edward, bouncing in excitement.

'Soon. Next week. Maybe,' I say.

BONED CHICKEN WITH PEACHES OR CHERRIES

This is my quintessential dinner-party/picnic/guests-to-impress-for-luncheon dish. If you've ever had it at my place you know I'm trying to impress you or I like you or I'm just feeling gluttonous. It's one of my favourite foods but too fiddly to bother cooking it for myself – which is a mistake. Wasn't it Norman Douglas who said 'Nothing is too good for every day?' And he's right – life is far too short to be grudging with pleasures …

To get back to the stuffed chook. It looks impressive; it tastes impressive; it can be made at least three days beforehand; it slices well (but should be carried unsliced to a picnic).

Serve it on cold days with spuds sliced in a baking dish and covered with cream and *slowly* cooked till thoroughly brown on top; eat it on hot days with excellent brown bread and a salad of chopped beetroot (not the canned stuff), peeled orange segments, walnuts and mesclun lettuce and an orange vinaigrette (1 part orange juice to 2 parts olive oil; salt and garlic to taste; and a good dollop of French mustard).

Depending on how thinly you carve it and how substantial the accompaniments are, one stuffed chook feeds four gluttonous or ten abstemious people.

Use a home-grown, happy-lifed chook if possible. Each battery chook you consume probably sets your karma back two millennia.

1.8 KILOGRAM CHICKEN
(I.E. LARGISH)

1 ONION, CHOPPED

2 TABLESPOONS BUTTER

4 CLOVES GARLIC, CRUSHED

1 CUP BREADCRUMBS, PREFERABLY
HOME-CRUMBLED FROM GOOD
WHITE BREAD (BUT WE CAN'T HAVE
EVERYTHING, CAN WE?)

JUICE 1 LEMON

2 TABLESPOONS CHOPPED
PISTACHIO NUTS

6 LEAVES SILVERBEET, DIPPED IN
BOILING WATER FOR 10 SECONDS
THEN THEIR STEMS CUT OUT

1 CUP PITTED FRESH CHERRIES
(*or* 1 CUP CHOPPED DRIED PEACHES,
COVERED WITH BOILING WATER
FOR AN HOUR THEN DRAINED)

Bone the chicken by placing it breast-side down and cut the skin along the backbone. Gently squeeze the flesh each side of the chicken till you get to the legs and wings. Cut off wing tips; slice the outer edges of wings and legs and peel their flesh back; now proceed to peel the flesh down to the breastbone on both sides. You now have a messy flap of chicken. Fold the thighs and wings back into the chook. Set aside while you preheat the oven to 200°C and prepare the stuffing.

To make the stuffing, sauté the onion in the butter till tender. Add garlic and stir for 10 seconds. Add crumbs, lemon juice and pistachios. Mix well.

Place the chook in a greased roasting pan. Layer the silverbeet leaves over the chook. Top with an evenish layer of stuffing. Cover with peaches or cherries. Bring both sides of the chook up to the middle and tie with string every few inches.

Leave the chook stuffing-edge upwards and roast for 1 hour, basting with its own fat at least twice.

Turn it over and cook for another 30 minutes to brown the other side.

Wrap in foil till cool.

❋ November 9

I walked up to the Dragon Pool with Edward this afternoon. The sun is high enough now to reach between the cliffs, so the clamminess of winter has disappeared and the gorge is full of dapples.

There is a place there, a flat stone among the maidenhair under the backhousia trees, where I go to sit and think, or not to think really, just to absorb. It's just up from the cascades, smooth rock and smoother water which is a special place for Edward; memories of years of tobogganing down the waterslide, into the deep round pool under the native figs – the rock is slippery with waterweed and ten thousand years of floods, and you can slide for hours till your bum gets raw.

I don't know if the cascades mean more to Edward than that – special places aren't things you talk about, especially to your parents.

When I was a child I had a place I dreamed about, especially during maths lessons or on the way to school. It was a headland rising from the beach, half cut off from the land, carpet green beneath the wind. The sea around was purple blue, as though it sucked the colour from the sky. The rocks below were very black. As you walked closer you could see rabbit tracks in crossword puzzles up the slope. Wallabies blinked from salty bushes.

You had to walk to it. It seemed a long way when I was a child. My mother lugged the basket with towels and sandwiches and my brother and I rolled the watermelon over the sandhills. It should have been easy to roll it down, but it wasn't. It kept on burying its head in the sand.

There seemed to be miles of sandhills, all held by spider webs of grass. We'd heave the melon up one slope and kick it down the next. As far as I remember it never shattered; there were no rocks till you reached the tiny beach hidden in the elbow of the headland.

It was a very small beach for Queensland – a sharp sickle. The sand was very white and there was never the debris of shells and seaweed like other beaches had in a series of ripples from successive high tides. I suppose the headland sheltered it. There was no surf either, just dandruffy ripples that my younger brothers and sister battered their bums against while I climbed the headland.

It was the first natural area I ever explored by myself, probably because the entrance was so narrow. If bodgies or bikies arrived I suppose my mother could have barricaded the entrance with driftwood, Horatius like, wielding the watermelon rinds or slapping the intruders with sandy towels till I came down. It wasn't likely though. There was nothing there that would tempt anyone who didn't love the place, as we did.

I've never felt as free as I did on that headland, not even in the early years here, without house or family, wandering with a hat, hot feet and not much else from rock to rock; but even then I knew that place was mine (or I was its) and the responsibility to keep it safe was always lurking.

Back in my childhood there was only the balloon of the sky above, the wind and the sand, the seagulls, and the white tongues of the sea below, curling into the black rocks. If you kept your back to the land there was nothing landbased at all; even if you turned round there was nothing human to be seen. Even our picnic was hidden by the bulk of grass.

I went back there six years ago. I'd told my friend to expect a sacred place. Of course it wasn't.

The sandhills had been levelled by mining. You could park right above the bay, opposite a shop that sold fish and chips and magazines and black bananas. There was broken glass where we'd eaten our watermelon and tepid corned-beef sandwiches and my brother had lost a tooth in the white sand (and we couldn't find it, white on white, and he howled because the tooth fairy mightn't come, and we couldn't reassure him without spilling the beans that the fairy didn't exist). The sand was wrinkled and grey; another residue of mining. Even the rocks no longer looked as black.

We climbed the headland among the chip cartons and beer cans. There were black scars from fresh bonfires and eroded bald patches from older ones.

I tried to pretend the sea was still the same, but I'd changed too. Oil slicks and sewerage outlets and algae blooms had made us both lose our innocence.

I suppose everyone has a sacred place, one they had in

childhood that seemed magic; one that was associated with happiness, kept sentimentally in memory. I wonder how many sacred places survive a lifetime. I remember my mother taking me to one of hers, on Lake Macquarie, once bush (there was a hollow tree, she told me, big enough to climb into). It was holiday houses and bitumen now and I was incredulous: how could anyone possibly have felt anything there?

I don't suppose urban special spots are any safer. Familiar skylines change. Even if they stay they're invaded by more cars and more people every year. The feeling changes even if the skeleton remains. My grandmother's spot, I think, was lunch at David Jones – damask tablecloths and napkins, silver tongs and potatoes baked to snakeskin crispness under shining domes and silver sauceboat gravy – that's what a day's shopping in town was all about. They've got a cafeteria there now.

The Araluen Valley has been a magic place for at least two people I've met in the past few years. One was a taxi driver I met in Sydney. He was wounded in New Guinea in World War Two, among the mud and sweat and jungle, and woke up in hospital to see a watercolour on the wall opposite his bed. It showed a green valley with blue hills and a single tree. He asked the nurse where it was, and she turned it over, and it said 'Araluen Valley, NSW'.

He reckoned it saved his life. All he had to do was live, and he'd get back there … and so he did live, and bought his wife to see the place after they were married, and then his kids. He reckoned he might bring his grandkids here soon too. They'll stay down at the pub with Stan and Margaret, and they'll fossick in the river …

The other was a woman in her eighties in Victoria. She wrote to me last year after reading a review of one of my books. It mentioned that I lived in Araluen. She'd lived here as a child, and the place has lived in her memory ever since. She wanted to hear about the valley. Had it changed? Did the casuarinas still grow along the river? Were the cliffs still silver when it rained? In her last letter she said that she has been privileged, in her last years, to be able to send her love back to where it began.

The valley may have been a special spot even before white settlement: it was certainly a place of feasting and ceremonial battles, and variously referred to as the valley of peace, place of waterlilies, place of running water. I suppose it was all three.

Like many 'sacred places' – some far more threatened than here – the valley's place in people's hearts has lasted for so many generations, black and white, that it's frightening to think that this generation might be the crucial one, the one that destroys it. There are so many things that threaten even 'safe' areas now – mining or clearing upstream, overgrazing, fire.

I know fire is supposed to be natural to the bush. It isn't here, not at this end of the valley anyway. There's no sign there's been a major fire in the lifetime of the trees, though there are scars on the ridges above. It's probably been too wet to burn. But in the past fifty years so much land has been cleared upstream that the ground no longer carries the moisture it used to.

The springs run dry quicker, the moist air of the gorge gets drier every year. It was tree ferns and backhousia forest once, but when the remaining pockets are destroyed they don't come back again. If a fire came through now the gorge wouldn't recover, and the surviving wildlife – many of which have disappeared from the more populated bush above – would go as well.

The fire would almost certainly be man-made too; most likely from the State Forest's regular 'accidents'. We've eaten smoke here for the last month, from Forestry 'cool burns' that turned to roman candles in the sky, leaving the land as black and dead as any bushfire. Fire could come from a picnicker's campfire, a farmer's burning off, a trail-bike's exhaust, from an empty hearted arsonist. Only a very tiny proportion of fires are caused by lightning.

Maybe it's safer not to have a sacred spot now, unless it's a church. Churches are man-made and relatively safe. We accept man-made things as sacred. The rest are expendable, easily lost for temporary jobs or profit, or simply from carelessness, worn out before we notice.

Perhaps I'm wrong to encourage Edward to love the valley. Maybe banks or ballot boxes are safer love objects. Maybe I should teach him to love a TV screen or admire the evenness of a stretch of asphalt instead. Though I won't.

We may be one of the last generations to know many of the sacred spots of the world. It's too soon to turn our backs on sites in bitterness at their potential loss. And I will continue to take Edward up the gorge.

❋ *November 11*

Gabby's skin is suddenly worse, although the hair is growing back. She's thinner too – a sharp ridge along her back and the ribs prominent under her fur. The flies are annoying her; the vet is stumped; even cortisone doesn't seem to help.

She spends some of her day in the wombat hole, but most is spent under the truck to be near to Bryan in the shed, or asleep among the wattle bark in the wood shed. At other times she's sniffing round the flat trying to find a trace of human scent, till the exhaustion of daylight overtakes her and she falls asleep where she is, often in the middle of the road, and nearly always in full sunlight – so we have to search for her every quarter of an hour, and take her into the shade.

I think the world frightens her. It's so much bigger than the kitchen where she grew up. She ignores the other wombats, even the most recent droppings. And, while she eats a little grass, her staple diet is still rolled oats and carrots, wombat nuts and Womba-roo, fed to her in the old shampoo bottle twice a day. She is really too old now to be handfed, but every time I've stopped it she has got thinner – even hunger won't tempt her to a diet of mostly grass, though at least she's munching it for part of the night.

✳ *November 12*

The kiwi fruit are flowering – fat-fleshed, white petals that turn yellow with age, then drop off into greasy heaps on the paving. There are millions of them and there'll be millions of the fruit too. But luckily the bowerbirds and the honeyeaters and the silvereyes and red-browed finches will eat most of them, and the ground below will be sodden again, with fruit instead of blossom. We never have to worry about getting rid of the harvest, we just watch the birds' acrobatic displays as they turn upside-down to poke their beaks into the juiciest end of the fruit.

No sign of Gabby all day. I'd assume any other wombat had wandered off, investigating other holes. But not Gabby. I'm worried.

❉ November 13

No sign of Gabby. I called at the entrance to her hole, and banged the rock at the entrance and stamped my feet so she might hear the vibration in the ground. We searched the flat and the road, but no sleeping wombat.

I feel guilty, though I'm not sure why ' – for being human perhaps, of the race that killed her mother, so even with all our best intentions, best attempts, we couldn't make it up to her.

I'm speaking as though Gabby is dead. I think she is, though I won't admit it to Edward yet. He's used to wombats wandering off, for food and sex and territory (and maybe the wombat equivalent of adventuring too). I'd rather he thought she's gone adventuring than died.

❉ November 15

Maggots crawling from the hole behind the bathroom; conclusive enough. Edward ran to tell me and of course he is less upset than I am. He's grown up with much more life and death than I saw in the suburbs of my childhood.

'Can we look after a kangaroo this time?' he asked, pouring more salad dressing on his asparagus. 'Like Fuchsia. Remember how she and I used to race?'

✳ *November 16*

The first day of real heat; the sort of heat that sucks the moisture from the air and the water from the creek and even the leaves seem to pant, and the ants stay deep underground. We sat on a rock at lunchtime and watched the waterline shrink back between the rocks. The water seems to get darker as it retreats, almost as though it has thickened. You'd think the creek would get lighter as it grew shallower.

I remembered how I'd tried to get Gabby to drink from the creek; but she wouldn't drink. She just kept walking into the water as though she couldn't work out what was happening and thought if she kept going she might get away from it, so I'd had to race in, jeans and all, and lift her out before she drowned. She drank from the bowl by the kitchen instead (attached to a thick piece of wood to stop her shoving the bowl over). I miss her terribly; and the sense of guilt remains.

✳ *November 17*

Peaches. Finally. We called in at the shed this afternoon on our way home from the bus. Edward got the first, crunching into it as I drove up the road; I restrained myself till I got to the kitchen; the whole car smelled of peach.

It's hard to describe the first taste of peach every year. You forget it till the sweetness hits you – infinitely soft, entirely juicy, succulent green flesh that bruises as soon as you touch it, so you have to eat it, you really have to – it's no good keeping it for later.

The first peaches are tiny things. They're packed like fragile china. No, that's an understatement – china is much more robust than an early peach. The later ones are tougher, firmer and those later firmer and meatier yet.

Sometimes I think it's a mistake to get the first peaches of the season in a box – almost excessive. The first peach should probably be plucked and savoured – but a boxful is impossible to resist.

Noel's shed is the first in the valley to open – still pristine and tidied from last year, the concrete swept, the grass mown, 10,000 virgin boxes piled to the ceiling. There are neat trays of firsts and boxes of seconds out the front to tempt the passing trade – except it rained this weekend, so there weren't any cars, just Bev and Bess discussing picking times and rosters. Neither knew how much the trays were; whoever was in charge was down the back; but Bess knew how much the seconds were, and that's what we wanted anyway.

Seconds are the peaches slightly too ripe to get to market, split peaches, double peaches, ones with just a faint small bruise or those that are too small or too big to fit in the trays. They're usually excellent, often picked slightly too late so even sweeter than the firsts. The overripeness doesn't matter as long as they're going to be hauled straight home or eaten on the way.

The rejects sit in giant boxes down the back – really squashy ones and very split ones; and on hot days the scent of fermenting peach reaches down to the road. It would be a fruit-fly's paradise, if any had survived the spraying.

Edward took one look at the boxes of seconds – dull red and shiny – then fixed his gaze on the nearest box of fine fat firsts and didn't take it off it till he'd got back into the car.

The wind is sweeping cold and leafy through the shed door, tossing bits of bark onto the sign (in French) 'In summer it's a sin not to eat a peach'. Ned picked it up on his tour of Europe a few years ago. It is a little incongruous buying peaches with our jumpers clutched round us. Bev and Bess duck further round, out of the wind.

'Can I eat one now?' and Edward sighs ecstatically at the first bite of peach, the biggest and the reddest. He fell in love with it five minutes ago and has guarded it ever since in case someone else got it first.

He eats another three on the ten-minute drive home and another dozen (at least) during the day; but it doesn't matter – his digestion has evolved with peaches, it'd take a solid peach diet to make him sick. By mid-afternoon he'd experimented sucking the smooth red skin (Wisbey's bought a polisher to get rid of the fuzz a few years ago) to make a juice bubble, then sucking it gently to make it burst, peeling it gently with his tongue so the flesh is smooth before he even tastes it; chilling them first so it's both cold and sweet on his tongue.

The front lawn is dotted with peach stones; the chooks' bucket is full of peach skin; Bryan has taken three of the best (he spends minutes poring over them too) down to the shed to eat while he makes a new nozzle for the fountain; the kitchen smells of rotting peach from the box on the kitchen table, right where I put the mail the rest of the year (I'll have to find another spot now).

Our peaches won't be ready for at least a week – they're earlier down the valley where they get more light. The first home-grown peach of the season is, of course, for eating warm from the sun, right under the tree, where you've discovered it before the birds have, the next peach is one you've taken inside, one of a handful grown cold on the dining table; you eat that peeled, on a plate, slice by slice and lick up the drips.

By the hundredth peach you're looking for variety. Peach season has begun.

PEACHES IN CHAMPAGNE

'Tis is an idea rather than a recipe. Some people complicate it with a few drops of Cointreau or Curacao or brandy; but this is a pity, and necessary only if you don't have very good champagne and perfect peaches — peaches ripened on the tree and so strongly scented your hands smell of peach after you've peeled them — and without either there's really not much point to the recipe.

Slice your peaches — firm and yellow, soft and white, or green with that sort of sugary stringiness — it doesn't matter, all are good, though the results will of course differ. Just as it doesn't matter if you use sweet or dry champagne — whatever is your pleasure.

Just be sure that the champagne is poured as soon as you slice the peaches; and that it's drunk as soon as it is poured; and that the slices are fished out (with your fingers) still with the last of the bubbles on them and slipped between your lips.

EARLY PEACH JAM

Peach jam is a temperamental thing at any time — it moulds and runs and ferments in a few weeks, or months at the very best, which is no loss as peach jam loses its scent in a matter of weeks. Peach jam is a luxury to be spread in summer, not hoarded in a dark larder for winter; an exquisite gift for Christmas to be gluttonised before New Year.

Early Peach Jam is perhaps the hardest to get right – later meatier peaches are much easier to jam. But it is definitely worth it.

2 CUPS SUGAR

2 CUPS WATER

JUICE OF 2 LARGE LEMONS
or 4 LIMES

SUFFICIENT PEACHES TO GIVE
4 CUPS PEELED SLICED PEACH FLESH
(DON'T SLICE THEM YET!)

Boil the sugar and water and lemon or lime juice together for 10 minutes before you peel the peaches.

Slip the sliced peaches into the bubbles. Now stir it gently, just enough to break up the fruit and let the juice combine with the syrup. The jam will suddenly get much more liquid as the juice explodes into the pan. Keep stirring, test often; as soon as a little sets in a saucer of cold water, pull the jam off the stove and bottle it – in small jars, so you can eat the lot in one sitting. (A large jar is certain to go off before you feed on it – unless you have a lot of guests for breakfast.) Keep the jars cool and sealed till you need them.

This jam is incredible with cream.

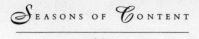

THE GINGER VARIATION

If you want a sort of breakfasty peach jam — I am more a pikelet or scone and jam person, and believe good jam is wasted on the coarseness of toast (but Bryan disagrees) — add half a teaspoon of peeled grated fresh ginger and cook it with the water and sugar syrup. Make sure it is as finely chopped as possible. This will give you a sort of ginger peach marmalade; the perfect summer marmalade, sweet and sour and spicy.

SUMMER

❋ *November 18*

Summer begins with peaches, no matter what the calendar may say, a sky hazed with heat and the cry of cicadas so omnipresent you no longer hear them.

Picked the first gooseberries today; but gooseberries aren't interesting if you've got cherries and peaches and the last of the navel oranges. They're tough and tart, but beautifully bulging – for decoration rather than eating. Not bad with cream.

The first strawberry is different – sweet as sunlight, hot on the skywards side and cold near the soil. No other berry will taste as good for the whole season.

I don't know what variety this strawberry is. I bought a yellow alpine strawberry three years ago, but this grew instead. It's not alpine and it's certainly not yellow – it's pointed, succulent and bears only for a few weeks in early summer, and it's spread all over what was once the lower vegie garden but it's too good to pull out even if we don't get many berries. A chance seedling I suppose, as yellow alpines are grown from seed, some wonderful mutation. I'm glad it's ended up here, with a good home where it's appreciated.

I used to grow carpets of strawberries; then the wallabies discovered that strawberry leaves taste good. (Wallabies are true gourmets, ever experimental. They like pungency and tang. I could never imagine a black-tailed wallaby eating anything from McDonald's, though they might lick the salt off a chip or two.)

So now we only get a few berries; which is okay, as red-bellied black snakes adore strawberry beds, and your back aches after ten minutes' picking and your face burns with the reflected heat of the soil.

Luckily Giles grows them commercially up at Jembaicumbene – pungent, sweet, biodynamic strawberries. Even his everyday Toigas and Red Gauntlets taste good. So we buy them from him, or more often barter, as they can't grow avocados or oranges and we usually have a cauliflower surplus in spring too, when their garden is still shrugging off the frost.

There was a wind last night – a long, far off wind, moaning up the gorge and gusting as soon as it hit wider land. The grass is now pink with fallen rose petals and the terrace waxy with kiwi-fruit flowers – great fat petals that stick to your feet and decompose into sludge. At least leaves dry and blow away.

There were fallen peaches between the trees when we drove down this morning, bright red against the clover or herbicided brown. We felt like leaping through the fence and rescuing them, though what we'd do with all those peaches I don't know – I suppose the geese might like them. But Jason was spraying the trees with fungicide – a dense and deadly cloud of white, so we didn't. Anyway, our first tree will be ripe in a week or so and we'll be giving the things away.

※ *November 20*

More rain, heavy drops clanking on the roof just before the moon rose as I was getting Edward to bed. The moon was smoky behind the cloud, the ridges dressed in yellow fog. I went outside to check for hail but the drops were just water, cold and splodgy on my neck, and Chocolate wombat smelly wet and squeaking behind the powerhouse.

The creek had freshened this morning; gushing where it had trickled, currents instead of stillness. Probably not a good day for the first swim of the season.

'You first,' I said to Bryan.

'No, you,' he said politely.

So I slid down the rock, linen smooth after centuries of water, and the first shock of coldness froze my genitals and nipples, an instant so painful it sent me lunging for the closest rock to clamber out, but by the time I'd got there I was numb instead.

The second plunge is easier. Your body expects torture then, and so the water feels infinitely warmer in contrast. I swam for about a minute, then lay on the rock.

The granite here drinks in the heat, and holds it, and fills you up with it if you lie on it; but you have to be naked for it to work. You feel like you're glowing for hours afterwards. Possibly I am – granite is radioactive. How much radioactivity is present down here in the valley I really don't want to know. I'm not moving, no matter how bad it is – and I'm sure the stress of worrying about it would be worse than the effect of the radioactivity.

Bryan's testicles were frozen small and hard again, just as they'd started to droop for summer. They're still semi-frozen now, hours later, as I write. The creek packs a solid wallop.

AN INFALLIBLE ROSE LOVE-POTION

(Otherwise known as Rose Mulled Wine.)

Pick three rosebuds (if any roses have survived the rain) – red, pink and white. Wear them over your heart for three days (you can take them off at night). Then toss them in claret. Add honeysuckle flowers, a few borage flowers, lots of clove scented (and tasting) carnation petals, sliced lemon and a few sprigs of lavender. (Don't worry if you can't get all the flowers in this recipe – just use as many as you can. The roses are the essential ingredient.)

Add a little brown sugar or honey for a (perhaps) mild aphrodisiac effect. Steep for another three days. Heat or chill, according to taste.

*Don't be tempted to add cinnamon or other spices –
this is a subtle and very lovely drink, and spices coarsen it.*

*Don't use yellow roses – they're the symbol of infidelity.
(If you want to tell if your lover has been unfaithful get
him or her to wear a red rose over the heart, then dip the
rose in a river. If the rose turns yellow, he or she has been
unfaithful. If the rose stays red, stop worrying.)*

*Honeysuckle used to be known as 'woodbine' or
'love's bind'. A few honeysuckle flowers on the dresser
are supposed to bring erotic dreams. Carnations were
reputed to spring from the graves of lovers.*

.... ✿ ....

MEDIEVAL KISSING SWEETS

(Also known as Sugared Rose Petals.)

*Take perfumed petals, cut off the white base (it's bitter).
Dip in beaten egg white, then in caster sugar. Leave to
dry in the sun or a very, very slow oven. Store in a
sealed jar – but they don't keep long.*

*Note: If you have any powdered ambergris handy,
mix it with the sugar. There is a shortage of sperm
whales (and their ambergris) in the swimming hole, so
I've never tried it.*

.... ✿ ....

❋ *November 21*

The corn is aiming for Jupiter, with stalks as fat as my
wrist, and the silverbeet is growing crinkly. The tomatoes
are almost ripe, which is probably how they'll stay for the

next month – *almost* getting there, then sulking till January and strong sunlight. But at least I can dream we may get one next week.

Picked the first tiny carrots today (in gumboots – there's a red-bellied black snake in the vegie garden). They're the size of my little finger and as sweet as sugar and almost as tasteless. Even the wallabies don't bother with them now. Young carrots are best left whole and stewed in chicken stock with lots of chopped parsley, to give them some bite.

❊ *November 22*

Edward was bubbling with bad news when I picked him up from the school bus – hail destroyed the Harrisons' peach crop last night. A narrow swathe across the valley, missing our place and Wisbey's, heavy enough to break branches from the trees and leave the leaves in tatters. (All I saw were bruised clouds down our valley.)

The Harrisons have lost $100,000 worth of peaches, states Edward, though how accurate that is I don't know. But it's a tragedy nonetheless – the long winter of pruning and mowing and feeding, the spring of thinning and spraying, and now an empty harvest. Bare trees and a bare year till next year.

They are kind people, the Harrisons. I remember when our black sheep Dunmore used to traipse down to their place every time the ewes were in season – he'd been castrated but he hadn't noticed – and every time they'd catch him and call me and I'd lure him into the truck with a couple of Milk Arrowroot biscuits. (He loved Milk

Arrowroots.) And they insisted we use their shearing shed gratis too …

It's sad the world can't be kind to them as well. But there's no malice in a storm or a drought or a fire and I hope that they can survive this too.

❊ *November 23*

Saw the first brown snake today, pink as the granite, winding its way around the rocks by the cliff. I jumped back and it glanced at me, neck up, obviously annoyed. It was hungry, not long out of hibernation and I was disturbing it. So I tiptoed away, and let it get back to hunting lizards.

There are a few mulberries on the tree. Edward, his friend Lucas, and the birds have got the rest of them so far. Edward and Lucas climbed the tree after swimming in the creek, and raced up here blue and naked. The mulberries turned them even bluer, like ancient Britons preparing for battle.

So I made Mulberry Crush with the remnants.

MULBERRY CRUSH

It's almost as good as real iceblocks, says Edward.
It works with other berries too. It's fantastic with
slightly green frozen mango – yes I know it sounds
horrid, but try it. Mango is one of the few fruits we
can't grow here. Ditto pineapple.

*Freeze the mulberries whole. For every cup of berries
take half a cup of caster sugar and the juice of a lemon.
Simmer the lemon juice and sugar for 10 minutes in*

*half a cup of water. Freeze the syrup, then bung it and
the frozen berries in the blender and whacko …*

.... ✢ ....

✳ *November 24*

Sue is back from shearing again. The phone rings at
9 a.m. – just time for her to get her breath after getting the
boys to the bus.

'You home, love? I'll be down for a cuppa in an hour
then.'

Sue is thinner – too thin – and browner. Being a shearers'
cook is hard work. 'But the men are darlings. Everyone says
all shearers are awful but they're really pussycats when you
get to know them. Most are young – just like kids. They've
got nothing to do but look at sheep's bums all day – and
they think any mucking-up's the greatest fun.

'I made them a lamb and onion pie last Monday, and I
put bay leaves in it, and one of the blokes called out to me:
"Hey, Cookie, what's this? You trying to make koalas out of
us?" He was holding up the bay leaves. He thought I'd put
gum leaves in their dinner.

'Then it rained Wednesday, so they had the Thursday off,
and they decided they'd go yabbying in one of the great
dams on the place. So they came and asked me for some old
meat, and they came back that afternoon with a whole great
sack of yabbies. They cleaned them and cooked them, and I
made sauces. I'd already cooked the dinner but I put away as
much of it as I could to eat cold the next day. Someone had
gone in to town for beer and we sat outside and drank cold
beer and ate fresh yabbies, and it was wonderful.

'You can really stretch out there,' says Sue. She looks out the window as though the walls of the valley are just too close.

* *November 25*

Bess Wisbey brought her grand-daughter Tammy down to the school bus stop this morning. Tammy's mother is down at the packing shed. They start work now in the cool of the morning, and will keep going till it's dark.

Bess was seventy this year, but you wouldn't guess it – as the song says she might very well pass for forty-three in the dusk with the light behind her (or when she's working in the packing shed). The whole family has been hard at it the last two weeks with the first of the peaches in, but the main body of pickers are still at uni or high school – it'll be another fortnight or so before the valley fills up with this year's mob of workers.

Meanwhile Noel's first crop is picked and packed and sold, and Rod's is coming on. Bess looked at the sky and sighed at the heat haze already over the valley. If we have a week of cool weather Noel's next lot of peaches will be delayed and there'll be a bit of a break for everyone. But we probably won't.

Bess is going up to Sydney for four days to see her grand-daughters in a concert and she wants Ned to go too. He says he's too busy, what with the sheds and his garden. Bess thinks both would survive for four days without him. He'll say he missed her when she gets back and she'll feel guilty. She's still working on him, she says. He might change his mind by Monday.

The swimming hole felt glorious for the first time today — liquid silk slowly spreading over your skin as you slide in. (The rock slide is a wonderful, gradual one; it takes twelve seconds to slowly submerge.)

PEACH SORBET

You need pale greeny white peaches for this. It can be made with yellow ones at a pinch, but it won't be as delicate.

10 WHITE PEACHES

2 TABLESPOONS WATER

JUICE OF TWO LIMES (*or* SMALL LEMONS IF LIMES ARE IMPOSSIBLE)

4 EGG WHITES

4 TABLESPOONS CASTER SUGAR

Peel the peaches and mash the flesh well — it should be soft and squashy and easy to mash — then add the water and juice.

Whip the egg whites till stiff, beat in the caster sugar till it's shiny, then add the peach mixture. Blend in lightly, place in a covered dish in the freezer and stir three times while freezing.

Serve just — or even not quite — set. If it sets too hard, melt it a little before you serve it.

Like most sorbets, this'll stay edible for years in the freezer; but you'll lose the fragrance after a day or two.

A few sun-warm strawberries go well with it too; dip them in and suck them.

GRILLED PEACHES

Very quick – a good appetiser or accompaniment to grilled or cold meat.

4 FIRM YELLOW PEACHES (THEY MUST BE RIPE AND FRAGRANT)

4 TEASPOONS BROWN SUGAR

Halve the peaches; remove the stones. Turn on the grill so the base is hot when you put in the peaches. Scatter the sugar onto the cut peach halves and grill at once till the sugar bubbles. Serve at once.

....

❉ *November 30*

My birthday – so I spent the day planting out the edges of the fountain, instead of stuck indoors at the computer.

The fountain began as a fantasy – as all good projects do – a dream last summer on a hot day, when the creek (all of twenty metres down on the flat) seemed too far away and you couldn't smell the creek or hear it whisper or feel the sudden coolness as the air swept over the water.

We need a creek up here, we said. A water garden like the Alhambra, a fountain indoors (we could heat it in the winter and watch it steam). But the dream compacted to a fountain outside the kitchen window where we could watch it while eating breakfast.

It's turned into a birthday present – but whether for me or Bryan or the birds I don't know. The wombats haven't discovered it yet, hopefully the sides are too steep for them to climb up and it's too rocky on the top for them to sunbake. I've planted it out with mint – apple mint and ginger mint and curly mint and water mint and white and black peppermints, Corsican mint and creeping pennyroyal and a few others that I've forgotten, with ferns and scented geraniums round the bottom. You can hear it from the verandah outside the bedroom and from the kitchen you can just see the interweaving rings of water.

❋ *December 1*

Aphids on the roses. Edward and Celine (Giles and Victoria's daughter) were passing, so I showed them how to eat them. A few years' time and they'll say 'yuk'; but they're still adaptable and believe what adults tell them (and don't necessarily condemn all information from their parents, yet). So they ate them, and sure enough they were sweet ...

Food is habit. Parliamentarians who scorn the harvest of nutty, rich protein on their doorstep (bogong moths) lunch on the coagulated mammary secretions of cows (cheese).

A good many pests are edible. They're just not very attractive. Actually, what is a pest to someone might be a feast to someone else – it just depends on how you look at it and if you know how to prepare it. A Martian coming to Australia might assume that sheep are a greater pest than rabbits if they didn't know how good a leg of lamb could taste (and even with the joys of leg of lamb and mint sauce I suspect the Martian may be right).

When it comes to eating pests there's a wide range to choose from. Some are better than others.

Scale and red spider mites actually taste sweet and good – but you'd have to be pretty desperate to scrape off enough to make a meal (don't try them if the leaf they're on is toxic). Lerps taste acceptable – a bit like maple syrup. Lerps are those tiny waxy casings over psyllids, one of the main pests on gum leaves. The psyllids suck the sweet sap – that's why they're so sugary.

If you're really into bush tucker you can scrape off a cup of lerps, cover them with water, then leave them in the sun. They'll ferment into a sort of lerp beer – it's, well, interesting. Don't try it in a bad season – it could be deadly.

One of the most evident edible pests at the moment are the grasshoppers – not plague locusts yet, thank goodness, but little sticky things that lurk on the backs of leaves. There's a Middle Eastern delicacy called locust bread that's made with grasshoppers, not honey-locust seeds, every nine years when the locust plagues are due. I've never made it … or eaten it (not knowingly at any rate).

Grasshoppers taste okay, at least when they're cooked. I admit I've never eaten them raw (except a small one accidentally that flew in while I was puffing up a hill, but that didn't count).

You don't eat the whole grasshopper – at least not on purpose – just the abdomen with the prickly bits removed. The Romans had a popular dish of grasshoppers fried in butter. You had to make sure that they were browned to a pale gold colour. If you fried them too long you apparently spoiled the flavour. I've also come across a recipe for chocolate-flavoured grasshoppers. Again the abdomen is fried, then dipped in chocolate. I haven't tried them either.

The best recipe I know involves wrapping them in bacon, then egg and breadcrumbs and deep-frying them.

You can omit the bacon if you don't know a source of free-range pig. If anyone wants to know what they're eating tell them it's fried brains. In fact if you can get over the initial shock, grasshoppers are really good deep-fried.

(It's also a good idea to make sure the grasshoppers haven't been eating anything toxic – keep them penned for a week to make sure.)

Probably the best way to eat grasshoppers though is via a mob of chooks or turkeys. Let the poultry feed on the grasshoppers – then eat the chooks.

One of the most commonly eaten pests are snails. Eating snails is a virtue. Most are feral pests; and I've known even fervent vegans to scatter snail bait. So why not eat them, and use the protein? (It's also an excellent excuse for garlic butter.)

I remember going to the meat markets in Athens years ago. Amid the fly-encrusted lamb carcasses were half a dozen giant barrels filled with snails – and they were crawling out all over the place and heading down into the gutters. Unappetising, even for a snail lover.

I adore snails – in garlic butter, not among the seedlings. But even people who love snails in restaurants get a bit twitchy if the snails don't come out of cans – and they'd never think of harvesting them themselves. Snails are easy to catch and easy to prepare.

THE EDIBLE SNAIL

You have to be careful with snails – and grasshoppers and other pests too – in case they've been feeding on something poisonous. First of all you have to either let them starve for a month or feed them on lettuce leaves or

*vine leaves. After that either feed them on flour for a
couple of days, or be prepared to gut them. I'm not into
gutting snails, so I put them in a box with a lot of flour
at the bottom. The Romans fed them wine-soaked wheat
to fatten them.*

*After you've starved them, throw them into a pan of
boiling water, shells and all, then add a little wood ash.
Boil them for 20 minutes, then toss them into cold water.
They'll have shrunk from their shells and you can pull
them out with a toothpick.*

*Now you simmer them in white wine and water with
a bit of garlic and some herbs till they're tender. This can
take up to 3 hours, depending on the sort of snail. You
can either thicken their sauce with a few egg yolks or toss
them in garlic butter or homemade tomato sauce or garlic
mayonnaise or anything else with a strong flavour,
because by now the snails haven't any.*

*If you want to disguise them, mince them and fry
them in butter and garlic, as snail patties, and call them
(small) game rissoles. And you may never think of snails
as pests again.*

❋ December 10

Suddenly the whole valley is peaches – the scent of
peaches; the plop of peaches in the night; pickers' cars
scooting round the corner in the early morning as we dash
down for the school bus; pickers already sweating by eight
o'clock filling buckets; trays of peaches on overladen utes
crawling down to the packing shed; tractors pulling trailer
loads of peaches, and semi-trailers of peaches; peaches lying

red and bruised below the trees; peaches red and furry in the green leaves, weighing down branches or nestled next to the trunk; the smell of peaches everywhere, almost too sweet but mitigated by the scent of hot dry soil.

You can buy peaches now all along the valley, not just at the Wisbeys' and the Harrisons' sheds but from smaller growers like Ray Spriggs (he's built half of Araluen and now they call the mid-valley Spriggsville, and if there's any justice in the world the name will stick) and at another half dozen road stalls. The varieties vary from grower to grower; so of course the knowledgeable know exactly when to come down to the valley to get their favourite, and who to buy them from.

I picked our first peach this morning. (Well actually the bowerbirds got the first half dozen.) I've just remembered why I stopped growing peaches commercially – the peach fuzz makes me itch. And itch. And itch.

As soon as I've written this I'm heading down to the creek to swim it off. (Peaches nowadays are defurred before you buy them.)

Chocolate wombat was drinking from the fountain this morning, with a satisfied look on his face as though to say: I don't know how this pool got here, but it's convenient.

Fresh Peach Melba

This is not the stuff you get in most restaurants – commercial white-as-anything icecream with a few tinned peaches and raspberry (but not really) topping.

The essence of Peach Melba is the marrying of hot peaches and tongue-burning sauce with cold icecream – so that Madame Melba, who loved icecream, could eat it without her throat freezing (or so the story goes).

I adore Peach Melba, and hardly ever have it – mostly because it's fiddly to make – and I don't dare order it in restaurants as I have *never* found one that does it right, and then I get annoyed and start hectoring the waiters, which is not an ingredient for an agreeable night out.

2 CUPS FROZEN *or* FRESH
RASPBERRIES

8 FRESH PEACHES, PEELED AND
SLICED (*or* EVEN BETTER, *GENTLY*
POACHED IN HALF WHITE WINE
AND HALF WATER, SWEETENED IF
NECESSARY WITH CASTER SUGAR)

GOOD VANILLA ICECREAM

1 TEASPOON ARROWROOT MIXED
WITH 1 TABLESPOON WATER

1 TABLESPOON CASTER SUGAR

Heat and stir the raspberries gently till the juice starts to run. Mash roughly with the back of a spoon. Add sugar and arrowroot. Stir till thickened.

Place the warm or cold peaches on the icecream and cover with the hot raspberries. Eat at once.

❄ *December 11*

'Hallo there,' announced Jeremy, darting out from behind the baked beans. 'How are you then? Did you hear about old Joe last week? How much rain did you get? What's been happening down the valley?'

When Jeremy asks you that, it means he really wants to know. I mean *really* wants to know. It's Jeremy's right to know everything that happens in the district – from who's said what to whom, to the environmental risks of the new garbage site – and as he owns the grocery where just about everyone goes at least once a week (unless they go to the 'top shop' instead), he is in an excellent position to find out. He also owns the bottle shop.

Some friends of ours arrived from New Zealand a while ago, and booked into the Doncaster, the guesthouse up in town, then ambled down to the bottle shop for a bottle of something for dinner.

'And then this great tall man sort of jumped on us from behind the counter,' said Alice, still in shock twelve hours later, 'and he knew where we came from and where we were staying and that we were going to visit you today – and we'd only been in town half an hour – and he wanted to know where we were going next and did we know such and such … I felt like I should give him my birth certificate and passport and three references.'

Jeremy is married to Helen, whose paintings move me more than most art I've ever seen, though I don't know enough to understand why … they're not the literal works I usually love.

Jeremy writes verse, to be recited publicly, preferably after three bottles of something extremely good; his greatest is perhaps 'The Man Who Brought Mascarpone from Leichhardt to Braidwood' – about himself, naturally.

Jeremy too understands food, though in a different way

from the valley; and Helen treats it with as much discipline as her art.

✳ *December 12*

The golden skinks are sunbaking on the stone wall around the herb garden. They really are golden – if they could be snap frozen and keep their glow they'd be jewellery you could wear scattered around your neck. Though you'd never get that pulsing aliveness with a jewellery lizard, and the joy of these are that you never quite know where you'll see one next.

A new wombat has moved into Gabby's hole, and shovelled out her bones. I haven't shown them to Edward.

He'd demand a grave, or retribution. There is something very right about the bones in the heap of wombat-trodden soil, as though Gabby has finally achieved wombathood.

I still feel guilty, thinking of her – not because there was anything else we could have done for her, but because she suffered … through human sentimentality? Lack of knowledge? She should never have been returned to the wild. I know having wild 'pets' is against the WIRES philosophy; but I think that's what she was.

❋ *December 13*

Roos pounding away into the night when I came out on the verandah for a pee last night. The roos only come down when it's dry. Which it is. Concrete dry. If you hit the earth too hard it shatters.

UNCOOKED RASPBERRY JAM

This jam has one of the strongest and best flavours and colours of any jam I know. Sunlight doesn't have just one taste – it has millions, and this is one way of capturing it.

Choose a stinking hot day (which today was). Go down to the end of the garden and see if the wallabies have left any raspberries. If they have, pick an icecream container full. Carefully pick out all beetles.

Now take a plate of raspberries and a plate of caster sugar – the same weight – and take out into the sun. Leave for 4 hours – they should both be very hot. Mash them together, spread in the sun and leave another hour. Bottle and seal.

This 'jam' is of course likely to ferment after a few weeks. It should be eaten fresh.

....&...

❊ *December 14*

I tried to dig a hole for a new grevillea this morning – two centimetres of dust then concrete. There've been showers; enough to keep a green flush on the grass, not enough to wet the soil.

The river has stopped above the bridge and Noel hasn't any river water at all for the trees. He's been digging the dams out again, but every time he digs it gets too muddy to pump and it's days until it clears.

We've still got water here – a thin silver trickle greening gently between the rocks – but Rod's orchards drink it before it gets down to Noel. At least the swimming holes stay full of water, no matter how dry it gets – they just get thicker, green and full of duck shit and a thousand ducks …

Ten thousand flies are sheltering from the heat against our windows, giving themselves concussion as they bump against the glass, and waking with a confused buzz as we walk out the door.

The fly traps are also buzzing, and the back door is littered with flies' wings from the nest of swallows above. (Swallows don't eat wings – just the juicy bodies – and they do make a terrible litter with the wings.)

❊ *December 15*

The sky's a hard deep blue, so dry you could knock it and it would flake before it would seep. All the sky gives us at the moment are beetles, hard brown-backed things that don't come inside till you turn off the light. Then they crawl underneath your pillow and tickle your cheeks – we must have had half a dozen last night, the light semaphoring on and off as we tried to find the beetles in our hair (and other more intimate places).

The ground smells dry, and the trees have that particular scent that dry gums get, as though they are niggardly with any moisture they release. (It's true – the oil in gum trees does change consistency with weather and with pests.)

The butterflies are waltzing in thin air as though they can only dance when it is dry. Too much sunlight, unchecked light, so you are always imagining someone out of the corner of your eye, and turning and catching shadows flittering round the garlic flowers or in between the gladioli.

The rosellas are suddenly bright between the leaves, having lost their camouflage – they are so much more vivid than the heat-stricken leaves.

Birds love peach season. The rosellas have grown canny – swooping through the grass like low-flying aircraft, hoping for invisibility, settling among the fallen peaches or grasping the lower peaches in their hands and eating swiftly, silently, till they hear the noise of the tractor or the ute (me they don't respect at all: I'm no threat). But no matter how canny, they rarely last the season. There is always a peach grower more silent than they are, waiting among the greenery with a shotgun.

Up here in the sanctuary of the gorge the birds are more open – larrikins holding onto the branch with one leg while the other grasps a peach. You can see them savouring it, the juice running down their feathers, they don't hurry their eating up here, one bite and then survey the world and another bite and listen to the wind.

We are no threat at all – even if we try to scare them they just yell at us, angry at the disturbance to their meal. Birds are good judges of character; or at least those that survive a season or two are.

Once the rosellas and the parrots have bitten into the fruit – broken the ground as it were – the smaller birds move in, silvereyes and even spinebills and honeyeaters, sipping and poking delicately at juice as thick as nectar. And after them the bees, clustering among the beak-marked peach holes, so you see what you think is a perfect peach and find a dozen angry bees on the other side.

Birds are no fools – they always go for the best of the fruit and as they prefer wild fruit (sourer than our domesticated versions), they eat it just before we pick it. A rosella will make do with a peach of perfect ripeness, or even an overripe peach, only if there isn't a slightly green one to hand.

Luckily we have a lot of wild fruit here too, nestled in water seeps among the rocks and cliffs, fecund along the creek: kurrajong fruit and wattle seeds and bursaria berries (tiny and purple but worth plucking along the track to the swimming hole) and pittosporum fruit which humans can't eat and emu berries (long and purple orange green – some are quite good if you get one fully ripe, and some are like bitter cardboard) and wombat berry vines and Port Jackson figs and sandpaper figs, which can be wonderful.

There is a giant wild fig above the pool near the water slide (fifty metres of sloping smooth rock with an even smoother channel of water – irresistible but your bum gets red after a few slides).

The pool is almost a perfect round, incredibly smooth and deep and shimmering green. It is a darker green in winter when the light hardly penetrates the gorge, a silver green in summer when the rock below seems to reflect the light in crazy patterns through the water.

The pool is always cool, often freezing, like silk on your skin in midsummer when you edge into the water (each centimetre a shock to hot flesh) and slide through that line between creek and air. Half the pool is under the fig tree, so you have a choice of sun or shade – dappled at the edges, and deeper shade further in where the pool shallows to a ledge where you can sit and pluck the fruit and spit the seed up into the maidenhair above. The figs aren't bad; not as large or succulent as domestic figs, but quite soft and sweet.

The lowest fruit are picked first. If you're agile you can pick the fruit further out as well, but you have to be able to lunge and grasp like a merperson or a cormorant, at home in both water and air.

And the rosellas sit above us in the tree top and slurp at the fruit and laugh at us.

MIMOSA

This can be wonderful but only if drunk in summer,
when the smell of peaches drifts down on the wind
with a hint of bushfire behind it.

*Purée your peaches – they must be smooth and liquid.
White peaches make perhaps the best-tasting Mimosa,
but thick-fleshed yellow are more spectacular as they
swirl through the champagne.*

*Pour half a glass of champagne – it is important that
the champagne goes in first or you'll just get peach and
champagne cordial. Now pour in the peach purée in a
neat swirl through the bubbles, so it winds and twirls and
hangs there, supported by the effervescence. Sip it slowly,
so you can watch the way it changes. This is the glory of
Mimosa, this trail of peach and bubbles – a well-mixed
drink of peach and champagne isn't the same at all.*

DRIED PEACHES

You need dry hot days for dried peaches. Apricots
dry easily, as do tomatoes, but peaches can get furry
and rot in high humidity.

*Peel your peaches (peach fuzz is even worse dried), stone
them and slice them thickly. Wipe them with lemon juice
so they don't go brown (because the brown bit in dried
peaches is rotten, soft and sticky; brown, dried apricots
are sticky, hard and good). Lay them out on netting trays
in the sunlight; or just on aluminium foil. On netting
you can leave them out all day; on foil they get hot
quickly and you have to turn them every hour or so or
they cook before they dry. Netting over foil might be even
better, but I haven't tried it.*

*Take them in before the dew (or if a hail storm lurks
over the horizon) and put them out next day. Three days*

of heat should do it — chewy and rubbery and intensely peach flavoured.

Any peach can be dried, but the juicier they are the more rubbery the result; white peaches shrivel into thin rubber bands. Fat slices of meaty yellow late-season peaches are best — full of subtle rich flavour that caramelises well on drying. The more delicate essences of early peaches are lost in drying. You just get sweetness and an almost artificial taste of peach.

❀ *December 16*

Chocolate has discovered the new wombat. We heard his howls last night. I adore animal howls: great long shrieks into the night. We dashed out and there was Chocolate bellowing into the hole, his sides puffed like someone had stuck a bellows up his bum and these great ululations echoing down the valley … and tiny whimpers from inside the hole.

I presume from this that the new wombat is a male. We haven't given him a name. From last night's performance I doubt we'll get a chance to.

❀ *December 17*

No sign of the new wombat.

❀ *December 18*

The frogs have discovered the fountain. No more lapping water at midnight. All we hear now is *riggor riggor riggor unk* — always out of sync.

❊ *December 20*

Bryan's daughters Liz and Cath came down for a few days before Christmas. We have at least two Christmas dinners, one on Christmas Day and one for family who'll be Christmasing elsewhere, so I made Peach Crumble.

Peach Crumble is what you make when you've been cooking for three weeks – all the social necessities of Braidwood pre-Christmas social life, when it's bring a plate parties (adults) or bring a plate parties (kids), and everything from art class to ballet has an end of year event at which you *eat*. Peach Crumble is impossible to muck up, no matter how culinarily burnt-out you are.

Edward ate three helpings; Liz and Cath only two. Liz is the elder, organised and laughing; Cath a bit wide eyed, and sometimes verging unexpectedly into incredible beauty, which I think she is quite unaware of. We played silly table games, sticking labels like President Lincoln or Blinky Bill onto other people's foreheads so they had to guess who they were supposed to be; which Bryan refused to join, and did the washing-up instead.

PEACH CRUMBLE

1 CUP SELF-RAISING FLOUR

HALF A CUP BROWN SUGAR

HALF A CUP BUTTER (MARG
DOESN'T MARRY WELL WITH
CARAMELISED PEACHES)

12 PEACHES, RIPE BUT FIRMISH,
AND DEFINITELY NOT BRUISED

A DROP OF COINTREAU *or* A FEW CLOVES

Preheat the oven to 200°C (this is important – if it's stuck in a cold oven it can turn gluggy).

Rub the first three ingredients together till they look a bit like lumps of breadcrumbs. Peel the peaches and lay the slices in a baking dish with the Cointreau or cloves, sprinkle at once with the crumbs (if you leave it more than 5 minutes the peaches will start to soften and brown).

Bung the dish into the oven and cook till browned on top – about 30 minutes, but this seems to vary according to all sorts of unpredictables, like if the month has an R in it and whether it's raining, so keep checking.

It smells wonderful. It tastes even better.

Serve with masses of good cream, or an excellent, preferably homemade vanilla icecream. Any left over you can eat for an extremely sinful breakfast.

There is now a distinct wombat track up the edge of the fountain, and a squashed wombat 'sit' on top. I wonder if the wombats connect us with the fountain, and are grateful. But I doubt wombats feel gratitude. Wombats are the centre of their universe. You can never make a wombat feel ashamed – as you might make a dog feel ashamed – or embarrassed or grateful either. Say 'Bad wombat!' to a wombat and it'll just wait for its carrot or maybe run from the sound of your anger.

I've never known a wombat to learn its name either, or even to understand a single word like 'Dinner!'. Not that wombats are dumb – no one who has ever lived with wombats thinks they're stupid – they just don't think the way we do, so they flunk every 'intelligence' test humans give them. But a wombat-created intelligence test – now, that would be different.

✳ *December 21*

The apricots are ready. Actually they've probably been ready for a week, but I've been too flat out to scramble up the hill. Not that it matters – the wallabies have been stuffing themselves.

There's a particular family of wallabies who live on the apricot hill. We call them the apricot-guts clan, because they are. They sit under the trees and cram the fruit into their mouths so the juice runs down their stomach and looks disgusting. At dusk they hop away, slowly, across the hill, bellies bouncing, and looking slightly seasick.

You couldn't miss the apricots today – the smell floated in a great wave down the hill, hot fruit and baked soil. The girls gathered the fallen fruit under the trees and Edward clambered up and threw fruit down (which squashed it, but it doesn't matter; I've saved those cases for jam) and the apricot-guts clan watched us disconsolately as we purloined their Christmas dinner.

There are still six trees left for the apricot-guts. Hopefully we can persuade friends to come and pick and eat, as I don't want to spend two more days picking. And then selling, which takes even more time. (I used to make my living selling fruit and veg, but it's a hell of a lot easier writing about it.)

The back of the truck is lined with cases to give away as Christmas presents to anyone we pass. I feel a bit like putting up a sign 'free to a good home' – even the girls are a bit aghast at the incredible plenitude of fruit.

The new wombat is lurking down the end of the garden among the avocado trees. It hesitated as I approached last night as though to gallop back to its hole, then kept on eating.

HOMEMADE PEST REPELLENT

(Doesn't work with wombats.)

This is a good way to transfer the pest-repelling qualities of plants onto your skin.

1 PART LAVENDER OIL

1 PART EUCALYPTUS OIL

1 PART METHYLATED SPIRITS

10 PARTS CIDER VINEGAR

If you've got your own lavender growing, pick the flowers and fit as many as possible into a bottle, then pour the eucalyptus oil, meths and vinegar over them and leave to steep for a week before using.

If you use your own flowers, the repellent turns a wonderful translucent purple – it makes a wonderful Christmas gift strained and poured into a fresh bottle, with a few new sprigs of lavender inside just for decoration. But be warned – the incredible colour fades on exposure to light, and after a few months the liquid will be clear again.

❊ *December 22*

Liz and Cath came home giggling after shopping with Bryan in town.

'How many women kissed you this morning?' asked Cath in wonder, after he'd happily been bussed by Jenny, Mary, Natalie, Sue, Netta (who demanded sternly when he was coming to the next Historical Association meeting), Kirsty, Virginia …

The girls have now realised why it takes Bryan three hours to get the groceries: even without Christmas embraces you have to talk as well as pile things into your trolley.

Jeremy leapt on them from behind the frozen-fish fridge and interrogated them swiftly; he needs to be swift at this time of year as there are so many visitors to find out about.

The girls found it a novelty to have to be introduced at every shop they went into, and several they didn't go into as well: to Gordon Shorrock sweeping the footpath outside Muttons (where you can buy anything, though it can take a month or two to find it; Gordon will see you passing and dash out to say he's got it now); to Rose Wehby outside the draper's; to the Robbos, two backs in overalls under a bonnet at the NRMA (another fool Canberra motorist with a leaking radiator) though the backs didn't move from the bonnet as they passed; to Mr NomChong, who you rarely see outside the shop unless he's unloading a washing machine on the footpath (you can buy anything at NomChong's too, as long as it's electrical; for some reason goods from NomChong's always behave well). And the girls found it hilarious, and unlike anything they'd known before, an hour almost just to walk down the street …

They left this afternoon with cases of peaches, apricots, pots of herbs, jars of apricot and peach jam, bunches of parsley, silverbeet, lavender for Cath's potpourri, a dozen eggs each, a pot of hand cream (chamomile and lavender scented) and their Christmas presents.

CHEAT'S CHRISTMAS PUDDING

1 CUP DRIED FRUIT

SLICED MANGO PULP (OPTIONAL)

CHOPPED FRESH APRICOTS
(OPTIONAL)

2 CUPS SLICED FRESH CHERRIES

1 CUP BRANDY *or* RUM *and/or* FRESH
PASSIONFRUIT JUICE WITH A LITTLE
GRATED ORANGE ZEST

1 LITRE GOOD VANILLA ICECREAM

1 TABLESPOON TOASTED SLICED
ALMONDS

1 TABLESPOON TOASTED GROUND
ALMONDS

GRATED ZEST OF AN ORANGE AND
LEMON (NO WHITE, AND USE THE
FINEST GRATER)

On Christmas Eve soak the dried fruit, mango, apricots and cherries in the liquid. (If the dried fruit looks like its spent six months in the Saraha, simmer it for 10 minutes in half a cup of water first.) Put the lot in the fridge to keep it cold.

Before you eat the main course of Christmas dinner

take the icecream out of the freezer. Just before serving
mix all ingredients into the slightly soft icecream, then
serve at once, in chilled bowls so the icecream doesn't
melt any further before you eat it.

Don't refreeze or the icecream may get ice crystals in
it. Not to mention interesting bacteria.

.... 🍂 ....

✳ December 23

Bryan went down to Noel Wisbey's shed to get some
peaches and nectarines to take to Noöl and Geoff's on
Christmas Day (our next lot won't be ready for about a
week.)

Noöl used to be my boss during the short and
claustrophobic time I spent in the public service, saving up
for this place. The valley is Noöl's spiritual home – or one
of them – but she and Geoff and Fabia rarely get down
here; so the peaches will at least be a scent and a memory.

Bryan left at 3.45 p.m. and was back with the peaches at
5.00 p.m. (the shed is twelve minutes' drive away).

When Bryan got there Ned and his brother Jack were
sitting out the front gazing at the mountains and
reminiscing. Ned scrambled down the back of the shed
(about a three-acre walk) and hauled back another chair,
and Bryan sat there listening to memories – the hail storm
in the '60s that wiped out their orchards but left the
Harrisons' alone.

'Do you think the Harrisons'll stick it out?' asked Bryan.

'They'll give it a go again next year,' says Ned, 'they've
got too much tied up in the place to give it up now …'

And it wasn't just packing shed, machinery and spraying gear he meant either.

Noel protected his crop this year with a wind machine to beat the frost. (Wind machines are like giant fans — they mix the air so the cold layer mixes with the warm and it never gets quite as cold as it might — even two to five degrees is enough to save the crop.)

'They're good boys,' says Jack of his nephews. 'We taught them all they know, remember?'

Jack and Ned gazed out at the industry their father started and they established, the kilometres of bright peach trees, only slightly drooping in the heat, the heat haze lifting to the mountains filled with the scent of ripe peaches. Then Ned hunted out the very best peaches in the shed for us to take on Christmas Day, and a case of seconds for us, on the house; and Bryan came back, eventually, like a hunter bringing home the Christmas feast.

Around here Santa comes in a white ute, a bit dusty, with a strong smell of sheep (Santa doesn't shear that afternoon). He's already been to the Araluen Christmas party. On Christmas Eve he'll be hovering with the sea mist above the valley. Christmas will be a good day. It always has been, no matter what disasters have danced on either side of it.

RUM AND ROSES FRUIT CAKE

There is no spice in this dish — just roses. Christmas cake, after all, used to be a harvest cake, made in times of plenty and eaten in winter. At least the roses in this recipe will be home grown. Avoid using roses from the florist and filled with pesticide, fungicide and preservatives.

This cake tastes nothing like a bought one. (Don't let anyone kid you that any cake in cardboard tastes like the real thing. Nothing with preservatives really tastes good.)

The Marinade

Shove some extremely stinky rose petals into a large jar. Top with 1 cup of rum. Shake once a day. After 3 days decant, and tip the now fragrant rum into yet another jar of petals. Repeat till the liquid smells like a perfume counter should but never does.

The Cake

250 GRAMS BUTTER

1 CUP BROWN SUGAR

5 CUPS SULTANAS

1 CUP CURRANTS

3 DESSERTSPOONS COARSE-CUT
MARMALADE

4 EGGS

2 CUPS *PLAIN* FLOUR

Preheat the oven to 130°C.

Beat the butter and sugar together till smooth. Add the sultanas, currants, marmalade and half of a cup of marinade. Then cream in the eggs, one at a time. Stir in the flour.

Pour into a cake tin lined with 2 layers of greaseproof paper (don't bother to grease the pan).

Bake for $4\frac{1}{2}$ hours, or longer if the top doesn't spring back when you press it lightly with a spoon.

Remove from the oven; sprinkle with the other half cup of marinade (blokes like this cake).

Wrap the whole lot in a clean tea towel till cool —
this will take hours.

This cake can last for up to a year, but probably won't.

....❦..

❋ *December 24*

Christmas has a smell, like all festivals do I suppose; and the smell varies, depending who you are and where.

Here Christmas smells of hot grass and burnt roo droppings and algae threads in the creek and the scent of the sea mist lifting. The sea mist always rolls in after hot summer days and drifts back up the gullies with sunrise, and by the time the shrike-thrush is pecking at the window in the first flash of sunlight the mist has evaporated and the heat is closing its fingers over the valley again.

Christmas smells of summer, suntan oil, dead grass, pudding boiling (of course), Pimms with cucumber (the girls had never tasted it before), and chocolate and muscatels.

When I was a child it smelt of roast potatoes in the dripping that my mother reused from roast to roast till it had a mother's vintage cooking smell. (The dripping was finally discarded after perhaps twenty years when my mother moved into her flat, and no other scent has matched it.) There was the smell of brown paper too, still over the Christmas wrapping – most of our relatives lived elsewhere and gifts were posted, bundled round the tree still in string and stamps and cut and torn and wrestled with on Christmas morning. (Do organised homes exist where someone gets the scissors *before* they start opening presents?)

There've been dry Christmases here, when the ground was too hot to walk on in bare feet and the wombats huddled in the damp sand of the creek.

Winter is a time of shadows, swallowing colour in deep purple. Christmas is too bright for colour, everything diminished in white light.

COLD PEACH AND CURRY CHICKEN

This is excellent – a luxury dish – rich enough so all you need with it are fresh bread or hot new potatoes, and a good salad (slightly bitter to counteract the richness), none of which accompaniments take much time to get ready. The chicken dish can be made a day in advance. A good celebration dish when it's too hot to cook. (If you ate it every day, you'd get gallstones.)

1 TEASPOON GOOD CURRY PASTE

1 EGG YOLK

1 CUP OLIVE OIL

2 TABLESPOONS LEMON *or* LIME
JUICE

4 DRIED PEACHES, SOAKED
OVERNIGHT

SALT TO TASTE

1 TABLESPOON OF FINELY CHOPPED
CORIANDER *or* GARLIC CHIVES *or*
PARSLEY (IN ORDER OF PREFERENCE
– CORIANDER IS BY FAR THE BEST)

THE MEAT FROM A COLD ROAST
CHOOK, CHOPPED

*Place the curry paste in a deep bowl with the egg yolk.
Whip well with a whisk (apparently it is possible to
make mayonnaise – which this is – in a blender, but I've
never managed it). When the mixture is pale, add a
dribble of olive oil and whisk 20 times. Add another
dribble and whisk 20 times. Continue at this extremely
slow rate till the oil is gone and the mixture is thick and
incredibly shiny, the texture of a fresh cowpat after rain.*

*Add the lemon or lime juice; whisk again. Now add
the squishy peaches and mix till they are spread
throughout the sauce. Add salt to taste, then the
coriander, and then the chicken.*

*Don't keep this more than 2 days, and keep it well
chilled – aerated egg yolks are wonderful breeding
grounds for bacteria.*

❋ *December 25*

'It must be twenty years since I've seen peaches like that,'
said Geoff's mother. 'They're perfect peaches.'

And they were. They just sat there in their box like
prize racehorses who know their worth and lift their heads
in pride. They'd be stud peaches, if there were such a
thing, and I felt like one of the three wise men bringing

gold and frankincense to the manger (I bet Mary would rather have had a good box of peaches).

Later, driving home, we watched the hills of Canberra like golden skulls fading in the dusk, and the Tablelands growing green as the day receded, as though dead grass fades into lushness with the light. The smell of trees and soil was a shock as we plunged down the mountain into the valley with the moon behind us ringed with light, as the moon is when it's dry. (Not with the misty ring of damper weather.) And there below us were Rod's fruit-bat-scaring lights, red and yellow flashing through the valley like Christmas ornaments gone mad – no Christmas dinner for the fruit bats tonight – and when we opened the front door the smell of ripe peaches washed over us like a tide.

※ *December 27*

Bryan and I first met at a cafe called the Pot Belly, then ignored each other for the rest of the night. I was dressed in my go-to-town best. He thought I looked very urban and besides I wrote books (the sort he never read), and he told me how he'd been doing some walking in the Netherlands, where he'd been posted for a year (and I thought:'Good grief, he thinks *that* is bushwalking … ?').

But it was nearly Christmas and that year I was having open house, so I invited the whole table, including him …

I remember how he walked up the steps as we sat under the kiwi fruit drinking yet another cup of tea. He looked like he belonged to the valley, and he does …

That was December 26 and we all walked up the gorge with the heat and the golden skinks, and bottles of champagne in our pockets. Bryan slept on the sofa – there were makeshift beds all over the place. And the next day we walked up there again. The others left as the mist rolled down, but Bryan stayed and we went platypus hunting in the mist and moonlight, and that night he didn't sleep on the sofa.

Every year after that we walk the gorge on December 27. We call it National Platypus Day … and if neither of us can remember exactly what date we got married (sometime in January, the year after we met), we never forget the anniversary of that day in the gorge.

And in those months before Bryan and I were married, when I sometimes wondered if I was doing the right thing – one failed marriage behind me, and what did I have in common with this man who loved computers and had never read a novel in his life – I would walk up the gorge with him again, and then I'd know …

The gorge is a place out of time. The sun glows from the cliffs on either side, the wonga pigeons bellow around the corner, the wind winds across the water and smells of rock and waterfalls, and you could be walking twenty thousand years ago or twenty thousand in the future, and it would still be much the same …

The local Aboriginal tribe used to feast here, on waterlilies (roots and stems and seeds); but they were hunted out last century with dogs and guns and righteousness, and sent down the coast, though a very few remained.

They called the last to live in the valley Big Maggie. I don't know what her real name was. They called her drunk and disorderly, too. Finally they said she had to go. If she left the district, they said, nothing would be done to her, the grave men of the court scribbling compassionately and the hatted, corseted women nodding agreement.

They say Big Maggie screamed in the court at the just, tidy men and ran down the steps of the Braidwood Courthouse. She was a large woman, but she ran down the mountain road towards Araluen still screaming, yelling in the valley, into the hot air and cicada buzz, over the blue haze as the heat rose from the trees, long wounded shrieks across the country they were exiling her from.

They found her body two days later.

There's an oil dump now at the foot of Jillamatong, the crouching hill behind Braidwood that was once a sacred site perhaps, who knows for certain now. Pine trees crawl up one side of it and joggers pound to the summit on Heritage Day.

The occasional tourist pamphlet states that Araluen in the local Aboriginal dialect means valley of peace or place of running water or valley of waterlilies.

Probably it didn't mean any of those things. There was an Araluen in Scotland and various Araluens are dotted around Australia, including an Araluen National Park. Probably the valley was never called Araluen until white settlers arrived, but a name that sounded a little like it to foreign ears.

The waterlilies that the Aboriginal people feasted on disappeared with the gold miners, when the river was dredged for the small flakes of alluvial gold, and the creek flats turned over to find the gold vein that never existed, and the dark still pools diverted to flush the shining grains from sand and gravel on the lower ridges.

The water barely flows through the valley now – there's always a drought or the water is sucked up for peaches or vegetables or gardens of roses and geraniums. Clearing at the headwaters up above the valley means there's less deep forest litter, less humus to hold the moisture. The creeks flood and dry up more readily now than they did two hundred years ago – or even twenty years ago.

The old sacred sites have gone with the people they belonged to. Now they are gone it's safe to call them sacred sites. There's no one to object to whatever you do to them. A sacred site is just a footnote in a history book or a titbit for the tourists, probably wrong, like Clark's Lookout on the road above us that was too near town for any self-respecting bushranger to ever have stopped there for a gander, and anyway, you couldn't see much till the Lion's Club cut down the trees to improve the view and built the concrete platform. But tourists are meant to park there and imagine the Clark brothers gathered, like them, on a neatly fenced viewing platform waiting for the stage coach to curl up the road from the valley.

Black sacred sites are accepted now even if we don't respect them. I wonder how long it will be before our culture accepts there may be white sacred sites too – not man-made ones, not churches or parliaments, but parts of the land that we too hold sacred, that we are part of, that are part of us.

Conservation battles are often about economics, which is safe – most large projects have mistakes if you look into the accounting close enough – or about preserving resources for our grandchildren, places for them to play or investigate or exploit in their turn. We are rarely prepared to say: 'This is my land, I am custodian of it, I would rather kill or be killed than have it violated. I am my country, there is no separating us.'

There is no language to talk about it. Even to say 'this is my land' is a simplification, and not quite accurate. It is more identification than ownership.

It's not just the land. It's the patterns around it, the million complexities, the golden skink licking the fat from its lips, the hard bare ant trails up the hill, the arrowheads of fish motionless in the water while the red casuarina roots flash above them. The total of these things can't be restored. There is no possibility of multiple use with these. You tread softly or you change it all and if your steps are loud enough you may not even notice.

The rufous bettongs on the hill behind the house disappeared a few years ago. Their nests and land were trampled by the sheep. Bettongs are soft and small and kangaroo like. You only see them with quiet luck and waiting – and rarely as you round up sheep. There were no grass orchids this year in the areas where the sheep roam, no sudden flame of indigophora bush sweeping down the cliff in spring. You need to know a place well to see the changes when new animals are introduced.

Half of me watches my garden here, prunes the roses, glories in ripe apricots and tomatoes, lies on fresh green grass, and plays with words and music. The other half watches the ridges, too steep for more than minimal human impact. Always the gorge behind, waiting.

Sometimes it is the centre of the world.

Near the house it is rockpools and rapids and places for kids to laugh. Further up it is quieter. Sometimes only the water moves; not the air, not us, not the other animals trapped in the silent heat. If a breeze flows it is a local breeze, trapped by the walls of the gorge, and it smells of water and lichen and casuarina and deep forest litter. The wind from above rarely penetrates down here, the heat is trapped in summer and the wet chill in winter. The air is hazy, sheltered by the cliffs – cliffs so high, so deep, so near that the sun penetrates only at midday. The light is clear green shadows till the sun hits, then suddenly golden haze.

When the wind does pour down here it gusts, huge buffets that knock rocks from the cliffs and send the lyrebirds cowering. It roars out of the gorge into the wider area near the house, throwing trees and bark and webs of dust. It sounds like a Boeing 747 crashing through the thorn bush.

The pools are deeper here. The further up the gorge you go, the deeper they get, etched out by floods pounding down the chasm, cracking boulders, carving hollows even in the granite – deep still pools now with smooth cascades or sharper raceways falling into them.

The pools are so green they're blue. You can see the clouds floating in them, still in the summer heat haze, so to swim across them you are flying as well as floating.

Here we are predators among other predators, the small dragons scuttling after dragonflies, the foxes scenting frogs, the leeches humping forward for our blood. We are large animals among the small.

You start up the gorge from the house with backpack and lunch, clothed and hatted and suncreamed. But the cliffs are too sheer for climbing. Finally you have to swim and after swimming clamber from pool to pool.

You realise that even loose clothes confine you. Your breasts swing out from rock to rock. You need to find a new balance for your body to counter them, a new rhythm for walking; and the sun feels different on the separate parts of your body.

Some of the wonga-vines are thick enough to swing on, to build a basket or a bridge. They twist around each other, a three or four strand rope, perfect circles drooping from trees to cliff to water. The perfume is trapped here when they flower.

The air is golden with pollen, rich with moisture as the water falls and falls again, as you walk from sun to shadow, slide into the water like white lizards, break the warm surface and the cold water underneath rolls along your stomach.

The water is never warm. Often bitter, sometimes cool. But the rocks breathe heat, cast it through your bones, radiate it deeply, so lizard-like you're warm again and the gold flecks glow from the granite.

You can sit for hours in the gorge. Time is only the darkness growing from the cliffs till only the pale rocks and downward slope guide you back. Watching the leaves slip over the water of the silent pools till they are caught, collected in eddies as the creek falls further. Listening to the sharp alarm calls of the lyrebirds, till they grow calmer, forget you, come to dance, bums up and legs out. Watching rainforest dragons bask in coolness under water, the hot air turning liquid in the dark. Sitting here in the blue light smelling the waterfalls.

Outside the world spins and rumbles. Here there is sand, air, water and rock and the wildlife of the gorge and you. This is the still heart, the centre of the world.

Years ago, when I was teaching English to some Aboriginal women, one told me: 'You forget how to listen in the city.'

Cities are human. They are simple because they are only human, everything created or modified. There is too much going on, not quite linked together. You have to shut things out. When you finally get back to the bush you have to learn again to use your senses, to learn to listen to everything, not just one or two things that are loudest or most interesting. It took me years of living in the bush to hear again and see. The sudden shock as the peripheral vision widens and you learn to accept and not shut off.

I am as much ruled, as much modified by this place as it is by me. Probably infinitely more. How many generations does it take for us to become aboriginal?

❋ *January 3*

The hills are brown now, not golden; the last few days' heat has sucked the last of the green away.

The maples on the flat are losing their leaves ('Do you think they'll die?' asked Mrs Clyste in Jeremy's; 'With luck, no,' I replied). They lose their leaves as a defence mechanism to save moisture and it's usually a successful one. If we get rain in the next month or so – and if the temperatures are reasonably kind – they'll come back.

'Bet you're getting lovely rain down your way too,' said Terry at the post office, 'buckets and buckets of the lovely stuff. I bet you're knee high in grass down there.' He shook his head slowly over the stamps. 'Makes you sick, doesn't it? All that rain in Melbourne washing out the cricket when we could have done with a bit of it here.'

We drove home from town through what we regard as traffic: six cars on the road, and another two on the mountain road. (A woman came trembling to the front door yesterday, pursued by gleeful geese – she and her husband had lost their brakes on the mountain road, and could she use our phone. The brakes had recovered by the time the NRMA arrived.)

The valley is at its busiest now; anywhere you go you pass at least one car. There are more humans than at any other time of year – fossickers hopeful in the dry river bed (if they puddle for a day or two they might just see some colour) or even more optimistic with metal detectors (the only metal down here big enough for detectors are the packing sheds or old tools washed down from Major's Creek). Some are just perambulating, seeing where the roads go and why, and discovering that once they've wandered onto the mountain road (affectionately known as the goat track; and ironically it does attract wild goats), it's hard to wander off it – it's a brave driver who'll do a three-point turn, though I've done it a few times when Edward has forgotten his lunch or the project he just has to have for school.

Some strangers drive slowly, watching. Others drive fast – teenage or macho would-be rally drivers who haven't yet learnt how to drive (from a sub-species perhaps that never will). Sometimes they roll off the corners; more often they hit other people, but usually not locals, who are wary throughout the holidays.

Ginger Beer

Homemade ginger beer is perhaps the wettest drink ever on a throat-parching day. (*And* a great way to trap fruit-fly – just leave it in jars among the tomatoes with a thin film of oil on top; when it stops bubbling it'll stop attracting, so replace. Note: fruit-fly don't taste of anything much, just a sort of tickle as they stick in your throat, and don't add savour to the recipe.)

4 WHOLE LEMONS, SLICED (JUST
REMOVE THE PIPS)

16 CUPS WATER

1 TABLESPOON GRATED GINGER

A PINCH OF DRIED YEAST

2 CUPS SUGAR

Heat the water. Then boil the lemon with the ginger till soft. Cool to wrist temperature; add the yeast and sugar. Leave the lot for 48 hours. Bottle.

*Release the pressure every day. The beer should be ready
in a week. If it tastes too sweet, leave a few days more.*

*If kept too long this becomes alcoholic and not suitable
for kids (they become giggly, boisterous and tell rude
jokes). And if it smells odd or grows interesting flora,
throw it out (not onto the geraniums — it will kill them).*

✱ *January 4*

The cockatoos have arrived — buxom, white and feathery. I
can see them out my study window as I write.

The first one lands in the grey-trunked Araluen gum by
the house. It lurches, then falls off. The next one falls off too.

The third bird stands there teetering, watching its
comrades lie on their backs, flapping their wings against
the grass and trying to claw their way back into the air. If
it was human you'd say it was hiccupping. Maybe white
cockatoos don't hiccup, no matter how drunk they get.

White cockatoos only get drunk when Christmas is hot.
Cool Christmases, when the mist sifts softly over the
ridges, mean sober cockatoos. Sultry weather means
fermenting peaches down at the dump.

White cockatoos are fond of fermented peaches. The
juice dribbles onto their feathers and their black eyes
gleam even brighter. By the time it's dark they've found
their way back onto the branch, yelling and snapping at
each other's crests. By midnight they're asleep, burping
gently on their branches. They wake up at about ten,
grumbling and bleary; by midday they're on their way
again, winging down towards the peaches.

The binge takes roughly three weeks, which is about all even a white cockatoo's constitution can stand; then they're off for a health cure to the apple orchards up the mountain.

❋ January 5

There are people everywhere; the sounds of motors in the distance and light aircraft in the sky; there are cars all down the road and panners in the river (which still isn't a river, so maybe they've brought their own water for panning).

We spent last night with Giles and Victoria, up at Jambaicumbene, twenty minutes and 1,000 feet upwards. They live by a series of swamps that merge into waterholes; it's only in dry times like these that you can see the real stream itself, deep between high banks of grass. We used to stop on the 'three bridges' and watch the platypus, but not since the wooden bridges were replaced by a concrete one. Two years of damming and heavy machinery eliminated the platypus, and none has been bold enough to recolonise the spot.

Giles is French, which is perhaps the reason their house looks like a medieval French farmhouse. All owner-builder's houses around here announce the character of their owners (Angela's is a rammed-earth mansion, a hospitable sort of house, with a fireplace large enough to roast an ox, though I don't think she ever has); mass-produced houses never tell much at all.

Giles and Victoria built their house of pisé. It's cool in summer, and in winter it keeps out the wind at least. Jembaicumbene seems always windy or frosty or hot; there are no trees to shield it from any passing weather, except the ones that Giles and Victoria planted ten years ago which are finally rising above the house.

Giles grows strawberries and garlic (both are superb) and Victoria pots and draws and makes linocuts and woodcuts. (She also illustrates some of my books.)

Theirs is the sort of garden that will look magnificent in 200 years time, when the trees are lichened and twisted and shelter tiny courtyards, and even now it is something of an oasis.

I have made Jembaicumbene sound ugly. It isn't; just exposed. It has a touch of Lombardy about it, green stretching to far hills and stands of poplars above the stream and watermeadows full of brilliant enamelled buttercups. It is very beautiful, especially in the frost, when the spider webs are frozen between the barbed wire and even the great oak by the bridge has turned white, and when the mist hangs over it in soft drifts so the world is white and green and wet.

But I am glad to live in the valley.

We ate rooster, youthful and still tender, cooked in red wine. Giles is the only person I know who can make coq au vin that isn't stringy; maybe you have to be French or have a wood stove for long *slow* cooking. And we ate fresh chapattis because they'd forgotten to put the bread in the oven. Giles made flat cakes of the risen dough and laid them for a few seconds each side on the top plate of the wood stove, then Victoria held them just above the coals in the fire box, so they puffed up and were crisp.

They were excellent, especially with the rich wine gravy and the greens from the garden (except that only a few of the leaves were green, brown too, and red, and cress and roasted sunflower seeds to scatter on top so they wouldn't get sodden in the dressing) and the first of the potatoes – the crop is late at Jembaicumbene – two or three sorts so you could scavenge in the bowl for the ones you liked best. And a late plum pudding with raspberries and cream for us and strawberry icecream (homemade, home grown) for the kids, who eat plum pudding under protest once a year and felt they'd done their annual duty already.

The raspberries were fat and firm – you need a fresh, cold climate raspberry to appreciate its texture – ours are Wettex-like, just a hint of what a raspberry can be and dotted with grass seeds. Giles had picked them in the half light as we arrived. (They gave us raspberry jam to take home too; set firm with its own pectin, and unbelievably red and seedy.) Usually Jembaicumbene raspberries are withered by the wind; but this year they're in abundance (some kindly freak of the Weather God who lives in the mist on the mountains) and they're making the best of it.

Somewhere in all the eating the conversation turned to peaches. Why were the peaches in France (they spent the winter there this year, staying with Giles's family) universally good? Even the supermarket peaches in France were fragrant. Why were the ones in the shops here so lousy – tasteless and often textureless?

I think I have the answer: it's the early peaches that are lousy, sold for early lucrative November, when peaches haven't much flavour – they haven't had enough sun – unless they're eaten pretty close to where they're picked, before the first faint blush of scent and taste has faded. Your average peach buyer buys early peaches, is disappointed and doesn't buy any more till next year and the whole pattern is repeated.

Of course there are also the peach buyers who demand that every peach has a red skin, which is why it's almost impossible to buy superb old-fashioned peaches like Golden Queen any more – they're dull greenish yellow skinned and furry, not smooth and red blushed white at all. Consumers get what they deserve.

But there are magnificent peaches around, except in wet years when everything – peaches most of all – tastes of rain. This isn't one of them.

✳ *January 6*

The trees are green shadows in a brown land; the grass so dry it sounds like cornflakes when you tread on it, thin fragile brown stuff that literally turns to dust.

The creek stopped flowing over the crossing yesterday; then last night it began again, a fine trickle like a cold green thread; and this morning was gone. It'll probably keep doing that for weeks till it stops altogether.

You start ascribing feelings to nature in times like this – the sky really is pitiless and today's wind relentless, tearing, gusting, throwing up leaves as though waiting for a pyromaniac to throw down a match. The avocados look like hysterics throwing themselves around the flat.

There's a big fire over past Captains Flat, but the smoke hasn't reached here yet, and there are fires all along the New South Wales coast. No respite in sight, just more blue sky and wind.

The peach trees are drooping along the road; but the fruit is good. The whole valley smells of sweetness, richer than honey, deeper than blossom.

Picked our first egg tomato today (in gumboots, as the snake still roams the vegie garden; red-bellied black snakes adore the scent of tomato leaves – it masks their own.)

A real egg tomato. Not the little cherry tomatoes we've had for months this time – one sharp mouthful and they're gone, too much skin to do much with – really just a touch of brightness after too long with winter green salads.

This one was wonderful, incredibly deep red, perfect except for the bottom where an eelworm was nestling so I cut that bit off and we ate the rest. The eelworm had good taste; the tomato was superb. Tomatoes, like other fruit, taste best in droughts.

I picked a few not so ripe (and not eelworm infested) to cook for dinner – half a dozen chopped roughly (home grown never have such thick skins as bought ones) and threw them in the cast-iron pan (I love my cast-iron pan; it'll be one of the things I'll try to rescue the day the fire comes across the ridges) with lots of olive oil and some roughly chopped nearly red capsicum, and seethed them for a few minutes with some very fresh garlic, then threw on lots of basil – torn, not chopped – ten seconds more and took it off the heat to add the pepper (if you cook pepper it gets bitter). We ate it with roast chook and creamed potatoes mashed with chopped garlic chives, and even Edward ate some.

The fresh garlic came from Giles. Fresh garlic is different from older garlic – crisper, sweeter, less sulphurous, and dissolves when it's sautéed. I can throw a dozen cloves into the pan with the butter and the chook, and they'll turn to mush and gravy. Later in the season when the garlic has toughened and dried out I'll either have to fish them out when I strain the gravy juices, or ladle them onto my plate – I love roast garlic (dark brown and sweet like raisins), even if it's slightly tough.

I bought twelve garlands of garlic from Giles yesterday – about twelve kilos. With luck it'll last all the year, supplemented by what I remember to pull up of ours, which won't be much – I never get around to it till the whole lot withers from the ground and disappears till next year, to come up in a host of tiny garlic stems.

We do eat the stems. Garlic stems are delicious, much better than leeks if you pick them when they are fattest but before they begin to go to seed; just bake them with a drizzle of olive oil and maybe a few dried tomatoes or a scatter of parsley and a very little lime or lemon juice.

Even when they do go to seed, the stems are still good – peel them and slice them thinly – a cross between garlic and a waterchestnut. You can pickle the flowers if you've got spiced vinegar on hand and if you eat a lot of capers – they're better than capers – but once I discovered the recipe and we wolfed down the first three bottles I didn't bother with it again. Which probably means it's not one of life's great culinary discoveries.

* *January 7*

The air is so dry you can feel your skin withering.

There are fires all over New South Wales, and the sky is totally cloudless, the sort of featureless blue that almost invites smoke to smother it.

Every summer we wait for the fires here, wondering 'Will this be the year ...?'

Twice in the past ten years I've gathered up possessions in case we have to evacuate – documents and photographs and basic clothes and Edward's old toy wombat and my favourite of Grandma's paintings.

It's terrifying but also strangely cleansing to work out which of your accumulations you really do love and which are just a matter of money and replacing.

Bryan was up at the Fire Control Centre all of yesterday and part of last night. They had fed him a steak sandwich from the Burger Barn; he looked deprived when he came home and glanced wistfully at the leftovers: a few pieces of fresh corn still in a bowl with the new potatoes, some chicken with mango and a hunk of pavlova.

I'd made pavlova because Edward complained he'd never eaten one (not surprising – Bryan doesn't like them, which was why I made one last night). I used the egg whites that have been accumulating from my icecream binge and put chopped nectarines and banana and banana passionfruit on top – yellower fleshed and drier than normal passionfruit, but almost as sweet in summer, and even better on pavlova which is too sweet anyway.

TINY ONIONS IN MANGO CHUTNEY

A variation on sweet and sour onions.

*Pick your onions young and sweet; peel them; drip
some olive oil in a pan and cook the onions slowly and
carefully for 10 minutes, till they are almost
transparent, then add a good dollop of mango chutney,*

keep cooking slowly and stirring often till thick and
sticky. Serve hot.
  Good with grilled chicken or meat on skewers.

.... ✿ ....

❋ *January 8*

The Lorings are in the shed down at Wisbey's.

Loring is an enormous peach with a yellow skin and
yellow flesh – a peaches in champagne peach. You can
make a meal of a Loring. The trees give huge crops. The
main problem with marketing Loring, says Noel Wisbey, is
that it isn't red. The secret is to refrigerate them overnight.
This turns the skins an even yellow, wiping out the
greenish tinge, without harming taste or texture.

People buy apples by name and season – early
Gravensteins, mid season Jonnies, late Granny Smiths. But,
to most people, a peach is a peach.

Not to the Wisbeys – or anyone who lives in Araluen.
Everyone has their favourite peach. This is the land of the
peach connoisseur. White fleshed or yellow, clingstone or
free, firm or juicy, blush red or sallow – each peach has its
season and its flavour.

Each variety holds for about ten days – a time of solid
picking, sorting and packing before the fruit spoils.

I miss the old peach varieties. I remember one old-
fashioned aniseed-flavoured sort that I haven't seen for
years; sliced up with peeled grapes and cream, it scented
the bowl. Others whose skin and flesh stays green even
when sweet and ripe and the bees are sipping at the juice
from a bird peck.

The flavour of peaches declines with storage. You can only expect a peach to keep its full fragrance in your fridge for about five days — and that's if you grew it yourself. No supermarket peach can ever taste really good — it's just the memory of lusciousness, a peach for those who've never guzzled a peach from a tree.

※ *January 9*

WIRES rang last night; they have another wombat needing to go bush.

I hesitated. The Gabby disaster has made me doubt my ability to care for a young wombat, despite the ones who've gone bush successfully from here before. (A young roo I was caring for died when I was pregnant with Edward — its injured foot developed gangrene — and for months I anguished over my ability to care for a child.)

I explained my fears — or some of them — to WIRES. But they were still happy for me to take her — she apparently failed to go bush in another refuge, and had to be brought back to the city; and if she fails here they'll take her back again.

So I agreed, and drove through the smoke to pick her up. (The fires are under control … till the next lot break out. I have rarely known the sort of fury I feel when I think of those that light them. For the first time I understand public hangings and displays of hate.)

She's dark brown, round and scared — the scaredest wombat I've ever met; starting at every noise and showing the whites of her eyes and needing to be cuddled all the way home, her nose in Edward's armpit.

I showed her the hole with some trepidation, ready to bundle her back into the car if she refused to go in. She sniffed, considered, advanced cautiously inside – then came out ten minutes later, dusty and for once relaxed, with just the hint of a wombat grin, as though to say: 'Dirt! Ah, dirt!'

She gulped down her bottle, fell asleep on my lap, woke up twenty minutes later, sniffed and trotted back to the hole. Five minutes later I heard digging.

Her name is Phoebe; but she doesn't really look like a Phoebe, and in fact hasn't had the name long. For some reason her other carers found it hard to give her a name too.

The world is still grey. I woke up gasping in the night; the air was almost too thick to breathe. I went out to the balcony, hoping the air would at least be moving there and there was Phoebe munching on the lawn, Chocolate a darker shadow under the persimmon tree.

✳ *January 10*

Bryan calls Phoebe Frisbee, because she keeps coming back; advances cautiously round the rose bush, then darts back in terror if the rooster calls. She's a good eater though; will finish a bottle in two minutes flat, devote some time to wombat nuts and carrots, then go at the grass – and she eats grass like it is a religion, something you dedicate yourself to – and then she goes to bed.

✳ *January 11*

Bryan gave me an icecream machine for Christmas (I craved icecream in the '78–'82 drought too, savouring

something cool and moist at least somewhere in the world
– I'd have holidayed at the Pole if I could have.)

I thought of making peach icecream, remembering the
first lot of icecream I ever made in '79, with the gum
leaves drooping and the air filled with hot eucalyptus oil –
you could smell that icecream from one end of the shed
to the other, and we all sat on the hot hill in the twilight
and churned and churned – but apart from Edward we're
sick of peaches already (he ate twelve yesterday; I counted
the peach stones by the video). So I made plain vanilla
instead, and we ate it with fresh peaches (Edward) or
sliced bananas (Bryan) and leftover Christmas pudding
(me). But I probably will make peach icecream again,
with bottled peaches, once the peaches are off the trees
and the peach fuzz out of the air and I start to crave their
sweetness again.

PEACH ICECREAM

*Chill 6 peaches in the fridge till very cold. Peel them;
slice them; roll in lemon juice to stop them going brown.
Make a custard with:*

2 CUPS CREAM

2 CUPS MILK

6 EGG YOLKS

6 DESSERTSPOONS CASTER SUGAR

HALF A CUP CHOPPED MACADAMIAS
IF YOU HAVE THEM

*Heat the custard mixture gently in a double boiler till it
thickens. Add nuts. Place in the fridge till cool.*

Mix the sliced peaches into the custard. Place in an icecream machine and churn till hard; or put ice and salt in a bowl and put the mixture in a smaller bowl and whip till thick (takes about 30 minutes, and is incredibly smooth and good).

Keep in the freezer, naturally, but not too long as the subtlety disappears and the texture flattens a bit too. Fresh icecream is by far the best.

.... ✿ ....

❋ January 12

Great thuds and reverberations down at the chook house – Lacy goanna's tail lashing on the roof. She can't get in to steal the eggs because we've closed the door. Instead the chooks fly in through a special chook window – with stripy plaster curtains to dissuade the bowerbirds from flying in as well to eat the wheat. (We found the curtains at the dump.) But Lacy goanna has never learnt to fly. So she sits on the roof swishing her tail instead and hissing at the chickens, who ignore her. Maybe goannas dream of growing wings and turning into dragons and investigating nests on high-up ledges …

Lacy goanna gets as drunk as the cockatoos some summers, but only if we neglect the trees and let the peaches rot on the ground. (If she had wings she could fly down to the dump.)

Goannas don't get obstreperous on fermented peaches. They just laze along the branches, burping. Apart from eggs and rotten peaches, goannas love decaying meat. They're the scavengers of the bush … and their burps smell like it.

❋ January 13

Took Edward up to town to have his foot looked at – he cut it on an oyster down the coast, but it's healing cleanly. Phoebe Frisbee Pudge was waiting to play when we got home.

Pudge is Edward's name for her, and it suits her because she is. She eats with dedication, like a vacuum-cleaner absorbing grass across the lawn. She's more contented now. It's been days since she showed the whites of her eyes.

We played The Wombat Game, which involves jumping out at the wombat from behind a bush; and then the wombat runs off and hides and jumps out at you … The game must be programmed somewhere into the wombat mentality, as all wombats play it – though come to think of it, Gabby didn't.

Phoebe Frisbee Pudge loves The Game, especially when we wrestle her when she's brought us to the ground, snapping and grinning and baring her teeth, which are long and curved and could be dangerous if she ever really gripped with them, but she doesn't. Just snaps and shakes and lets us go. (Ricki The Wrestler used to draw blood sometimes, grinning away and not realising that the shouts were agony not glee.)

❋ January 14

I love the richness, the sheer sun and dirtiness of summer garden smells – pungent tomato branches shooting out their bitterness as you water them; the hot sweet scent of mint, the cooler smells of carrots and beetroot and silverbeet.

You get the strongest garden scents in summer; and the most aromatic at night – even better when you've been hosing, as though the water brings the scents back down to earth. (I wonder if there are pockets of garden smells under the clouds; if eagles get a sudden whiff of cauliflower rotting from too much rain, or an echo of parsnips drifting with the wind).

The curry bush smells strongest of all the garden plants. It hangs over a band of rocks up above the bathroom – many times I've dashed from the loo to the kitchen to whip up a vindaloo. Of all fragrances, curry is perhaps the most irresistible. I mean that literally; once you've smelled it you've got to taste.

The curry bush is small and grey; the flowers are brilliant yellow pompoms all through the hot weather. The smell flows over the ground and up your nostrils; courtyards and garden edges seem to catch it and hold it, just like the bathroom does. (Don't try to cook with curry bush – it changes flavour. But it's good very finely chopped in vinaigrette over tepid vegetables.)

I've just come in from watering now. My knees smell of mint, where I brushed past the Egyptian mint as I came through the back door. My toes smell of thyme I trod on as I pulled out a bit of invading kikuyu from the thyme beds. My hands smell of lemon verbena and chamomile as I picked both for a cup of bedtime tea – tiny yellow flowers, pungent now, but insipid and composty when dried – I don't see how anyone can drink chamomile tea from tea bags. My hands probably smell of wombat too, from picking Pudge up from on the flat.

If anyone kissed me now (but Bryan is up at the Fire
Control, manning the radio as relief crews are sent to the
fires down the coast), I'd taste of the parsley I chewed
while I ran the hose over the ginseng first of all (cherished
for three years now and just starting to form roots) and
then the herb beds out the back. My hair probably smells
of scented geraniums that I brushed under watering the
parsley. And all of me smells of curry bush – it's almost an
oily smell, impossible to get rid of, pervasive as cigarette
smoke – it's a good thing we like it.

It's getting dark now; the sky is smoky with dusk, not
fresh smoke, I think, so there is no need to panic. The
wind is still in the wrong direction. The grass on the
Tablelands was bleached almost white as we drove home
tonight; the trees were pale green, the whole landscape
almost skeletonised by dryness. I have never seen country
fade so fast.

❋ *January 15*

We are craving cold things – iced watermelon, as fragrant
as good sherbet, you can smell it across the room (and hear
it calling you from the fridge).

Edward and I can eat a watermelon in two days, a relic
perhaps of my childhood – when we'd head off to the beach
with towels, Vegemite sandwiches and a watermelon, and
dinner would be corn on the cob (even my mother's
culinary powers stretched to that) or one of her stews
(whatever meat was cheap – usually mutton shoulder chops)
with whatever else we had on hand – pineapple, sweet
potato, tomatoes, always onions, bits of spud and sometimes

pumpkin too. Surprisingly good, or perhaps we were just ravenous. (Sometimes in the stew there'd be bits of string as well as paper, and once a sea-shell and another time a bit of wood – it became a joke to see what we could find.)

It's no accident that three of my mother's four children turned into avid cooks – we had to learn to cook to eat. Or perhaps I am unfair – my mother's cooking at least showed improvisation, a determination to use what was there, which is the basis of all good cooking traditions (of course, culinary skill should be there somewhere as well).

Mum has cooked well since she discovered microwaves – a bowl of mixed veg imprisoned behind the glass for three minutes. And the joys of yoghurt and precooked chooks. Cold chicken and hot vegetables or sardines on toast, and fruit for after, and toast and sugar-free marmalade shared with her Corgi for breakfast. Hers isn't a bad diet, after all.

Sometimes I dream of living in a city, being able to choose bits and slices from every tray in a neighbourhood delicatessen. Not in summer though. Last time I was in Canberra I went to a delicatessen but walked out without buying anything except bread (which was good for a change). But the local baker's bread is also good, as is mine ... and Giles's is even better.

✳ *January 16*

Rain – just enough to count the drops, and then a deluge – a full forty-five seconds of it. But at least today is cool and misty; for the first time in weeks we can draw breath deep into our lungs again. The world still seems bleached with heat – as though it's been painted by a watercolourist stingy with paint – but you can see the hint of deeper colours underneath.

The egg tomatoes are ready, and the first of the capsicum – long yellow dangles, like pop-art jewellery (they'd make good earrings). The first few went bad in the heat. It's been the first time in a fortnight I've really felt like rummaging in the garden – the extra breath of heat from steamy soil was too much to face.

There are a few late artichokes too, from the seedlings I put in this spring, and the rose hips are swelling on the rugosas – they'll be a lovely crop if the silvereyes don't get them first – and the basil has finally leafed enough to pluck big handfuls, and the zucchini are swelling so fast you'd think they'd burst, which means the chooks are being fed plenty of zucchini lately.

You can probably tell a lot from a household by its vegetable rubbish. The chooks get a giant bucketful every day – outside leaves of lettuce and silverbeet stalks and tough bits of marjoram and paper from the garlic; thick rinds of watermelon and bowls of peach and plum and cherry stones and crusts of yesterday's bread.

All our dinners are similar at the moment – meat or pasta or rice or spuds in some fashion. But always a great dish of veg – whatever gets picked from the garden first, tossed into the old black cast-iron pan with olive oil and garlic – spanish onions, celery, zucchini, tomatoes, the first of the butter beans, artichoke hearts, button squash, sprigs of cauliflower, torn-up basil leaves or marjoram leaves, chopped parsley, garlic chives or wild celery, spring onions, parsnips or tiny new onions from among the poppies (we pulled out the poppies because they were windblown in the heat, and pulled up the tiny onions at the same time).

Sometimes there's more tomato and basil than anything else, with a strong flavour of garlic; or more beans and onions, or celery and chives and artichoke hearts, or zucchini fried till brown with spanish onions and garlic, all soft and crisp and olive oily. Every night is different as well as being the same.

The young asparagus has survived the heatwave, and the new white fig is wilted but alive. Sing halleluiah and watch the weather forecast.

❋ *January 17*

I dreamt of Gabby last night: her slow helpless dying, the maggots from her hole.

I had to creep downstairs with the torch to check on Pudge, who was happily and steadfastly chomping across the lawn, round and silver in the moonlight. She didn't see me.

So I went back to bed, and inched closer to Bryan's furriness, and fell asleep.

❋ *January 21*

Dinner at Robin and Virginia's, driving through the dust and wilting peach trees along the valley to climb the far ridge to Fox Hill. The peaches are so fat they look ready to succumb to gravity, and many have, so the smell is a combination of freshly fermented peach hooch and hot soil. You could feel the echo of last week's heat sing from the earth, even though the air itself was cool, having meandered up the valley from the coast, softened by sea mist.

It was even cooler in the Fox Hill kitchen, tall ceilings and blue white walls, with paintings, sketches, lithographs, collages, photos all precisely placed, so you have to concentrate either on the walls (in awe) or on the people, and either choice seems rude (while Robin gleefully pounced on our 1985 torch, announcing that it was subject to a recall notice, had we seen, it was in the paper somewhere … as he rummaged in the newspaper pile).

Dinner was mostly via Conrad and Carol, who grow veg down the valley and bring them up to town once a week, rousing Virginia and Robin in the early morning to sing the praises of corn or beans or artichokes – much the same produce that we grow here, but it's fascinating to see what other hands do with it.

Virginia made chilled yoghurt and cucumber soup with chives and new potatoes and beans. And peach cake afterwards with cream, while Lottie the poodle sat at the table, in a posture infinitely more erect and elegant than ours (her manners are superior too), and ate the last of the rolls that Robin had baked this afternoon.

Pudge was waiting for us at the front steps, giving her own peculiar little yips which mean: 'I want food. Now.' So we fed her and she crouched in the darkness, paws on either end of her carrot. A dedicated eater.

We could still hear her gnawing when we went upstairs to bed.

* *January 23*

I've decided veg have voices. No, I'm not joking. Haven't you ever heard a zucchini yelp when you snap it? It's an anguished sort of sound, the cry of a zucchini cut off in its prime — which is the best time to harvest a zucchini. If a zucchini bends, it's too big. They should be finger thin and snappish.

Fresh corn squeaks when you thrust your teeth in, though it needs to be fresh. Supermarket corn just oozes. Peas pop if you steam unpodded young ones ... the air pressure builds up till you open them. It's a disgusting sound. Kids love it.

Carrots crunch (or they should) and tomatoes squelch — home-grown ones do at any rate. Most of the flavour of a tomato is in its juice, so if you can slice it without a wet patch on the bench you've either got a modern hybrid or cut into a pink tennis ball by mistake.

Edward's favourite vegie sound at the moment is the bang when I forget to prick holes in the jackets of the spuds before they're baked. It's a good solid boom — fun for youthful males, but I don't recommend it for the oven.

SUMMER VEG IN OLIVE OIL

This isn't so much a recipe, as a catalogue of what's in the garden or at its best in the shops.

Slosh some olive oil into a pan. Slice a bulb of garlic — yes, I do mean a bulb, *preferably just dug from the garden (at this time of the year it looks like a young onion, not papery and segmented at all). We cook them, bulbs and stems and all, like garlic-flavoured leeks, but nicer. It won't taste garlicky at all as long as you (a) chop it, don't crush it and (b) cook it till it's mush in olive oil. That way you get flavour instead of acridity. Elderly garlic tastes more sulphurous, and if it's turning brown or powdery the stench will last for days.*

When the garlic is soft, add chopped-up baby zucchini, still yelping, tiny squash, pearl-sized peas, miniature carrots, tiny artichoke hearts, thumbnail-sized cucumbers (don't peel), juvenile beans, asparagus heads, pickling onions (peeled but not sliced — if you need to slice them they're too big), quartered new potatoes … whatever you can get your hands on that's young. For this recipe you need things soft and mild and sweet.

Seethe the whole lot as slowly as you can, stirring as little as you can without it sticking, for at least 30 minutes (though this depends on the amount of veg), until the veg are just starting to amalgamate but are still intact.

This can be served hot or lukewarm, and is good with almost anything, or by itself, or with hot fresh bread (probably the best accompaniment) or as a pasta sauce.

❋ *January 24*

'Mum, what smells?' asked Edward. So I checked.

It's a dead rat in the hall ceiling. At least in this weather it will soon desiccate. Dehydrated rat.

❋ *January 26*

Four fat maggots inching their way to the bathroom, and the stink still lingers, a combination sweet and musk. (You could *almost* imagine it sliced thinly on focaccia.) Swept up the maggots and opened the bathroom window wider.

Bryan swatted three flies in mid-air this evening. An Australian record? Bryan swats flies with concentration and passion, and is extraordinarily efficient.

❋ *February 2*

Noel Wisbey was eating a peach as we drove past this afternoon, juice dripping down his chin. It has to be a Fragar. Noel says they're his favourite peach.

They were Grandma's favourite too. I remember her picking a Fragar off a tree, the peach still hot from the sun, with a blushed almost transparent skin, so large she had to hold it in both hands to bite it while the juice ran down fingers and trickled along her arms, and we had to take her down to the creek to wash off the stickiness.

That, said Grandma, is what a peach used to be like.

A Fragar should sit in a bowl on the table and be admired, fat round and perfect and eaten when no other flavour might distract from its perfection. Fragar is an old variety. Like old roses, blushed and fragrant.

But a Fragar is a white-fleshed peach and the public expects yellow. 'When you're selling Fragars you have to sell yellow peaches too,' says Noel. 'A shop may take a pallet of Fragars – but they'll have to have a pallet of yellows too. If a peach isn't yellow, most customers will ignore it.'

❋ *February 3*

Even the brown has faded on the hills now, as though the earth has been poured into bleached skulls with too blue sky behind. I asked Roger the Ranger (National Parks variety, now retired but the name has stuck) what the forecast was.

Roger is passionate about weather, and has worked out a long-range forecasting program for this area. He predicted an eighty-seven per cent probability of bugger all; and for a moment I found myself furious with him, as if it was his fault the forecast was so bad. If he'd just *tried* to make it better ...

The creek is hardly flowing now, though the pools will keep us and the animals going for months, as they did in the last drought (the pools shrank to weed-filled puddles, crammed with a hundred mountain ducks).

❋ *February 4*

Clouds – high, grey and even – but no rain. Not even the smell of rain, as though the sky is laughing at us. The swimming hole is filling with algae, and the valley is full of the dull drumming of the pumps, pulling water from the creek and water table while it's still there.

There were roos on the flat last night – maybe eight or ten of them. We could hear their thumps from the balcony. The roos only come down from the hills when it's dry. And it is.

Pudge has taken to pushing the rubbish bin over and rolling it round and round the paving to attract our attention so we'll come out and feed her. So we do. She's an intelligent wombat. She's trained us well.

❋ *February 9*

Jenny and Trudi – my cousins – came down from Sydney late last night, driving along the track in the darkness, which takes courage for the uninitiated, and were promptly attacked by Pudge, who ran up to the car with glee, and butted their heels as they got out, yelling *hip hip hip*, which is wombat for something or other.

Trudi naturally assumed she was rabid or manic or both – and leapt back into the car. I grabbed Pudge and slung her over my shoulder (which at least kept her still, though another good T-shirt now stinks of wombat).

We spent this morning trout fishing; then up to the packing shed to buy peaches for J and T to take back to Sydney (we are again between ripe peach trees).

Ned was there, shirt off, shoes off, sitting back in his chair and enjoying the faint tonguing of the breeze. He showed Jenny and Trudi around the shed – the conveyor belts and defuzzers and cooler and waxing device and peaches everywhere, great barrels and boxes and neat stacked cartons. And, like Edward, Trudi couldn't wait till we got home to eat her first peach; I think the two of them had eaten four by the time we rattled down our track.

The clouds were gathering over Monga this afternoon; but I don't believe them.

✳ *February 10*

Rain – so thick you can't see through it. The girls left in almost zero visibility; and I walked back to the house dripping, with a grin on my face.

No Pudge last night. Pudge is no fool and won't come out in the rain ... not the first night at any rate. (I suddenly realise that this may be the first rain she's ever known. Perhaps she's waiting for us to turn the sprinkler off outside her hole.)

❊ February 11

The grass must have grown an inch in the night. The flat is green, the gums have spread their leaves again so the hills are green as well. Pudge ventured out at eleven o'clock, hearing Bryan slam the door as he squelched down to the chooks; so we fed her oats and carrots in the shelter of the back door, then she went back to bed. (Edward wanted to bring her inside; but I pointed out her coat was thick and she was quite happy. Besides, she smells of wet fur.)

There was a leech on the bathroom floor this morning. I shoved it down the drainhole.

❊ February 12

Still raining – soft rain now. Ned had his shirt on as we drove past the shed to the bus – Ned wearing a shirt is the first sign of a new season. The first of the late-season peaches are ready today too – though too wet to pick more than two or three. Firm-fleshed ones, bottling peaches that stay firm in syrup all winter; but I prefer them fresh – peaches with bite.

The peach trees look thicker and greener than they did last week. Not just the dust washed off. They're standing straighter, the leaves pointing out instead of drooping; and the creek is galloping across the rocks.

❊ February 13

Sunlight when we woke up and a million birds yelling as though they'd been waiting to yell for days. The creek is flashing happily and swirling into corners; but it still wasn't enough rain for a flood; and certainly not enough to replenish the water table.

But at least the valley's green.

❋ *February 14*

Treated ourselves to a new doormat today. The old one is much chewed (Pudge consoles herself with it when she's waiting to be fed). When I lifted it, enough hair sifted out to knit another doormat. Or maybe another wombat.

Bought another case of peaches at the shed on the way back from the school bus; but even Edward's appetite for peaches is almost gone.

❋ *February 16*

'In Spain and those hot regions they eat the [Love] Apples prepared and boiled with pepper, salt and oyle, but they yield very little nourishment to the body, and the same naught and corrupt.'

So said Gerard, in his *Herball or Historie of Plants*, 1597, which I was reading this morning – he was a better writer and gardener than you might think from the quote. The love apple is, of course, the tomato.

A good tomato calls to you. I'm serious. Suddenly there'll be a baking hot day – like yesterday, all freshly washed sunlight, and which seemed twice as hot now that the dust has gone from the air – the sort that sends the cicadas singing and the magpies muttering in the shade. And you'll hear a voice from the vegie garden – well, not a voice exactly, a sort of song … a sort of scent … a hot soil and tomato smell ... and there among the pungent leaves will be the first ripe tomato.

A watched tomato never ripens – well, it does, but it takes a long time. We have long, cool springs here and the tomatoes stay green and swollen for months (this is not an exaggeration) before slowly blushing pink and finally, oh frabjous day, we have one stinker of a hot snap and they turn red.

We've been eating tomatoes for over a month now, I think, but the joy of them hasn't diminished. It is hard to imagine a world without tomatoes, though even early this century they still weren't popular in most of the western world.

A good tomato doesn't need vinegar, not even balsamic, or not more than two drops anyway. It should provide its own acid, its own sweetness, as well as that indefinable pungency that means fresh home-grown tomato.

Even decent varieties of shop-bought tomatoes don't taste like home-grown ones. A tomato has to be picked hot and soft and as red as it's ever going to be for the best taste. (So soft you can't cut it for sandwiches either – those neat round balls in the supermarket are good for something.)

Tomatoes were brought to Europe by Christopher Columbus (along with chillies, syphilis, slaves and a few other odds and ends). The Europeans regarded them with suspicion but liked the look of them. In those days tomatoes were sourish and golden. They were grown purely as ornamentals and went by the name *pomo dei mori*, meaning 'apple of the Moors' or 'apple of death', and later as *pomme d'amour* – 'love apples' or aphrodisiacs – and then *pomme d'or*, which was anglicised to 'golden apples'. Small kids were warned not to touch.

The suspicion of being an aphrodisiac lasted right up till the end of last century. Actually I'm not sure they aren't. There's something about a fat ripe red tomato …

If you're worried about the tomato's aphrodisiac properties – especially on the sandwiches of susceptible adolescents – just add a bit of lettuce. According to the medieval herbalist Culpeper (who was not a big fan of the tomato), lettuce is a sure-fire dampener of passions, especially when applied directly to the source – but that's another story. (It would be interesting to see what Bryan would do if I applied lettuce to parts of his anatomy. Laugh, probably.)

The whole garden smells of tomato at the moment – a scent reminiscent of my school days. Everyone seemed to have tomato sandwiches for lunch, and they all went soggy – but no one seemed to mind. (I *like* soggy sandwiches – especially when it's hot.) The fermenting rubbish bins were collected from the school once a week, for the pigs. By then they were probably a rather torrid blend of soggy tomato/ banana peel/meat-pie crust hooch. Did the pigs get drunk?

I'm drying tomatoes on aluminium foil at the end of the garden, then bunging them in olive oil with a bit of garlic and basil to keep till we want to impress visitors. None of us really likes dried tomato. Maybe you only really like them if you've never tasted that fresh concentrated flavour of a sun-ripened fresh one, and believe the only intense tomato flavour comes when they are dried.

I used to bottle tomatoes, but I don't bother now … which I will regret come winter, as home-bottled tomatoes have a richness that no canned tomato has. But the cans are so easy, and there's so much else to pick and process at this time of year.

We spend six months of year tomatoless (maybe it's just the sheer glut of tomatoes now that makes me feel like I'll never really long for a tomato again).

Classic Aussie Tomato Sandwiches

Do kids still eat tomato sandwiches? School bags used to smell of them. There's a particular pungency about tomato sandwiches baked in a Globite case in greaseproof paper for a minimum of three hours. Grandma's picnic hamper used to smell of them too.

The secret of a really good tomato sammy is to butter evenly, thickly and everywhere so the juice doesn't soften the bread prematurely. Add black pepper (pre-ground to follow the classic recipe) and wrap in greaseproof paper.

Store in sunlight for at least three hours so the tomato sweats. Eat warm.

A 1990s Aussie Tomato Sandwich

Take a thick slice of fresh Italian bread. Brush olive oil on both sides. Toast lightly on both sides, top with fresh tomato, with or without boconcino cheese and lots of torn basil leaves or a thick spread of pesto. Add a touch of grilled eggplant or capsicum preserved in olive oil, chopped garlic chives, thinly sliced artichoke hearts, french beans in vinaigrette ... the possibilities are endless.

Heat in the oven or under the grill till it loses its chill, no more – just enough to get the fragrance wafting off the bread. Eat at once.

························· ✌ ·······················

How to Peel a Tomato

Cut just through the skin, no deeper, from top to bottom and back again, so you've divided the tomato into quarters. Now pour boiling water – or even very hot water from the tap – over the tomato for a few seconds. The edges of the cuts will peel back and you can peel the rest of the skin off.

Peeled tomatoes are much nicer sliced on sandwiches and infinitely better in soup and stews unless they are going to be puréed – otherwise you end up with wrinkly bits at the bottom.

························· ✌ ·······················

Tomato Jam

Don't knock this till you've tried it. It's good.

2 KILOGRAMS SKINNED *REALLY* RED
TOMATOES (THIS DOES NOT WORK
WITH INSIPID ONES)

2 KILOGRAMS SUGAR

6 PEACH LEAVES *or* A FEW SLICED
ALMONDS

Boil till a little sets in a saucer of cold water. Bottle and seal.

························· ✌ ·······················

❋ *February 19*

An echidna was nosing up the paving when I came out to feed the chooks this morning … eating the ants in the crevices. It heard me or felt the vibrations of my feet and froze. So I froze too.

It relaxed sooner than I did, waved its nose around searching for my smell and then located it. Stopped, sniffed again, then pondered. Finally it lumbered slowly over to me (ready to freeze again if I moved) and shoved its nose delicately down my shoe. It sniffed again, but didn't like it; then waddled off to the nice anty bit behind the bathroom.

I'm not sure whether to be insulted or complimented that a creature who loves ants rejects my toes.

❋ *February 20*

Another storm – bruised clouds hovering at the end of the valley, then suddenly darting up; sharp angry drops that turned into hail in a few minutes, then thankfully melted back into rain. The ground was silver for about ten minutes with a fine sheen of water and then it stopped, as suddenly as it had come, and swept off to drop its offerings on someone else.

❋ *February 21*

Alan came to breakfast (omelettes with tarragon and cheese and a very little chopped tomato). He'd been visiting his son Cynan, who's spent the holidays picking down at Wisbey's till uni starts again. He's been doing it every Christmas since he was fourteen. (He pretended he was sixteen the first few weeks, and then confessed; but by then Noel had realised he'd got a good worker and kept him on.) Cynan has the sort of muscles you'd imagine a semi-trailer might grow if it went in for weightlifting.

Alan had left Cynan surrounded by capsicums – the whole shed is full of them – green and red and white and black. The hailstones bruised them so badly that if they're not picked now they'll rot. If they can get them to the markets in the next day or so they'll be right. And of course the fruit will be bruised too …

Some of the pickers camp out; some stay in the 'white house' – which Cynan says is pretty grotty, with who knows how many sweaty peach pickers there, all too exhausted to do anything after their day's work except sleep, eat or go down to the pub.

Edward takes it for granted he'll work there in the holidays when he's old enough; though I don't know how he'll feel about it then – the work is hot and peach fuzz makes you itch, and the scratches sometimes turn into great horrible blisters (I suffered from them at one time). The blisters are not, as is rumoured, caused from pesticides and herbicides, but from a bacterium in the soil. Mine re-occurred for months, gradually lessening in severity, and hopefully I'm now resistant, because they're lousy things to have.

Pudge came out to be admired – she has a sixth sense about visitors, knows just when to arrive to get an extra carrot, and lies there with her legs spread out behind her and her stomach spread along the ground, gnawing her carrot till she falls asleep with her nose in the carrot shavings. (We call it 'doormat position' – spread-eagled wombat.) Pudge never bothers with the carrot bits left over. Wombats aren't interested in things they can't get their teeth into.

The omelettes were good – bright yellow, moist and firm at the same time. (The hens have been foraging under the blackberries where it's still damp, so half their diet must be beetles – beetles transmogrify into good eggs.) I don't know how anyone manages to make an omelette with battery eggs – they don't hold together. The whites run all over the place when you break them, and the yolks are too anaemic to thicken anything.

ROSE PERFUME

Picked flowers in the afternoon – a basket of roses, so I felt almost medieval, and then hop flowers, which sent me giggling and I think I'm still floating from the pollen … hop pollen is a euphoric. The world is shimmering slightly and I still want to chortle at the moon.

The rose petals went into old Vegemite jars and were covered with vodka; which immediately went deep red. (They were delicious fat Papa Meilland roses – my favourite for deep colour and a scent you want to eat.) I'll add a few lavender flowers tomorrow too – but not too many, as it'll swamp the roses.

In three weeks I'll strain off the vodka, which will now be faintly rose-scented, add fresh petals, and stopper again. Then I'll restart the whole thing about six times till the vodka smells like Woolies perfume counter (but richer and much more subtle).

Homemade perfume really does have a tinge of the sun. There'll be enough perfume hopefully to add to lotions all winter, and enough to wear behind my ears as well.

✳ *February 28*

The car felt like a pressure cooker when I went down to pick up Edward – so hot even the air had escaped, and I was left gasping. Edward was hot and cross from too many sweaty bodies in the bus, and the heat glaring off asphalt playgrounds; so we raced for the swimming hole as soon as we got home (well, he raced; I wilted along).

Five minutes in cold water is miraculous; you don't feel hot for the rest of the day; at least not so oppressively hot you can't stand it any more. I'd hate to live without water to immerse myself in, just to float with eyes hovering crocodile-like at the waterline (crocodiles know how to use a good creek), so all the world is watershadowed and different and you meet the waterbeetles face to face.

Edward could have stayed there till it got dark; but I had dinner to put on (a young rooster to roast, just starting to crow, and the first butternut pumpkin) and he had homework.

So we left the green shadows of the creek and came back into sunlight and the scent of dust and trees.

AUTUMN

❋ *March 1*

Edward sees it first, a shock of red in dark green shadow. It lifts its paws through the tall matted grass and noses under the apple tree, into a patch of purple dahlias, the red disappearing among the petals so only the greyer tail is visible.

Edward whispers urgently: 'You won't shoot it?'

I shake my head. The fox pricks its ears up above the dahlias, then bends its head again.

'What's it doing?'

'Hunting. Shh.'

The fox lifts its paws like a well-bred horse, head poised and graceful. It trots out of the dahlia patch, and through the orchard towards us. It's definitely male. Long thin legs, surprisingly high taut body, the front very red, the back turning silver, thicker, bushier, for winter.

The air explodes behind it. Not a rifle. A cloud of red-browed finches leaping up into the pittosporum branches. They've been feasting on grass seeds and are disturbed by the fox.

He takes no notice. He's not after red-browed finches. Little beads of noise echo from the pittosporum, then the birds are off again to the grass on the other side.

The fox is nosing under the rosebush now, my full-blushed Countess Bertha, soft-cupped roses sprawling from the canes onto the grass. Roses become full coloured in autumn, glowing subtleties you never see in harsh hot light. But then everything loses colour in summer, the white light drinks colour, the air hazes in the heat and the world is bright and all the same.

Colours come back in autumn. The sky reaches deep blue and clear above you, the shadows thicken; there is clarity in the air again, each scent distinct. From where we sit we can smell the kiwi fruit, hard and furry and ripening above us, the clear water, damp soil smell from the creek, the bitter casuarina, softer red gum smell, the honey taste of roses and, sharply now, the smell of fox.

Foxes smell like dog, but more so, a concentrated essence. You can smell a fox a day after it has passed.

The fox is half under the rosebush now. Its tail sags behind it, not held upwards like a dog's.

Edward whispers: 'Do you think he'll prick his nose?'

'No,' I answer, and then he does, leaps back affronted and rubs it with his paw.

Suddenly he leaps, brushing the edge of Countess Bertha, so that soft pink petals sprinkle on the grass. But he's missed it, whatever it was. He leaps again. He catches it.

It's a lizard, a golden skink. We can see it in his mouth, one end still wriggling. Then it's gone. The fox trots back across the lawn. He stops, sniffs, bends down and snuffles over the grass.

That's where we walked this morning, picking parsley and fat tomatoes and fatter dahlias, yellow purple and globular pink. The fox can smell us. He follows our tracks over to the tap, then stops, considers.

We stay still. Edward's learnt stillness lately, at least when watching animals. Before he used to bounce with excitement. Now he just watches, quiet for a time.

The fox looks around. He sees us, considers, pads quickly over to the old tank we use as a woodshed and considers us again.

We don't move.

The fox bends down and starts to hunt again. It's after more golden skinks, more fat little crunchy lizards. There are plenty in the woodshed and on the paving around the house. Edward claims he's tamed one, it lets him pat it, though I've never seen it. But last Christmas we fed a somnolent golden skink up the gorge, Bryan and me, and the lizard lying on the hot rocks all eating slivers of turkey and plum pudding, the lizard greasy round the jowls and licking its chops after every offering of plum pudding or crumb of turkey fat.

I've watched foxes eat lizards before. They seem to be a large part of their diet around here. They like frogs too, leaping after them among the rocks by the creek. I once watched one fishing in the shallow pools, waiting in the water, paws wet, then snapping down suddenly, into the water, arching up with wet head and spray catching the light around its shoulders and the tail of a fish flapping out of its mouth.

Foxes like peaches as well, will snuffle out windfalls and even climb a tree, especially in a drought, so you find gnawed green peaches halfway up a tree and wonder, till one day you catch a fox up there, munching, having trotted up the rough vase-shaped branches, almost horizontal in places and easy climbing for agile paws. They adore avocados too, but foxes can't climb avocado trees (the trees are too straight), so they have to wait for the currawongs to knock one off.

One stalked away in disgust once after I shot a rabbit. It didn't want dead meat, though foxes will scavenge chook heads and roadkills happily enough – or maybe only if they're hungry. They eat the crimson rosellas too, pouncing out on them from the thorn bushes as they eat grass seeds, though most of the smaller birds round here seem relatively safe, secure in thorn bush and blackberry thickets, the daredevil male bowerbirds rustling and whistling under the bushes at the foxes as they pass. In a good season the foxes have easy pickings without prickles.

The fox has had no luck in the woodshed. Maybe we make it nervous. It wriggles under the netting and is out of the orchard.

'Will it come back?' asks Edward.

I shake my head. 'Probably not today,' I answer. We catch a last glimpse of red as it pads up through the stringy-barks.

Later we go for a walk ourselves. The bark crackles under our feet like old toast, the creek flows clear between warm rocks, brown-water lights this time of year instead of blue or green, the sky a distinct entity, you can almost slice it, you can taste the colours around you, fresh green, chocolate brown, air like boiled lollies.

There's a long sweep of goanna track on the path in front of us, elongated roo prints in the mud from last week's rain. There's a furious chattering, guzzling above us, female bowerbirds and currawongs en masse gorging on the last of the apples, the first quinces, the final crop of figs. The bowerbirds and currawongs mob together at this time of year, gorging the same harvests, but there's more than even they can stick their beaks into, no competition.

Edward picks the quinces; they look like knobbly footballs. I fold my jumper up to carry them and they leave it brown and furry and stretched out of shape. Edward dances beside me.

'Do foxes like quinces?'

'No.'

'Even cooked?'

'No.'

'Even with custard?'

'Not even with custard.'

'Neither do I,' decides Edward and takes my hand, so I have to hold up my jumper single handed, and we cross the creek again, under the she-oaks, through the shadows.

✳ *March 2*

I looked up at the hill today. I seem to be doing that more often; perhaps because the autumn light is kinder. The dead wound across the ridge is healing. There are green leaves among the brown. How much is due to rain and how much to gentler weather I don't know. I wish we could do more than just hope for more rain before winter. The fall last month was good – but not enough to fill the watertable. We badly need more.

Pudge's droppings are still soft and green though. She's an excellent forager, vacuuming up the grass. I've never met such a dedicated eater. I've stopped giving her wombat biscuits, but she still gets her carrots. She'll need the biscuits again soon though – there's not much protein in winter grass – but at the moment she looks like she'd burst if you pricked her.

Watched a lyrebird playing bicycle on a giant yellow zucchini this morning, rolling it down the hill, probably just to see what was under it at first; and then it liked it and kept on rolling . . .

✳ *March 3*

There were mushrooms on the track this morning. Not in the grass, but on the bare patch carved by the car's wheels. I suppose I tracked the spores in. And they sent me remembering, as mushroom picking usually does (there's something about the scent, sweet and too pervasive; you can't get rid of mushroom scent).

I remembered the first time I ever heard about wild mushrooms (you didn't find them in Brisbane suburbs in those days). It was Anna who told me about them first, then Olga, and Julie too.

Anna was Russian, tall as the saucepan rack above the stove, with bright blonde hair (the shade in the chemist's window) in thick plaits wound about her head. At the time I considered her verging on elderly; in retrospect she was probably fifty to my sixteen.

Olga was Yugoslavian, a country that existed in 1969 when I knew her but doesn't now, and didn't in her childhood either. She had buried two husbands. The third beat her on Saturday nights. She shrugged as she buttered the toast. 'He is a man,' she said, as though that explained it all.

Julie was Italian, shorter than Anna, taller than Olga and rounder than either. She had a daughter-in-law who caused her endless trouble, and four daughters who gave her endless joy.

I met them at 6 a.m., when I arrived to wash dishes in their kitchen in a Brisbane hotel (which had become a car park last time I looked). The garbage bins bubbled in the alley, the cockroaches ran in a black tide from the back doorstep (but never into Anna's kitchen, and who would dare?), and the debris of last night's smorgasbord still lay in the dining room. 'You must have breakfast,' declared Anna.

'I had some toast at home,' I said.

Anna said nothing and reached for the sausages. Julie snorted and pulled out eggs. Olga poured more water into the teapot that was always kept hot on the table.

Three sausages, two bits of bacon, two eggs, half a tomato and four slices of toast with marmalade later, I was allowed to start work.

It was Anna who showed me how to make an omelette. 'You cuddle the eggs, don't beat them. Eggs should be loved . . . like this,' as her hands scooped air into the eggs in a way I've never forgotten. 'Your husband will thank me for this,' said Anna. 'All girls should know how to cook eggs for their husbands.' (When I said I mightn't marry she only laughed.)

Julie showed me how to cook spaghetti till it stuck when you threw it against the wall. (If you cooked it till it was soggy it fell off.) 'Your husband will thank me for this', she said, and sighed. I gathered it was a lesson her daughter-in-law hadn't learnt.

Olga demonstrated proper bed-making. 'Your husband will be glad I taught you this,' she said.

Actually it's Bryan who makes the beds in this family. He was brought up by an aunt who was a hospital matron in the 1930s. Her beds, and Bryan's, never dare to come apart.

In between serving breakfasts (none quite as large as mine) and tearing up chicken for the smorgasbord, they sat with their teapot and piles of toast and strawberry jam and talked: about husbands and daughters-in-law, about early morning in the countries they had known.

'The spider webs froze to the fences,' said Anna. 'We caught them on our tongues and felt them thaw. And the strawberries – they were small as my fingernail. We'd hunt strawberries all day and come home and tell my mother, no, we didn't find any; it's too early for strawberries. And she'd laugh, because she knew that we'd eaten them all.'

'Mushrooms,' said Julie. 'Every morning in the season we would climb the hill and fill our aprons. My mother grumbled because they stained, but she took the mushrooms.'

'I would hold a hen in my hands to feel the warmth,' said Olga. 'We took the eggs right from the nests and held them till they cooled.'

The traffic howled outside, the garbage bins kept bubbling in the Brisbane heat, and the chef – who never cooked – carved mermaids out of dripping and drank rum and pineapple juice sitting among the watermelons in the coolroom.

This morning I saw a raindropped spider web on a fence and remembered Anna. I thought it would be cottony, but it melted on my tongue. I tried to catch a chook and hold it in my hands in memory of Olga, but it looked at me indignantly and trotted off. And there was a single giant horse mushroom in the middle of our entrance track. We had it chopped into omelettes for breakfast.

The women of that kitchen are perhaps one reason why I went bush in my early twenties. For which my husband thanks them.

THINGUMMIES

Anna, Julie and Olga all had different names for
these. I can't remember any of them. I've called
them thingummies for the past nearly thirty years.

4 CUPS PLAIN FLOUR

3 EGGS

A LITTLE WATER

SALT (OPTIONAL)

*Pour the flour in a mound on the bench, make a hole in
the middle and break in the eggs. Add salt (I don't).
Knead till the eggs are absorbed and add water if
necessary. Keep kneading till it starts to look transparent
(I know this sounds odd but you'll see what I mean — it
takes about 10 to 20 minutes).*

*Roll thin. Cut into squares, toss a few each time into
boiling water. Scoop them out five minutes later as they
start to float (they should just stick to the wall if you
throw them hard enough).*

*Anna ate her thingummies with sour cream, chopped
hard boiled eggs and caviar if she could find it. (I add
chopped chives and dill, neither easily obtainable in
1969 Brisbane.) Julie ate hers with skinned tomatoes
simmered to sauce, then a glug of olive oil. Olga ate hers
just with butter, but the butter wasn't as sweet as it was
when she was young.*

❋ *March 4*

Bess Wisbey was at the bus stop this morning, with her grand-daughter Tammy. I got out of the car to talk to her, though my hair was wet. (I always wash it in the morning and dry it by the stove — hair dryers don't work on our power system unless we turn on the generator or inverter — but of course there's not time before the dash to the bus.)

Tammy's staying with Bess while her parents are in Sydney (it's just a bicycle ride between the Wisbey houses). It's not a bad autumn so far for the peaches, Bess decided. Not much rain . . . but enough. Just enough.

The kids always get on the bus in the same order: young ones scrambling to be first and get the seat up front, the older ones behind them, watchful in case a forgetful parent kisses them goodbye and embarrasses them, and then the teenagers languidly loping, their stride a careful calculation of the maximum time possible before Mac gets annoyed and drives off without them.

The bowerbirds were eating the cabbages when I got back. Bowerbirds are gourmets — they peck and then consider, then peer at the leaf again. I haven't objected. Cabbages are winter delicacies. I mistimed these, and they've hearted much too early. It's got to be fully winter before I get a craving for cabbage; and then they're at their sweetest.

I spent the afternoon making chilli garlands, threading them with a needle and cotton then hanging them up in the kitchen. They look bright and deceptively innocuous. I reckon this lot'll last me through the next decade, and possibly part of the way into the next millennia. I wiped my left eye accidentally before I'd washed my hands, and it's still watering.

There's a box of giant zucchini outside the front door too. They look like yellow and green shillelaghs and are too pretty to give to the chooks – and they're probably too tough-skinned till they start to rot a bit. I've kindly offered them around town, but strangely no one will accept them. I think every chook house in the district is probably stuffed with overgrown zucchinis now.

The only use I've ever found for them is grating them finely and adding a touch of freshly grated horseradish, with or without a moistening of light sour cream. But you can't always be eating zucchini with horseradish and sour cream. They're not bad for stuffing either, provided you only eat the contents and ignore the zucchini. But we don't have a plate big enough to hold them – fifty person orgies are out for the moment.

Rain last night. Not much. Enough.

❋ *March 5*

A grey day. Clouds hanging over Major's Creek – not soft fog but dull thick clouds. The peach sheds were shut as I drove down to the bus; the last of the peaches went up to Sydney a few days ago. For the first time there weren't pickers' cars tearing round the corner as we waited at the bus stop. The valley is emptying again. The leaves aren't yet yellowing, but definitely paler than they were.

A new wombat has appeared by the back door, large and low slung, which if you look carefully is because her pouch is full. We've called her Three-and-a-half. She's wary but friendly, as though the word has got out: these creatures (us) are harmless and their food is good.

I gave her a bowl of oats, which she loved, and a carrot, which she liked even more. Then she wandered over and started tearing at the grass in front of the house. Pudge came by soon after, but after one suspicious glance they ignored each other. Pudge bashed up the garbage bin for a few minutes till her food was ready, then fell asleep on my foot as I scratched her back.

Picked the last of the hop flowers. My fingers still feel sticky and there's pollen in my hair and down my bra and again a definite lighthearted feeling. Feeling frivolous, I made a sleep pillow.

HENRY VIII'S SLEEP PILLOW

Henry VIII had his own Keeper of the Royal Sleep Pillow. Sometimes I feel there are similarities between Bryan and King H – not just the beard (and definitely not the girth or the series of spouses) but an interest in all sorts of things and a complete dedication to what they like. King H had his own Keeper of the Royal Salad Bed too and liked his salad to be just right, fifty odd ingredients, which is very Bryan-like.

DRIED HOPS (BUT DON'T ABANDON
THIS RECIPE IF YOU CAN'T GET
DRIED HOPS)

DRIED ROSE PETALS (FRAGRANT)

DRIED LAVENDER FLOWERS

DRIED CLOVES

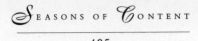
A DASH OF CINNAMON

DRIED ROSE GERANIUM LEAVES

ORRIS ROOT *or* A FEW DROPS OF
OAKMOSS OIL (AVAILABLE FROM
MANY GARDEN CENTRES)

*If you don't want to stick to the royal recipe, you can add
chamomile flowers, jasmine flowers or bergamot oil.
Combine. Insert into the pillow stuffing — assuming you
have a feather pillow — or make into sachets and slip
them inside the pillow case.
Dunno if I can persuade Bryan to sleep on one — his
republican sympathies might intrude. But I've stuffed
sachets into the cushions in the living room, so we should
get delicious whiffs through winter.*

.... ❦ ....

❋ *March 6*

Suddenly we're getting sick of rich red tomatoes and sweet
cucumbers and fat chillies. I even started looking longingly at
the frozen peas in Jeremy's shop the other day. But resisted.

The grass is good after the last shower of rain. Pudge is
even fatter (if that's possible). Even Chocolate has stopped
grazing like a lawn-mower scared to leave even a blade, and
is picking only the best.

I hope Pudge has enough flesh to keep her fat through
the winter. (I hope we get enough rain to see us through
the winter too.)

Three-and-a-half approached the wombat feeding zone
cautiously last night. Pudge and Chocolate were tucking
into their carrots and oats, so I poured a few out for her

too. She doesn't seem at all scared – just a trifle hesitant – as though Pudge and Chocolate have already told her: this place is good.

The vine leaves are starting to look drab – not because of autumn so much as downy mildew, which at this time of the year I don't worry about. But I picked a great swag of vine leaves to see us through the winter. I dunked them in boiling water for two seconds, dried them, then covered them in olive oil and into the fridge where they'll keep for months. Though if they start growing interesting flora I'll throw them out.

I'm not sure why I like vine leaves. They're tough, relatively tasteless, and become slimy as soon as you cook them. But like them I do; in fact, I adore them. It's probably the fact that there are so many of them, so easy to grab through most of the year, that makes me cook them so little – the disdain for something so familiar. I do *use* them often though: as platters for cheese or asparagus or even steamed veg with vine leaves spread on top. I think I'd rather serve food on greenery than on Royal Doulton china (though I wouldn't mind some Royal Doulton if someone sent me a set).

STUFFED VINE LEAVES

YOUNGISH, FRESH GRAPE LEAVES

RICE STUFFING

JUICE OF 1 LEMON FOR EVERY
10 LEAVES

TWICE AS MUCH OLIVE OIL AS
LEMON JUICE

HALF A CUP WATER *or* CHICKEN *or*
TURKEY STOCK

*Use any stuffing you like. I love rice cooked in chicken
stock with garlic, pine nuts, currants and lots of chopped
parsley – just bunged in a pot and simmered till the rice
has absorbed the stock. Though if I'm making it for
company I seethe an onion and lots of garlic in olive oil,
then throw in the rice and currants and so on, stir it till
it's covered with oil and has absorbed most of it, then I
add the stock – but the quick way is almost as good.*

*Once you have prepared the stuffing, take a youngish
grape leaf, pick off caterpillars, brush off beetles, and dip
the leaf in boiling water for 2 to 10 seconds – till the
leaves are limp, but not deceased.*

*Wrap the stuffing neatly in the vine leaves – yours
will probably look much better than mine. Place the
stuffed vine leaves in a casserole, sprinkle on the lemon
juice and olive oil and the water or chicken stock. Bake
for 30 minutes in a moderate oven.*

*Serve hot or cold. Vine leaves are one food that is
perhaps best tepid.*

❧

* *March 7*

The birds are coming back – red-browed finches pecking
at the grass seeds and poking their beaks into the rose hips,
silvereyes examining the kiwi fruit, the lyrebirds
investigating the moist places in the garden. We haven't
seen any of them for months, since before it got so dry –
there simply wasn't seed for them to eat.

We spent breakfast watching a lyrebird play with two giant zucchinis I'd picked this morning and left by the edge of the garden. It rolled them over with surprisingly dexterous feet – so massive when you see them actually grasp something – and perched on them and rolled them and rocked them in a fabulous balancing act, and pecked at the stalk, which I suppose was still damp with sap. Then a grey shrike-thrush startled it and it ran back into the dark under the kiwi-fruit vines, and then into the young asparagus to scratch and preen and play.

The chooks breakfasted this morning on Cheezels and things called Dinosnacks, which seem to be Cheezels in another shape, and candy-covered popcorn – all the goodies Edward gathered in his show bags up in Braidwood on Saturday and then discovered that he didn't like, and mooched out to pick a couple of cucumbers instead. Not that he doesn't like junk food – but his taste runs more to hamburgers than to cheese and salt and sugar-coated elderly corn.

According to Mistress Margaret Dodds (*Cook and Housewife's Manual*, 1829): 'to keep hens laying in winter the French give them nettle seed and hemp seed.'

I haven't tried it.

❋ March 8

The bowerbirds were pecking the Golden Queens so I ate one peach and then another. All ones the birds had pecked, as they were obviously the ripest. (Birds choose the best, and fruit ripens after it's been pecked too.)

There is no other peach like Golden Queen – firm but not crisp, so you think it's dry till you bite into it, then realise the juice is encased in the flesh, it doesn't drip onto your fingers but just oozes through your mouth. The taste is like essence of peach, three times as powerful as any other.

Of course it doesn't look like much, especially ours, because I don't prune the tree or thin the fruit so they're all small and fuzzy and slightly pointed at the bottom.

I thought there was only a light crop till I looked at the tree today. Peaches swell so much in the last week of ripening. Not that they're all ripe – we'll be picking them for weeks I think, the big ones first and then the tiddlers.

HARVEST TART

I haven't given exact proportions for the fruit and the pastry – how do I know how big your pie dish is or how fat your apples and peaches?

SHORTCRUST PASTRY TO LINE A PIE
DISH (DECENT PASTRY – DON'T
SPOIL THE TASTE OF THE INNARDS
WITH PRESERVATIVES)

1 *or* 2 APPLES, THINLY SLICED

1 *or* 2 FIRM-FLESHED PEACHES,
THINLY SLICED

CHOPPED MACADAMIAS *or* WALNUTS

3 EGG YOLKS

1 CUP CREAM

2 TABLESPOONS OF CASTER SUGAR
AND HALF A TEASPOON OF VANILLA

ESSENCE *or* 2 TABLESPOONS OF
VANILLA-FLAVOURED SUGAR
(*see note*)

Preheat the oven to 200°C.

Line a dish with the shortcrust pastry. Place it in a hot oven for 10 minutes, just to cook it slightly. It should still be mostly raw.

Fill the tart with the sliced apple and peach, scattering some chopped macadamias between the layers.

Beat the egg yolks into the cream and sugar. Add half a teaspoon of vanilla essence unless you've used vanilla-flavoured sugar.

Pour the egg-cream over the fruit. It should come up nearly to the top of the pastry (if it's too low the pastry will be overcooked and hard; if it comes right to the top it'll bubble over).

Bake about 30 minutes in a moderate oven, or till the custard has set.

Note: Vanilla-flavoured sugar can be made by sticking a vanilla bean into the sugar container; the flavour is infinitely more pungent, subtle and superior to vanilla essence.

* *March 9*

Sometime in the past week (lugging yet another bucket of apples up the hill or plastic bags of Golden Queen peaches or currawong-pecked avocados in my sweatshirt) I realised that the poem lauding the 'Seasons of mists and mellow fruitfulness' could only have been written by a man. A nineteenth-century man at that. Edward's school holidays were spent lugging cardboard boxes that invariably broke halfway down the hill, spilling apples into wombat holes and bouncing down the cliff into the creek. Bryan's fingers are (maybe) irrevocably purple – his contribution to the blackberry and apple jelly sitting on the kitchen table.

Only a nineteenth-century man would have had *time* to mutter poetry during harvest season. I can see John Keats languishing by the fire with a glass of fresh-pressed cider at his side while the women of his household scurried round with jam-stained aprons and strings of drying crabs (apples that is, I don't mean the crustaceans).

What we really need of course is a siege. A nice long one – long enough for us to *have* to eat the remnants of last year's plum jam, the seven bottles of pickled lemons that only a siege will force us to get round to, the apricots in rum from three years ago (potent enough probably to win a siege by themselves), the bags of slightly moth-infested red maize cobs that are too pretty to throw to the chooks …

I have sieges in my blood. I love the thought of sieges. Every time I fill a supermarket trolley or pick tomatoes I dream of sieges. Not of course that I actually *want* a siege – not one that would really deplete the larder shelves. I just like to dream of them.

The problem with self sufficiency is that you're stuck with it. Ten years and forty-four varieties of apple trees later, there are boxes of apples in the hallway, laundry, kitchen (not up the stairs however – the pumpkins reign along the stairway). The wombats are munching windfalls, the foxes climbing the more sprawling trees and the birds too fat to fly … and still we've got too many apples.

Not nice ordinary Jonnies or Golden Delicious either (both of which I believe are the queens of apples), but Lord Roberts and Prince Edwards and King Alfreds and French Crabs (planted mostly for their names – one for each member of the family ... though I couldn't find a Bryan), and now we have to eat them. And eat them. And eat them.

Old-fashioned apples sound better in the catalogue. Most need a colder climate to be truly rich and crisp. I remember my first Cox's Orange Pippin in Tasmania as a revelation – sweet and pungent at the same time and incredibly crisp (only apples and mornings and freshly ironed damask are really crisp).

Here they are sort of firmish, sort of sweetish, nondescript apples, not even a memory of what they might have been.

But back to the apple glut. I now realise why last century's recipe books are so hot on adding fruit and veg to cakes and puds. Not because they were starving, poor things, or grudged a little flour, but because they had too much ... too much ... too much ...

DESPERATION CAKE

HALF A CUP BUTTER

HALF A CUP BROWN SUGAR

2 EGGS

2 CUPS SELF-RAISING FLOUR

1 CUP MASHED PUMPKIN

A LITTLE MILK

1 TEASPOON CINNAMON

HALF A TEASPOON NUTMEG

AT LEAST 7 LARGE APPLES, PEELED
AND THINLY SLICED

*Preheat the oven to 200°C. Cream butter and sugar,
beat in eggs, add the other ingredients except apple –
the amount of milk you'll need depends on the
squishiness of the pumpkin. Pour into a greased cake tin
then press the apple slices deep and thick into the cake.*

*Bake at 200°C for 35 minutes or till a skewer comes
out dry.*

*Feed to family, guests and friends (makes good chook
food when you can't persuade anyone to eat another slice).*

❊ *March 10*

More rain, just as the creek stopped flowing again – so
heavy that as we drove home there was a sheet of white in
front of us. We never actually drove into the rain, only
where it had been. Runnels of milky water down the side
of the road, erosion gullies down the mountain and
collapsing edges on the mountainside. The creek ran –
well, not a flood, but more than a freshing – cloudy with
silt from the logging upstream. (So few city dwellers
understand that a good fall of rain doesn't break a drought.
You need lots of rain, for weeks …)

The rain has gone, but the clouds have stayed above us,
fat and stationary as though they've settled in for winter, a
true taste of the grey days to come.

I've started to pick the medicinal herbs for winter – hop
flowers and chamomile flowers and the last of the English

lavender (higher in oil, so better medicinally), all to be covered in brandy with lemon verbena leaves and a little peppermint for a relaxing brew: two teaspoons before bed, with honey in a glass of milk.

There are elderflowers too, for traditional cold and flu remedies – also supposed to be good for sinus problems, but I've never taken it long enough to tell. They get soaked in syrup; and rose hips to be picked and threaded and hung next to the chillies, and peppermint to be dried for tea before it dies down for winter and the last of the garlic to dig up, though we still have plenty of Giles's so it doesn't matter if I don't get round to it, it'll grow again.

It'll be time to dig the roots in a few weeks time, when the leaves have died down and the first of the frost has tenderised the bulbs – echinacea root, which is an immuno-stimulant and especially good for the bronchitis I'll probably get later in winter (an asthmatic remnant of a city childhood), valerian root for even more potent relaxation (if you want it for a sleep inducer, it's best fresh or dried to help long-term stress; but be warned – it can leave you as dopey as any commercial product), dandelion root 'for the liver', to be roasted and ground for coffee (which is disgusting, but some odd people like it), marshmallow roots for a cough remedy, and horseradish root so there'll be sauce to eat with the giant zucchini next season.

LOTIONS

(Written with pleasantly stinky fingers and the odd splodge of lavender oil.)

Sometime about now every year I start making potions. I know I should make them earlier,

when the petals are at their best, but somehow
I never do.

Maybe it's the sound of the bees. Bees are louder in
autumn – a sudden frenzy to store stuff before
winter maybe – or perhaps you just don't hear them
in summer under the noise of the cicadas.

Buzzing bees make some people feel drowsy. I get
envious, imagining them slipping from flower to
flower. Maybe I'm just naturally competitive and
want some of the nectar too.

The potion mood comes suddenly. One minute I'm
tapping calmly at the computer, the next I'm out in
the garden with stainless-steel bowls, picking, picking,
picking. (No, I don't pick my flowers by the full
moon – it's a nice poetic idea but you tend to pick
the odd caterpillar as well, which isn't much fun for
the caterpillar and is no good at all for the potions.)

Rosebuds, lavender flowers, echinacea petals,
calendulas, lemon verbena leaves – which is why I'm
writing this with stinky fingers and the odd splodge
of wax and lemon grass oil on my shirt. The jars
have been filled up, the larder's fragrant and I can
crane my head out my study door occasionally and
admire the produce lined up along the bench.

Most of the jars are handcream. There are … I need
to crane my head again for this … eight jars, two of
which I'll give away, and the rest I'll hoard. It's
enough handcream for the next decade, if not more.
(Perhaps I'd better leave an annotation to my will

too: and to my stepdaughters Elizabeth and
Catherine I leave my accumulation of lavender
handcream, jasmine massage oil, poppy face wash,
chamomile shampoo ...)

Six jars may not seem like much handcream for a
decade, and we do go through a lot of handcream.

But they're large jars and you only need the tiniest
smear of homemade handcream to do the job of
several large splodges of the commercial stuff. This is
because the cream you buy is mostly water –
customers need to feel they're getting something for
their money – whereas the jars you fill yourself are

crammed with concentrated essence of flowers
and bees.

There are two sorts of handcream sitting on the
bench. The first is heart's-ease handcream – made
especially for a friend with bad eczema. Heart's-ease
is excellent for eczema and this cream both protects
against irritation and helps heal.

The other stuff is more your generic handcream:
good for what ails you, whether it is chapped
fingers, scratches (my hands are always scratched),
swollen cuticles or just the creeping signs of age. It's
excellent stuff if you're planning to service the car,
dig the garden or scrub the bathroom – it really does
protect your hands.

You only need the tiniest smidgen on your hands –
literally a matchhead-sized blob. Any more and your
hands will be greasy.

I discovered today that Bryan doesn't know how to
rub on handcream, so if you or your near ones don't
(cross-examine your nearest male): place a little in
the middle of your palm, rub well, now rub the palm
of your right hand over the back of your left, then
the palm of your left over the back of your right –
and keep on going till it's all sunk in.

So this is the recipe. It's not set in stone – if you
don't have most of the ingredients there's no
excuse for not making it – just use what you do
have. As long as you have oil and beeswax it'll still
be good.

HEART'S-EASE HANDCREAM

1 CUP OLIVE OIL

3 CUPS HEART'S-EASE FLOWERS

A THIRD OF A BEESWAX CANDLE
(NOT PARAFFIN)

Blend the olive oil with the heart's-ease flowers till smooth. Melt a third of a beeswax candle in a saucepan, pull out the wick and pour in the oil. Mix with a knife (it's easier to get the scent off a knife than off a wooden spoon) till blended. Pour into small wide-necked jars (make sure you can get your fingers to the bottom easily or you'll either waste half the cream or dislocate a knuckle trying to get at it).

I'll probably mix 1 part of this with 1 part of the cream below.

BLOODY-GOOD-BEESWAX-AND-VARIOUS-STUFF-FROM-THE-GARDEN HANDCREAM

This smells incredible. Apart from the flowers, you'll need olive oil and some beeswax candles. (Make sure the candles are beeswax, not paraffin.)

Choose a day when the bees are sipping and the flowers are singing. Take a stainless-steel bowl (if you pick lavender into a plastic bowl your cakes will be lavender scented for the next two weeks; of course you may not mind this …). Strip off a collection of flowers:

LAVENDER FLOWERS
(ANTIBACTERIAL, SOOTHING FOR
ECZEMA, ANTISEPTIC, MILDLY
ANALGESIC, SMELL GOOD)

CALENDULA FLOWERS (ANTIFUNGAL
INCLUDING FOR THRUSH, ANTISEPTIC,
ANTI-INFLAMMATORY, HELP HEAL
SCRATCHES AND SCAR TISSUE)

CHAMOMILE FLOWERS (ANTI-
INFLAMMATORY, SOOTHES ITCHING,
GOOD FOR ECZEMA BUT CAN CAUSE
DERMATITIS IN SOME PEOPLE
THOUGH – TEST FIRST)

LEMON VERBENA *or* LEMON BALM
LEAVES (SOOTHING,
ANTIBACTERIAL)

ECHINACEA FLOWERS (ANTIBIOTIC)

MINT LEAVES (SOOTHING,
ANTIBACTERIAL, REDUCE
SWELLING)

ROSE PETALS (SMELL DIVINE, CAN
BE ANTIBACTERIAL, SOOTHING AND
ANTI-INFLAMMATORY DEPENDING
ON TYPE OF ROSE AND SEASON)

Take them inside and just cover with 3 parts olive oil to 1 part flowers. Heat slowly in a saucepan for 5 minutes with the lid on – otherwise you'll lose a lot of the volatile oils. (Don't worry. Even with the saucepan lid on, the house will still smell of lavender and roses.) Leave to cool.

Strain. For every 2 cups of oil add a melted beeswax candle (those rolled-up ones from health food or craft shops are great). Stir well. Pour into jars.

Note: If you don't have a garden or aren't herbally inclined, empty out some chamomile tea bags, rose-hip tea bags, mint ... well, you get the idea. The cream won't be as fragrant, but as I said – you have no excuse for not making your own.

.... 🌸 ....

✳ *March 11*

Grey light and wet grass. We walked across the ridges between showers: soft rain intercepted by the gumtrees, till the moisture ran in silver trickles down our backs.

It was the first time since summer that I've walked along the ridge. I've been clinging to the greenness of the garden and the shelter of the house. The grass is almost brilliant green now, fertilised with months of debris and wombat droppings gradually dissolving with the moisture. The hill is covered with wattle trees with dead tops and pale green shoots halfway up their trunks.

We sat on the old log halfway up (or I sat, getting a wet bum, while Bryan stood and kept dry). You could see the pattern of soil on the mountain opposite – wherever it is thin, along ridgetops or backs of rock, the trees have died; but most trees seemed to be coming back. It is still a piebald mountain though – gullies of green and stripes and almost squares of brown.

Then further up into the hills – me puffing, Bryan loping – the native raspberries are nearly finished. There's been so little native fruit this year (one reason we've lost so much down here) that there is only the odd berry to be found where the birds and wallabies and bush rats haven't found it. But the puff balls are fat and the wombat berries bright orange, and their roots would be swollen now, with all the rain. Wombat-berry roots are a bit like a sweet potato. It would be a good season to dig for roots now: soft soil and lots of new root growth as the trees wriggle into soft soil. Many of the trees here produce sweet roots – not to mention the bulrush roots, and the orchids – but I can rarely bring myself to dig any.

The last of the thorn-bush seeds (good to grind and bake), the last of the grass seeds – at least a dozen that are good to eat, probably many more if I only knew them – new green tips on many of the vines, very sweet. And if we wanted meat, the roos are fat.

About a dozen years ago I lived hand to mouth here – fed the occasional houseful of guests with food that got more and more traditional – great hunks of sheep roasted at nearly every meal (leg or shoulder or rib roast), with masses of veg from the garden (potatoes and pumpkins, peas, silverbeet, beetroot, zucchini and tomato), and stewed fruit for after, with maybe pastry from home-grown eggs and nut flour – everything home grown; incredible and easily achieved abundance, the living very cheap, and similar to what my great-great-grandparents probably ate. It would be easy to substitute roast roo for the sheep …

Sometimes, walking in the hills, I never want to stop. I want to keep going to that ridge and the next, though I know that eventually the hills would end, the roads begin and besides, I am a fair-weather walker, a nomad only in the gentle times, winter/autumn and spring. And then the heat arrives, or the cold, and I huddle back in the shelter of the stone walls and the protective greenness of the garden.

Grass-Seed Cakes

Take a cup of grass seeds – the oily ones on top of
the blady grass (*Lomandra* spp.) that rips through
your fingers if you're unwary enough to try to pull
it out. Bash the seeds with a rock or in a blender
till they're oily and mushy. Then bake on a hot
rock by the fire or in a non-stick pan, just a thin
scrape of mixture that slowly turns flaky and curls
up at the edges, then sets into a solid crisp pancake
which you eat hot and savour because there is
really no taste like it – like flour used to taste
maybe before we bred out the taste so we could
marry it with other things.

Almond-Flour Biscuits

Another recipe for when the aliens invade or the
meteor falls or the social fabric collapses and you
don't have wheat flour.

These are excellent with a dish of cold peaches
stewed in half water, half white wine.

2 EGG WHITES

2 TABLESPOONS CASTER SUGAR *or* HONEY

GROUND ALMONDS *or* WALNUTS *or* HAZELNUTS *or* GRASS SEEDS *or* WATTLE FLOUR (AT LEAST HALF A CUP — IT DEPENDS ON THE SIZE OF THE EGG WHITES)

Preheat the oven to 220°C.

Beat the egg whites until stiff. Stir in the caster sugar (or honey — different taste and texture but still good), then as much ground almonds (or walnuts, or hazelnuts or grass seeds or wattle flour) as you can, which will be quite a lot. Then place small dabs on a greased tray in a medium oven and bake till they puff up and just turn brown, which will be about 10 minutes.

Eat them hot or cold. They are delicate and lovely and you can pretend they're almost good for you.

.... ✿ ....

✳ March 12

The soil feels cool for the first time (probably won't last — we usually get a warm spell in April). I planted broccoli seedlings today. They won't mature till late spring. They'll be welcome then, after months of hauling the last of the silverbeet off the stalks and eating only the broccoli offshoots from autumn's plants.

✳ March 14

'It's me, love,' said Sue on the phone. 'You got time for a cuppa?'

This time she drives the truck down. It has more rattles than a day-care centre and has faded at one end — she had a fuel blockage one night back of somewhere, coming back from the pub, and one of the shearers decided to blow it out for her and lit a match to see what he was doing, and that was when he set the truck alight. Sue grabbed his shirt off him to beat it out. The truck still goes.

I make toast – lots of it – and bring out the plum jam. She's still too thin, but not as haggard this time.

'I've never seen such a miserable bloke in all my life after that. He just curled up on the seat till we got back. He's a real big bloke, tattoos all over him. When he first came I found him and his mates in the kitchen eating the stuff for tomorrow's lunch. He just looked at me, as though to say: "I can walk all over you." I suppose because I'm small, so I thought, I'll give him a rev. I gave him a real tongue-lashing.

'Half an hour later he was back again, sweet as pie. "Cookie . . . can I please have a bit of tucker?" And I looked up at him and I said: "Gary, stand back and let's have a look at you, you're a work of art!" And he flexed his tattoos and started giggling like a schoolgirl.

'There was one real bastard this time though. First one I've met. He had the room next to mine that first week and he was as deaf as a post, and his bed creaked all night, and so I yelled at him next morning: "Hey Bluey, do you know your bed creaks all night?"

'And he said: "I'll use yours then, ho ho ho."

'I just looked him in the eye, and he said: "Not funny then?"

'And I said: "No."

'Well, it must have been about midnight the next night. I'd just got to sleep, and I heard this rap on the door. There weren't any locks on the door so I'd pulled this old chest of drawers in front of it, and someone pushed the door open as far as they could and shone this great torch in my face, and this bloke said: "I've been into town and I've bought you back some icecream."

'I pulled the sheet up over me and started yelling my head off: "Go on, get out of it, go away!"

'I was really furious, because I'd been feeling so good with them and he'd made me afraid. I decided I'd talk to the overseer in the morning and get a lock on my door, but we were in the middle of nowhere, so I couldn't, and of course there were blokes sleeping all over the place and they'd heard everything, and this bloke told them that I'd led him on, and that he'd thought I said: "Come in."

'So I gave them my side of it, how he was so deaf he wouldn't have heard anything even if I had asked him in, he must have been lying, and they thought about it and said: "Yeah, yeah." They were really good about it. Then of course they turned it into this huge joke – it was all extremely vulgar – and from then on they referred to him as "Mr Whippy".

'He behaved himself after that alright.'

※ *March 15*

When did the cicadas stop singing? I can't remember.

※ *March 16*

Lunch at the cafe.

I didn't mean to have lunch at the cafe – I never do – but I wandered in there with my mail about 12.00, and there was Jeremy's unmistakable voice echoing over the coffee cups already, laughing with Angela about something: 'Aaawwww, how about that then!' (Some new hypocrisy by a local politician over the Welcome Reef dam – or Unwelcome Reef as it's referred to here – they were comparing anti-dam tactics over the melting moments.)

So I stayed for lunch (it is very hard to escape lunching with Jeremy), and Helen came in too, on her way back from an exhibition in Sydney, and custom was slack so Angela joined us, and Roger the Ranger at the next table abandoned his *Sydney Morning Herald* crossword and joined in the conversation, and Bjorn the Dane, wandered past for a minute and a half, whistling. (Bjorn always whistles, and never stops anywhere for more than three minutes. He used to live in a Mitsubishi van, with a TV aerial on the top. He's the only person I've ever known who drives from one side of the street to the other.)

Then Susan came in with another basket of duck eggs, greeny blue and perfect for sponge cakes (she works at the gallery weekends; knits and tends her menagerie and does stained glass the rest of the time). Carol works there during the week when it's less busy, with her patchwork on her knee. Then Mary, just back from sketching the Mongarlowe Bridge in case they knock it down like they did the Jembaicumbene ones, and Natalie's son Piers was playing his guitar in the courtyard, and Anders strolled by, still in dark glasses with a paper under his arm. Natalie's other son, Michael, was behind the counter, organising everything as Michael usually does. And it was four o'clock before I left, to explain to Bryan why it had taken so long to get the mail and bread and wombat oats ...

Picked the first red capsicum to stir fry for dinner.

❋ *March 20*

Another wombat – as though there aren't enough. It came up behind me as I was planting more snow peas in the hanging baskets outside the back door (they droop from baskets and mature fast in the heat above the paving by the house, so we get to eat them all winter).

I thought it was Pudge or Chocolate; then it bit my leg (just to attract attention, no malice intended), and I realised it wasn't.

I've named it Bad Bart the Biter. Bryan calls it Silvernose. It's the prettiest wombat I've ever seen – very delicate features and a pointed nose with silver fur about the snout and almost slanted eyes.

But it's a bastard.

(*No*, I'm doing it an injustice. Like most male wombats it just bites to say 'Hello, I'm here'.) And it isn't really the biting I mind so much (though I *do* mind the biting), but the surprise factor – there you are sniffing the last of the roses when *kerchunk*, something's ripping at your jeans.

I tried to shoo him away, but he wouldn't shoo. He was still hanging around when I fed Chocolate (who bared his teeth so Bad Bart retreated) and then Three-and-a-half (who lunged, head butted him, bit his balls, then went back to eating) and Pudge, who was terrified, so she showed the whites of her eyes again (it's been months since she did that). So I gave Bad Bart a pile of his own oats so Pudge could eat hers in peace; which in retrospect was a mistake, a sort of Munich appeasement of wombats. And now he'll expect food and hang round all the more.

❉ *March 21*

I was right. He is.

❋ *March 22*

Bryan was in an excellent mood when he came up for his midafternoon milk and chocolate. 'There's a truck overturned on Camden Road. They say the traffic's banked up for nearly four kilometres and it's not even peak hour yet!'

Bryan listens to the ABC Sydney traffic report every afternoon, down in his shed where he can watch the chooks as he works. And he always beams. After all, he's not in it. Listening to traffic reports is Bryan's secret passion. The worse the traffic, the more he smiles.

BAKED PEACHES WITH ALMOND MACAROONS

This is sort of Italian peach crumble – but a much more showoff-ish dish. You need deep yellow, firm-fleshed peaches, the sort you can smell at arm's length (if you can't, make something else).

8 PEACHES

16 ALMOND MACAROONS (EITHER HOME MADE *or* ITALIAN AMARETTI FROM THE SUPERMARKET)

2 TABLESPOONS CASTER SUGAR

1 EGG YOLK

1 TABLESPOON BUTTER, PLUS A LITTLE EXTRA TO BUTTER THE PAN

A FEW DROPS OF COINTREAU *or* VANILLA *or* NOISEAU (OPTIONAL)

Butter a baking dish and preheat the oven to 200°C.

Halve the peaches, then cut out the stones and just a little of their flesh (set aside), leaving a good-sized hole in the centre.

Chop the set-aside peach flesh; add finely crumbled macaroons, sugar and egg yolk (and optional flavouring, if you're using any), and dot with a bit of butter.

Bake at 200°C till the tops are just beginning to brown. Serve hot.

.... ✸ ....

✳ March 24

'What's the time?' asks Noöl idly, lying back against the rock.

Bryan looks at his watch. Bryan always wears his watch. It's waterproof to some incredible depth, shock proof and for all I know proof against black holes, daleks and space walks as well. And always accurate to the second – literally – a relic of his days in space tracking when a second's mistake could be fatal.

'Ten past one,' he says.

'We should go back for lunch,' says Noöl, trailing a toe in the water, but not as though she really means it.

Five minutes pass, or maybe more. Two wet heads poke up from the end of the swimming hole. Very wet heads. Kids can get wetter than any other creature.

'Aren't you cold?' asks Geoff.

Two heads shake, sending water spattering all over us. The wet-dog effect. They dive back in. They'd screamed at the cold water half an hour ago, but young metabolisms shrug off cold.

'We really *should* go back for lunch,' says Noöl, lying back on the rock like a lizard soaking up heat for winter.

We're drunk on sunlight.

Ten minutes later (maybe) Geoff opens his eyes again. 'Isn't it nearly lunchtime?' he asks.

'Mmm,' says Noöl.

The two wet heads are laughing at an echidna they've found at the other end of the swimming hole. It hasn't seen them – their scent is camouflaged by water – but its long black nose is sniffing curiously, and it knows there's something strange.

'Fabia!' calls Noöl. 'Aren't you getting cold?'

'No,' says Fabia. 'Look at his paws!'

'He might be female,' I say idly. 'We could turn it over and see.' But I'm not serious. It's too far down to the end of the swimming hole, and I'm too full of sun to move.

Three o'clock, maybe (no one has bothered to ask Bryan the time again) we wander back to the house.

I made soup yesterday, leek and potato, with the first leeks of the season – we don't bother eating leeks in summer. And there's avocado, lovage, tomato and basil salad with a few red mignonette lettuce leaves the snails haven't eaten – we're between lettuce crops at the moment, the winter one's aren't quite ready. We may as well use as much basil as possible, because it won't last past the first frost. And Noöl and Geoff have brought something rich and chocolaty.

'This place is always the same,' says Noöl. 'No, I don't mean it doesn't change. I mean it always feels the same. The spirit of the valley.'

I nod.

'Even the garden feels like it belongs here,' says Noöl.

So do we.

✳ *April 2*

It's a green drought again now – high clear sunlight and carpet-green grass, the first new fuzz from last month's rain kept short; not enough of it to get shaggy.

But the creek is dwindling again, the river still isn't flowing, and Bain's Gully is just a trickle – a week of hot days and they'll have stopped again, or even a few months of dry winter.

It's hard to worry about drought in the soft light of autumn. Autumn light is different – almost blue, the sky is higher, the shadows deeper, the colours more vivid now the harsh yellow summer light is gone.

The soil is cool, but not cold, the air is warm, the colours slowly swelling on the trees. It's a fecund time, even if the birds have eaten most of the autumn fruit and the bush rats have finished the last of the tomatoes. It's hard to believe the world around is harsh when the valley is so beautiful.

The valley is quiet now. The pickers have long gone (I saw Cynan in Canberra the other day, filling out an application for a work visa for England, and Giles's French niece who came for the fruit picking has headed back to Europe too.) The peach trees are drooping, in between seasons, not quite ready to turn colour and shed their leaves but having a disconsolate look, as if they don't quite know what to do to fill in their time. There are long brown strips along each row of peach trees, where the grass has been killed by herbicide. Even the cockatoos have deserted us for apple orchards somewhere else or a nut crop they decided to leave till last on the rounds of the district's fruit areas.

There are still peaches in the shops — small hard deep orange ones — and, contrary like, we're buying them (after having left the last of ours for the birds, and being totally sick of peaches, though I still have a dozen Golden Queens sitting in the fridge for a special occasion). But these are cooking peaches, incredibly meaty. I think the more sun a peach has had, the better it gets. I've made a note to try and get some of these very late peaches to plant here this winter.

Meaty peaches are best for baked peaches — they keep their shape as well as their taste. Baking and sugaring and lemon juice overpowers a delicate early season peach. Late-season, meaty peaches are perhaps the only peach to use for a peach mousse (otherwise you get all mousse and no sense of peach at all) — but definitely not the right peach for peaches in champagne. Late peaches are too selfish; they keep their juices to themselves, so you end up with two discrete entities in the glass, peach and champagne.

BAKED PEACHES

LATE-SEASON PEACHES

BUTTER

BROWN SUGAR

LEMON JUICE

Peel peaches, halve them by cutting along the 'slit' and wrenching the two halves apart. Lay them cut side down, their rounded cheeks upward, on a buttered baking tray (this must be buttered — no oil, no margarine). Sprinkle with brown sugar, then with lemon juice and bake in a moderate oven for 30 minutes. By now the peaches will

Seasons of Content

224

*be hot, soft, but still keeping their shape. The juice will
have run just a little, mingling with the sugar and lemon
juice and bubbling and caramelising.*

*Serve at once, with lots of cream, or vanilla icecream if
it's very good.*

.... ✿ ....

PEACH MOUSSE

If you wish to make a larger quantity, use the
ingredients in the same proportions. Don't make this
more than half a day in advance as it will lose its
incredibly light texture.

1 CUP LATE-PEACH PURÉE, COLD

2 TABLESPOONS SOUR CREAM

1 TEASPOON GELATINE

CASTER SUGAR TO TASTE

LEMON JUICE TO TASTE

1 CUP CREAM

*Heat the sour cream gently. Mix in the gelatine and
fold at once into the cold peach purée, making sure
there are no gelatine lumps. Taste — if it is insipid, add
a little caster sugar and lemon juice till it's vivid and
incredibly peachy.*

*Now whip the cup of cream, and fold into the purée.
Apportion into glasses — glass is best, to appreciate the
delicate colour, literally peaches and cream. Refrigerate to
set.*

.... ✿ ....

✳ *April 4*

Up to the cafe last night for one of Wilfred's rabbit and prune pies – or at least, Wilfred shoots the rabbits and skins and guts them, and either Natalie or Angela makes the pies. There's leek and potato soup on the menu too (which we're sick of) and red mignonette and tomato and avocado salad (that's the trouble with a cafe that relies on local fresh produce – we're sick of local produce).

But the rabbit pies are good. We feel virtuous as well as full, knowing that maybe another bandicoot may survive with at least one competing bunny gone.

Roger the Ranger and I once planned a restaurant called 'Ferals' where everything would either be a pest or a weed – prickly pear tart, wild boar and venison, feral goat and so on, not to mention dandelion, sheep's sorrel, cardoon, blackberry, hawthorn berries, briar heps, watercress . . . Of course sheep, wheat, rice and cotton are probably greater ecological disasters than any of the 'pests', but I'm not sure how a restaurant called 'The Great Ecological Disaster' would go.

✳ *April 6*

The creek has stopped flowing over the crossing. It's dropped quickly, despite the coolish weather. Another hot day and it might stop flowing altogether.

✳ *April 9*

All the wombats turned up for dinner tonight. Three-and-a-half first, then Bad Bart trying to shove her away (but she bit his balls again and he yelped and then behaved himself);

then an hour or so after they'd finished Chocolate arrived, then Pudge … and then just as we were about to go to bed Ricki turned up too.

Ricki was another WIRES product. We hadn't seen him for at least a year. He's lost an eye, as wombats often do – being short-sighted they probably run into thorns etc, but partial loss of sight doesn't seem to bother them. I suspect Bad Bart doesn't see much at all. His eyes are milky, and he relies on scent and sound almost entirely – but it certainly doesn't slow him down. Or his teeth.

Ricki didn't seem particularly glad to see us; but he made it obvious he did want carrots and oats – and fast. So we fed him, and gave him a back scratch for old times' sake, which he accepted. We left him to a second helping of carrots and went to bed. He was gone this morning.

✳ *April 13*

Rain.

The soil is sodden, the rain falling in a thick and even stream. It started last night, with lightning that turned the whole eastern sky yellow and thunder that grumbled over the mountain for five minutes.

The creek is running bank to bank now, foamy milk-chocolate water, thick with the smell of pine needles and several months of wombat droppings; the flats down the valley are riddled with brown-flushed streams, and the road so thick with wet clay I had to take the four-wheel drive down to the school bus.

The peach trees looked drenched, their half-autumn leaves without the stamina to stand up to the rain, drooping over puddles. And the river under the bridge is really a river again, waves and currents in a fury of dirty water.

You can smell a flood. It's a smell of rotting, fresh decay, debris accumulated from the last one. It's a wet smell, strong enough to creep into your clothes and every crevice, so strong you forget it's a smell and accept it as part of the world of flood. You forget it in the dry times. It's only when the water rises again that you remember.

I remember the smell from my childhood. Floods were adventure then – four kids and my mother hauling her brown Mini back as it floated down the street, tying it by the bumper bar to the fence where it bobbed amongst the tide mark of lawn clippings and dogs' bones and bits of lunch-wrapping washed down from other suburban gardens (I never asked if we were insured for flood damage; never wondered how long it took adults to turn the world back to normal).

We would sit on the verandah with the brown water lapping round the stilts of the house, watching cars sweep down the hill to the submerged road, betting which would ignore the barriers and crash through, to disappear under next door's diluted strawberry bed and dog turds. Mostly teenage boys who laughed as they struggled out of their cars, Brylcreem dissolving in suburban soup; or suited men unable to realise that any barrier meant them and who sat in their stranded cars and yelled as though someone must be responsible, some authority must be around to complain to and rectify the matter pronto.

There were floods at the beach too, on the island where we went for holidays – even more romantic. My mother remembered when she was a child and a storm washed a shipwreck ashore as well as a chest of money (to pay the crew, perhaps, or a pirate's horde, or the semi-mythical export of Australia's copper and silver coins to Hong Kong whispered through my childhood – the metal value was supposedly greater than the exchange rate).

She'd tell us that story every time it rained, and we'd listen under the thunder of water on the tin roof and fat drips from the gutters and the wet smell overcoming the holiday scents of damp towels and sand and watermelon and white bread and Vegemite and last night's stew – how the whole town was out on the beaches picking up coins, mostly small coins but some larger ones; she got over two pounds and her father more than five, women with handbags, shopping bags, kids' strollers and men with fat leather work-bags or hessian sacks with the coins rolling among the remnants of hen food or chaff.

The waves rolled the money in for three days, shifted sand on the silver so you had to grub for it with your toes, wedged the coins among dead seagulls; then it rained again and the waves crashed and the beach was clear again, just white sand and rolling water and no copper and silver freckles of humanity at all.

We'd run to the beach after every storm, of course, with wedges of bread and honey so as not to stop for breakfast, and the dog dragging its wet ears through the sand as it sniffed dead fish, but we never found any money or even broken chests or captain's chairs at all. Just cuttlefish that we stuck in our pockets for the cockatoo, jellyfish like half-chewed jubes, salty watermelon rinds even we wouldn't touch, the half skeletons of fish, and coral branches sometimes still with a wash of purple in the crevices but mostly flat and grey. And the dog would get sick on some innards it found draped round a rusty bucket. These were the days before drink cans and plastic bags; the days before you wondered if dead penguins and seagulls had succumbed to storm or humans and pollution. In those days bottles were rare, a prize to be carried off even if they didn't have a message in them – the deposit back on two bottles meant an iceblock.

This is a small flood of course. Not even enough to top up the watertable – the valley will be dry again in two weeks. (I still remember listening with rage to a woman in a city cafe in the last drought. She was watching perhaps twenty drops of rain scatter from the sky, and said: 'Maybe the farmers will stop complaining now.' She had no idea just how much water you need to fill the soil again, to buffer you from drought, to make things 'normal'.)

This flood was still fun. Edward and I went down to poke in the debris this morning. I'd told him Mum's story and it took hold, of course, though the chances of chests of money coming over the falls at Major's Creek and spilling into our swimming hole is even more remote than coins between the beach flags when I was a kid.

Silt between the rocks and rusty lumps left over from a tractor, old shirts (you find them every flood – bushwalkers casting off their clothes and then forgetting them? Campers washing in the creek? Or bags of rags dumped by the road and somehow washing down?), thongs – always at least one thong – if we'd collected them over the fifteen years we might have a pair by now. Thongs breed in floods, even now when more people wear jogging shoes than thongs (I have yet to find a jogging shoe washed down by floods).

Edward wanders back across foam-tipped rocks. He's found a wet feather, a bit of yellow waterproof that was too tangled around a rock to move, four rocks that will lose their colour when they dry, driftwood (we could make a raft but by the time the flood settles to safe levels there won't be enough water to float it on), and a bit of quartz with a flash of pyrites.

'Is it gold?'

'No.'

He throws it in the water with a fat plop. There'll be other floods. Perhaps the gold will come in one of them.

We head back to the house. The kitchen air is warm after the damp outside. It smells of cooking apples and boiling kettle, stronger than the smell of flood. Tomorrow or the day after we'll start repairing the water system, mending the water gouges in the road. The air will thin out and dry again, the ground won't suck and shiver as we walk on it, the creek will turn silver instead of brown.

Floods are a different world, as different as the sea.

❋ *April 14*

It's cold suddenly – that sort of bone-winter cold and even overnight the colours of the world have changed, wet green, deep green, the sort of green you get with lots of water and no sun to bleach it out. This is the start of winter: even if the air warms up again, the soil will stay cool.

It's a silent day – no birds, no wallabies, just a few wet roos up on the hill. Even Pudge has sheltered somewhere (I hope). Usually she just chomps her way through rainstorms and wonders why her biscuits are wet.

It's the sort of day that makes you check the store cupboard for winter preserves, the chilli and garlic garlands, the dried and bottled fruit, the boxes of apples and jars of jam and chutney. (I don't know why I make chutney — we rarely eat it — guilt I suppose at 'wasting' fruit, though it's never wasted with the chooks and compost.)

I hauled out a bottle of peaches this morning; probably a waste to start eating bottled peaches so early, but I feel like them now — it's a peach-soup day and nothing else will do.

HOT PEACH SOUP

1 LARGE WHITE ONION, CHOPPED

1 DESSERTSPOON OLIVE OIL

4 FIRM-FLESHED PEACHES

4 CUPS CHICKEN STOCK

1 CUP WATER

A SCRAPE OF CINNAMON

HALF A CUP GOOD WHITE WINE
(UNLESS YOU HAVE WHITE WINE IN
THE STOCK, IN WHICH CASE DON'T
USE ANY MORE)

2 CLOVES

1 TEASPOON VERY FINELY CHOPPED
PARSLEY

Sauté the onion in the olive oil till soft, add the other ingredients except the parsley and simmer for 20 minutes. Strain so that the soup is quite clear (eat the sludge with your fingers).

Reheat if necessary. Serve very hot with a sprinkle of parsley. (Though it's not bad cold.)

PEACH AND GINGER PUDDING CAKE

COOKED *or* RAW PEACHES –
ENOUGH TO LINE A CAKE TIN *or*
SOUFFLÉ DISH

HALF A CUP BUTTER

HALF A CUP BROWN SUGAR

2 EGGS

1 CUP SELF-RAISING FLOUR

1 DESSERTSPOON GOLDEN SYRUP

HALF A TEASPOON CINNAMON

4 TEASPOONS GROUND GINGER
(*or* MORE IF THE GINGER IS STALE)

STRONG BLACK COFFEE – ABOUT
HALF A CUP, DEPENDING ON THE
SIZE OF THE EGGS

2 DESSERTSPOONS CRYSTALLISED
GINGER (OPTIONAL)

Preheat the oven to 200°C.

Line a cake tin or soufflé dish with the cooked or raw peaches.

Cream butter and sugar, add the eggs, beating well between each one. Fold in the other ingredients. Pour over the peaches, bake in a moderate oven for 40 minutes or till the cake is firm on top.

*Turn out carefully onto a serving plate, or spoon out of
the dish in which it has been cooked. This is probably
best hot and fresh, but it's still good cold, or reheated
gently in a moderate oven.*

Serve by itself or with cream or good vanilla icecream.

❋ *April 17*

The trees are yellowing — not just the autumn leaves on
the European trees, but the new shoots on the pittosporum
after all the rain. The new gum shoots are red or rusty
green, and the casuarinas still sparkle silver with raindrops
on their branches. The last of the roses are incredibly fat —
autumn roses are the biggest and sweetest of all.

It's still too early for the red autumn leaves and the deepest
of the yellows. But the rose hips are reddening — great fat
ones on the rugosas and Climbing Ophelia (I always feel a bit
odd about Ophelia climbing up to our bedroom. Ophelias
shouldn't climb — languish maybe, but then 'languishing
Ophelia' doesn't have quite the same ring for a rose).

I pick the rose hips sometimes and bung them into a pot
of herbs in whisky to sweeten them. At the moment there
are jars of chamomile flowers, lemon verbena and lavender
brewing with rose hips in the larder — I just stuff them in a
jar and pour on whisky (brandy is the herbalist's usual
choice — I like whisky better).

The rose hips give a sweetness and tang. They may also
add vitamin C but I'm not sure about that after steeping so
long in whisky. (The whisky preserves and extracts volatile
oils and I'm sure Grandad would say it does you good in

its own right too – especially with the aforementioned brew of chamomile, verbena, lavender and rose hips, which is taken by the teaspoonful to relax you before bed.)

EGLANTINE SAUCE

This was Queen Victoria's favourite.

3 CUPS ROSE HIPS (PICK DEEP RED
ONES – BRIARS ARE BEST)

SUGAR

A DASH OF LEMON JUICE

*Simmer the rose hips in a very little water till tender,
then press through a sieve to get rid of the seeds.
Add half a cup of sugar for every cup of purée and
a dash of lemon juice to taste. Bring to the boil, take
off the heat.*

*You can eat this with roast lamb (as Queen V did), or
even on muesli or on top of icecream (as she didn't). It is
much better than you might think.*

*Last century's herbalists acclaimed this as a tonic
for chronic diarrhoea, cystitis, gall-bladder problems and
other 'female disorders'. Dunno if Queen V suffered
from any of those or not. After all those kids, perhaps
she did.*

❧

✳ *April 20*

Picked pumpkins today — two barrows full. I always go
overboard with pumpkins. Flat grey Crown Princes and fat
Queensland Blues and a few hard-skinned and thin-fleshed
Golden Nuggets, and an odd warty variety I can't
remember the name of, and a few Turk's Caps and yellow
squashes (don't know why I planted those, as we never eat
them; the siege mentality again I suppose — if the aliens
invade we'll live on pumpkin).

Pumpkins are supposed to cure on the chook-house
roof (curing really does harden pumpkin skins) but I
can't be bothered climbing up there, so they're on the

hot paving instead, where we trip over them every afternoon. Then all I have to do is find a place to store them …

❋ *April 26*

No sign of Bad Bart for a week, or Chocolate either – they're filling up on grass. Pudge hadn't been around for a while, but she visited last night. She looks like a brown beach ball with four legs and a nose. Three-and-a-half pads round the house looking hopeful as soon as the sun falls behind the ridge, and if we don't feed her straight away she tucks into the green stuff instead.

The grass looks almost good enough to graze myself at the moment – water fat and autumn lush.

Someone once called these blue and gold days. And they are.

❋ *April 27*

Down to Tilba to camp with Noöl and Geoff. Wind and sea biting at the cliff and ruffles on the lake and it was wonderful, just that wonderful stretching blue and it *doesn't* end, you can keep on going forever around and around the world

Geoff hauled home firewood, like a hunter proud of his prey, and then made damper, which was like most dampers I've eaten – small and hard and round (rather like a wombat, come to think of it) and doughy in the middle (which a wombat isn't).

HOW TO MAKE DAMPER THAT WORKS

No, I didn't smugly tell Geoff this, and I hope he isn't reading this; and luckily Edward shut up too and didn't say 'When *we* make damper' … . Maybe he's getting tactful or, more likely, was just more interested in the dead crab the other kids had found in the firewood.

Damper making is an art. It's not just what goes into it that makes it good – if it's not made the right way it'll be tough or, even worse, raw inside and burnt outside.

2 CUPS SELF-RAISING FLOUR
or PLAIN FLOUR WITH 2 TEASPOONS
BAKING POWDER

ABOUT 2 TABLESPOONS BUTTER *or*
MARG *or* OIL

SALT, IF YOU LIKE SALT

AS MUCH WATER AS NEEDED TO
MAKE IT DOUGHY – ABOUT HALF A
CUP, BUT THIS WILL VARY

Optional

BUTTERMILK INSTEAD OF WATER
AND BUTTER

HALF A CUP ROLLED OATS INSTEAD
OF HALF A CUP FLOUR

MIXED SPICE *or* CINNAMON

MIXED FRUIT, GRATED PEEL, ETC.

Combine all the ingredients. It's best to add the water a little at a time and knead well – the more you knead, the less water will be needed. You may end up with a soggy mess if you add it all at once.

Now butter a camp oven – the thicker the metal, the better a camp oven is. Flatten out the damper till it is about half the diameter of the oven and press a largish hole through the middle – a hole about the size of your fist. If you don't do this, you may end up with a doughy middle.

Leave the dough in the oven with the lid on for half an hour to 'rest', and tend to your fire. It should have plenty of coals.

Scrape the coals away and place the camp oven on the bare ground where the coals were. Then, with a spade or bit of green bark, scoop the coals up and onto the camp oven so there is a good layer on top of it as well as around it. If you don't do this, or if you leave coals underneath it, you'll get a burnt bottom and pale top.

The damper will take about 30 minutes to cook – check it after 20 minutes and stick a bit of grass down the centre. If it comes out doughy, put the lid and coals back again.

A good damper should be brown and shiny on top – the combined steam and melted butter dripping onto it will give it a good glaze. It should be eaten hot, with golden syrup or plum jam – or even strawberry jam and cream if you don't want to be traditional.

If you don't have a camp oven, you can use a billy. If you don't have a billy, you can use a terracotta flowerpot with a rock on top of it as a lid. When we were kids we made damper in an old fruit-juice can – we bent back the lid to drink the juice, then bent it back down again as a cover to keep the coals off the bread inside. If your tin can *doesn't have a lid, stick a large rock over it instead. Don't overfill small containers or you'll get heavy soggy damper.*

FRIED BREAD

This could also be called 'flat bread' – though most flat breads are cooked in the oven. It's a form of hearth cake, and variants on this recipe can be found in most cultures around the world, wherever seeds can be found and ground for flour. It is *much* easier than damper and very good indeed; also good made at home if you run out of fresh bread. (Come to think of it, flat bread has probably been eclipsed by supermarkets. Who needs to make flat bread now when most people can dash down to the shop at almost any time of day or night? Scones ditto probably – Grandma's emergency food if a horde arrived. Come to think again, hordes probably don't arrive unexpectedly in the city either – just out here, when they bowl up and say: 'We were just driving past and thought we'd …')

3 CUPS SELF-RAISING FLOUR

2 TABLESPOONS OLIVE OIL (PLUS EXTRA OIL FOR FRYING)

1 CUP WARM WATER (*or* A LITTLE EXTRA IF NEEDED)

Optional

FOR A SWEET FRIED BREAD, ADD HALF A CUP BROWN SUGAR, LOTS OF CURRANTS AND SOME MIXED SPICE

*Mix all the ingredients. Knead for about 5 minutes –
it should be elastic and rubbery or the resulting bread
will be scone-like. Cover with a tea towel and leave for
20 minutes.*

*Divide the dough into small balls, about the size of a
very small egg. Pat them flat – don't roll them with a
rolling pin – the constant patting with your hand gives
the best results.*

*Heat a heavy frying pan; add enough oil just to cover
it, and wait till the air above the oil begins to shimmer,
then put in your rounds of bread dough.*

*Fry each side for about 5 minutes or until golden.
Drain and eat hot.*

*I've cooked fried bread on a hot stone by an open
fire – it's a good standby when your camp oven is full
of stew.*

*Fried bread is good with hot kebabs and yoghurt
sauce, curry, vegetables cooked in olive oil (especially
tomatoes and artichokes) – and lots of other things.*

Sweet fried bread is good by itself, very hot and fresh.

❋ *May 1*

Pumpkins under the stairs, in the larder, along the laundry
passage – and of course the wretched things don't even
taste particularly sweet. We just don't get enough sun down
here in the valley, not enough for the lovely, dry, close-
textured pumpkin taste anyway. The best pumpkins are
grown in a drought (well, we had that most of the
season) … but not in a deep valley …

❋ *May 6*

Peach leaves droop before they turn colour and most don't colour much at all, though some varieties are more spectacular than others – although even then 'spectacular' is probably flattering them. Most of the leaves are dirty rust, and lying limp against their twigs, as though crushed by the weight of autumn shadows. They are much prettier on the soil, splayed around the tree, looking richer and redder against the dark soil.

PEACHES POACHED WITH VANILLA, GINGER AND CHILLI

FRESH PEACHES

A BIT OF VANILLA BEAN

HALF A DRIED RED CHILLI
(*see note*)

THINLY PEELED RIND OF A LEMON

6 THIN SLICES ROOT GINGER

1 CUP SUGAR

3 CUPS WATER

Pour boiling water over peaches for 5 seconds, till their skins wrinkle. Rub off the skins.

Place the peaches in a casserole with the vanilla bean, chilli, lemon rind and ginger.

Make a syrup with the sugar and water, simmer for 10 minutes, then pour over the peaches. Bake in a slow oven (150°C) for 2 hours, turning the peaches every so often if their heads are above the high-water line.

Scoop out the vanilla bean (dry it – it can be used again), and the chilli, lemon rind and ginger (which can go to the chooks).

Serve hot with cream, or good-quality icecream, which goes even better with the heat and tang.

Note: If you haven't got dried or fresh red chilli, fresh lemon rind, fresh root ginger and so on, don't substitute – vanilla essence, chilli powder and powdered ginger won't do.

························ ❧ ························

❋ *May 9*

Finished the last of the hoarded Golden Queens this morning. I had to force myself to eat it, as it won't keep any longer – it was already shrivelled and suspiciously soft on one side – but it was beautiful. Simply beautiful – a sharpness and meatiness to savour and remember for another ten months until I taste another.

❋ *May 17*

This is the magic time, the shadow and light time, the hills deep purple and the sky a high clear blue, as though free of the weight of summer's sun. Even the trees are at their most beautiful, the sodden dull leaves dropped off and the bright red new wood glowing against the sky.

Most of this will be pruned off soon – in fact the lower orchards have already been pruned. With so many to get through, pruning starts very early.

Peaches fruit on last year's wood and this supple red wood is the growth from last season that will bear fruit

next summer; but if all of it is left to bear, there'll be masses
of tiny peaches – mostly unsaleable to consumers who like
great fat soccer balls of fruit – and because of this great
harvest, there'll be little new wood the following year. So
to even up the fruit supply, about two-thirds – and often
more – of this new red wood is pruned off and the trees
are left as harsh skeletons throughout the winter.

The red wood more than makes up for the lack of
autumn leaves, though you only realise how spectacular
it is en masse. The wood of a single red-flushed peach
tree in your back garden probably stays unnoticed. You
need thousands of trees for the true beauty, the delicate
tracery of thin wood, complex and complexing, like
ordered spider webs. The more rows there are behind,
the brighter they look. Perhaps you need this clear blue
sky as well and the soft light of the sun low on the
horizon. A valley light, as well as autumn light, the
brightness reflected off the trees and cliffs and changed
in doing so.

BASIL AND OLIVE MEZZE

I keep picking my basil before the frost gets it –
great fat leaves, the sort of succulence you only get
in autumn. The recipe below is one thing to do
with the almost-last-of the basil. It keeps for
months. In fact it's all the better if you do keep it for
months, makes an excellent present when you've
forgotten Aunt Delilah's birthday, or to impress not-
quite friends who come to lunch expecting
something home grown, home cooked and looking
like it burped out of *Vogue*. (You never mean to

invite people like that to lunch, but they ooze their way in anyway — then demand a tour of the garden for three hours and a photo with their dog. Note: from now on I'm just going to tell them to piss off and to hell with the hospitality Grandma taught me.)

CHUNKS OF CHEESE (FETTA, MOZZARELLA *or* ANY FIRM CHEESE)

LOTS OF CHOPPED BASIL

BLACK OLIVES

RAW CAPSICUM STRIPS

A LITTLE LEMON RIND

WHOLE BLACK PEPPERCORNS

A LITTLE CHOPPED ONION

A CHILLI *or* TWO, IF YOU LIKE CHILLIES

Combine all ingredients in a jar and serve as an appetiser. It should keep for at least three weeks, but throw it out if it smells odd or grows wildlife or turns cloudy. (All preserved food is liable to grow interesting bacteria — eat at your own risk.)

A BASIL APHRODISIAC

Dunno if this works. If I tell Bryan I've just given him an aphrodisiac I'd like to test, he giggles.

Take a bottle of good hock or chablis. Insert a bunch of basil. Leave it at room temperature for 24 hours, remove the basil and chill. Pour out a glass for the object of your desires … and remember aphrodisiacs are far more effective if you tell the person you've dosed that they have just drunk an aphrodisiac.

✳ *May 20*

We ate massaged hare last night.

It's Giles who says they're massaged. His daughter says they're squashed. Edward says the last one they picked up was maggoty and even the cats didn't want it, though the chooks ate it happily enough.

Victoria is philosophical. If her husband wants to pick up flattened wildlife – sorry, massaged game – she's prepared to eat them, provided that he cooks and cleans them, both of which he does extremely well. After all she says, in France, where Giles grew up, you never get a chance to pick up the game that you ran over. By the time you've stopped, the car behind will have grabbed it first.

Wild food in France is a delicacy, whether it's trapped, shot or … massaged. And besides, she says, it's easy to judge the freshness of a roadside corpse. Just avoid it if it's maggoty.

Giles's speciality is hare, though rabbit is still welcome, and if I ever run into a deer, wild pig or feral goat I've promised to wrap it in a blanket and deliver it to him pronto. The hare was one I ran over last week and it's been marinating ever since. I didn't mean to run it over; I swerved, and it swerved too. And then the bump that means it didn't make it. The guilt stays with you for

days … though I wouldn't have felt guilty if I'd killed it
deliberately. Maybe it's just that cars are such dull, brutish
implements and killing should be a conscious act, with the
consequences weighed and accepted.

It was early morning; the mist still shivered over
Jembaicumbene. I was on my way to the ABC. So I
carried the corpse to Giles and Victoria's. (Giles feeding
the chooks in gumboots, jumper and nothing else.)

Giles's hare casserole is delicious, incredibly rich, so you
only need a few tablespoons for every mound of golfball-
like new potatoes grubbed out of the garden ten minutes
before they are cooked. Giles's massaged hare evokes some
race memory of the real taste of meat. The succulence
stays with you for years afterwards.

Nowadays we like to keep our food at a distance, so it's
sanitised as 'ingredients', preferably shiny or on trays,
bought by the kilo or in 200 gram portions so it fits neatly
into recipes.

No one in their right mind would *buy* the sort of foods
I've gathered in the last few days – sodden lettuces with
rotting outside leaves, tasting of the rain, spotty silverbeet,
cracked tomatoes oozing juice so you have to cut off at
least one side, pears with two small bird pecks at either end.

This year's peaches were smaller and tasted of hot soil
and sun. The apples had the dark red blush of drought. In
these supermarket days only wine has vintages. Only those
who grow their own remember the cherries of 1982, not
many but sun perfect, the leeks of 1988, fat and sweet …

Like Giles's massaged hare, even broccoli going to seed
or soggy lettuces are good – if you know how to cook
them. Turn the lettuce into soup (purée with rooster stock

and just a little cream), peel the broccoli stalks and stir fry them with young garlic bulbs – just like an onion before they grow the paper between the cloves, only sweeter and milder, but you must use lots of olive oil …

Besides, I think I like the taste of blemishes. Like my wrinkles, each blemish tells me where it's been – the late frost that dimpled the peaches, the stink-bug plague that sucked pale patches on the limes. Shop-bought food is grudging, because that's all you get. There's a world of memories in every blotchy leaf out of the garden.

Sometimes I feel that this fetish to tidy up the world is just a neurotic response – as our air, water, forests, resources are fouled and exhausted, we're fanatically sanitising the few bits left under our control – like a kid who believes the exam will come out right if every pencil is sharpened and lined up beforehand. But this 'tidy up' moves us even further away from the non-human world.

Besides, scabbed apples do taste sweeter, birds peck the ripest strawberry. If botrytis is 'the noble rot' on grapes, so is brown rot on apricots, which only attacks the richest ones of all – just scrape off the bad bit on the side.

One day I'll even find the courage to cook a massaged hare.

GILES'S MASSAGED HARE

If you don't have a hare – massaged or otherwise – this recipe is good with a hunk of wild pig, a leg of goat, pork leg chops at a pinch, or even chicken, which is what I usually use (yes, even a frozen chook if you must, but it'll be stringy and not as succulent). You need meat that *tastes* of something for this dish

to be really good – say a youngish rooster,
introduced to the axe just as he starts to crow at
maybe twelve weeks. (If you think I'm hard hearted,
remember that even Giles's massaged hares have a
better life and death than any meat you buy at any
butcher's. Those who eat meat need to shoulder the
responsibility … and anyone who keeps chooks
knows you can't keep *all* the roosters, they fight
amongst themselves and terrorise the hens …)

1 HARE, MASSAGED, SKINNED AND
GUTTED, *or* OTHER MEAT AS ABOVE
(IF YOU ARE USING A FRESH ANIMAL,
SAVE THE BLOOD AND LIVER)

FLOUR

GOOD RED WINE (NO, NOT A
GURGLE FROM A CASK – USE THE
STUFF LEFT OVER FROM THAT
DECENT BOTTLE LAST NIGHT – THE
POINT OF THIS RECIPE IS THAT ALL
THE INGREDIENTS ARE GOOD)

SHALLOTS

A FEW SPRIGS OF FRESH THYME
(*see notes*)

A COUPLE OF FRESH *or* DRIED BAY
LEAVES

OLIVE OIL

2 TABLESPOONS CHOPPED FATTY
BACON

12–20 CLOVES GARLIC, ROUGHLY
CHOPPED, NOT CRUSHED (*see notes*)

1 LARGE ONION, CHOPPED

12 TINY ONIONS (OPTIONAL) – IF
YOU'RE RUTHLESS, HAUL THEM
IMMATURE FROM THE GARDEN; IF
YOU'RE LUCKY, YOU'LL FIND
PICKLING ONIONS FOR SALE
SOMEWHERE

MUSHROOMS (OPTIONAL) – EITHER
FIELD MUSHROOMS (THEY'RE
SPROUTING UP ALL OVER AS I
WRITE, PRODUCT OF A LOVELY
DRIZZLY AUTUMN), WHICH WILL
GIVE YOU FLAVOUR AND A DARK
BLACK JUICE, *or* COMMERCIAL
CHAMPIGNONS, WHICH AT LEAST
WILL ADD TO TEXTURE

PEPPER

Joint the hare or rooster. Roll meat in flour. Place in a casserole. Cover with red wine. Add shallots, thyme and bay leaves and a tablespoon of olive oil. Leave covered overnight or for up to three days in the fridge. (In my fridgeless days I once kept a leg of pork for three weeks in a marinade. It was the best I've ever tasted but I haven't dared repeat it since.)

Place a little olive oil in a pan, brown the bacon, then sauté the chopped garlic and onion as well as the tiny onions till the chopped onion is transparent. Take off the heat.

Drain the meat (reserving the marinade) and pat it dry.

Fry the meat in olive oil till browned. Take out the meat and add 3 tablespoons of flour to the pan. Stir over a low heat till the mixture in the pan browns. Add the meat again, the marinade, and the sautéed bacon, garlic

and onion. Simmer for 45 to 60 minutes or till just
tender, with the lid off so the sauce reduces to rich sludge.
Add more red wine if necessary.

Take off the heat. At this stage you can bung the
whole lot in the fridge and finish it tomorrow or the next
day. If you've got the time and energy, continue now.

Add sliced mushrooms. Cover the pot, place in the
oven and cook at 150°C for an hour. Don't be tempted
to add more wine at this stage – the mushrooms will
yield up their juices to the sauce, and the wine will taste
too raw if you add it now.

A few minutes before serving, add the pepper (it'll
turn the sauce bitter if you add it too soon) plus the
finely chopped liver and reserved blood to enrich the
sauce.

Serve with a mound of tiny new potatoes, fast boiled
with parsley and butter added at the end (take them off
the heat when they're not quite cooked and cover with
the lid so they steam the last few minutes and don't
burst); or thick chunks of toasted or fresh French loaf for
mopping up the juice. Nothing else.

Serve a salad afterwards: either a mixture of green leaves,
some sweet and just a couple bitter (what the French call
mesclun), or the harvest of the garden – lettuce hearts made
pungent with a little dandelion (the newest palest leaves
and yellow dandelion flowers), tiny sow-thistle buds, sheep
sorrel from the cracks in the brick wall (the sweetest and
most succulent of weeds), with just a drizzle of good oil.
What else would you serve with massaged hare?

Notes: Don't use dried THYME – if you haven't
any growing, mooch down to the nearest garden centre

and buy a pot (it'll cost almost the same as a packet of green dust); you can pick up a bay tree when you buy your thyme. Secondly, 12–20 cloves GARLIC isn't a typo. I do mean 20 cloves, and the final result won't smell of garlic either – but don't even let a metal garlic crusher near this recipe or you'll be burping stale garlic for the next two weeks (a Teflon-coated crusher is probably acceptable). Chopped sautéed garlic isn't acrid, and it thickens the sauce as well. Crushed garlic put straight into liquid smells (and probably tastes) like a Marseilles navvy's armpit.

....🐝...

❋ *May 22*

Pudge has discovered the vegetable garden. Heaven preserve us from intelligent wombats. The carrots have been replaced by large brown holes, and all the tops of the parsnips have been eaten (she couldn't be bothered digging deep enough to get to the rest).

Bryan spent this morning fencing off the vegetable garden with reinforcing mesh – a case of after the wombat has eaten, as there's no point planting any more carrots and parsnips till next spring (they'd just go to seed without producing bottoms).

At least that answers the question of how many carrots Pudge could eat at a sitting: at least two square metres worth, and probably more. And she still turned up on the doormat wanting her oats this morning.

Sandra from down the valley called in to pick up someone's jumper this morning (it's been sitting on the chair by the door for the past month waiting to go home) and left a bucket of milk.

One of my dreams when I first came here was to have a cow. I then realised that while I love cows – they smell nice and are very cuddly first thing in the morning – and I quite enjoy milking, I really don't like milk much (or even cheese for that matter) and five odd gallons of milk every day was enough to turn anyone off Devonshire cream and butter.

So I gave up the cow idea though I'll happily share if someone else is doing the tending – fresh milk actually tastes of something, instead of that vague dairy taste that just reminds me of drink-that-milk-girl school days, when the tiny bottles coagulated in the sun till 'little lunch' at recess.

Sandra's milk had at least three fingers of cream on the top, almost solid so we had to use a spoon to scoop it off. Bryan is having it on his porridge tomorrow, and if there are any raspberries I'll make a fool. But even though Bryan loves milk (drinks a glassful every afternoon with two pieces of Lindt chocolate before he starts to tidy the chooks back to their roosts and put away the tools), we can't cope with a bucketful.

FRESH CHEESE

These aren't cottage cheeses, they aren't cream cheese – they're simply fresh cheese. They are one of the few cheeses I really like – probably because they're not particularly cheese-like.

Fill a bowl with milk, leave for two days at room temperature (this assumes your room is comfortable – if it's stinking hot, keep the bowl in a cool cupboard). The milk should thicken slightly without going bad. You can hasten thickening by adding a junket tablet, but there's no need if you have patience (though a junket tablet might be an idea if you're using homogenised milk). Pour into a cloth – I use a clean tea towel, doubled over – and hang in a cool place, like over the bath (if you don't mind the temporary but odd yellowish streak), till the liquid has run out and the cheese is firm.

Serve with fresh fruit, fresh fruit purée, cream or sugar.

VARIATIONS

If you wish, you can flavour your fresh cheese before it is placed in its cloth.

For a savoury cheese: add pepper (black or green), chopped herbs, garlic, chopped olives, chopped capsicum, chopped chillies in whatever combination you want.

For a sweet cheese: add sugar, chopped candied fruit, vanilla, cinnamon-sugar, etc. My favourite cheese has added grated orange zest and a little Cointreau, and it's served with fresh cream and a raspberry purée (there's no need to add sugar – the raspberries are sweet enough).

MATURING

Fresh cheeses can be kept to mature – rub them in wax and leave for six months, or keep in brine made with 3 cups of water and 3 cups of salt. They don't have the same texture as a 'proper' matured cheese – but they're very good. I like them best after about three weeks – firm, sliceable, slightly soapy, but still with a fine fresh flavour.

.... 🜩 ....

CALENDULA CHEESE

This is bright yellow and rather soapy – a sort of Jatz crackers and sliced tomato sort of cheese, definitely not for a connoisseur. I am not, and I like soapy cheese.

1 CUP CALENDULA PETALS

JUNKET TABLETS

MILK

Chop the calendula petals and cover with 2 tablespoons of boiling water. Leave to steep for 20 minutes. Strain into a bowl.

Make 2 cups of junket according to directions on the packet, adding the calendula juice to the milk before you heat it. *Leave the junket to set.*

Now take a knife and slice the junket back and forth till it is cut into as small pieces as you can – but don't mash it up. Pour into a sieve and leave overnight to strain.

Wrap the curds in a clean cloth (such as cheesecloth). Put the curds and cloth back into the sieve, and cover with a saucer with a small weight on top – this will press out more liquid. Leave in the fridge or a cool larder for three weeks. It'll be soft but firm. And soapy.

.... 🜩 ....

✳ *May 24*

Large holes all around the veg garden fence but Pudge hasn't got in yet. And besides, the silly twit has eaten all the carrots already. Maybe she thinks they've magically regrown. (I don't suppose you can really expect a wombat to understand the finer points of carrot cultivation.) We've left the holes as they are – she'll only redig them if we tidy them up, thinking she's found some undug dirt. As Bryan says, wombats have only two neurones, and only one works at a time – the ultimate single-minded animal. It is almost impossible to reprogram a wombat.

Picked the pomegranates today – mostly because I couldn't resist them – fat and red faced like they'd done something terribly naughty and hoped I wouldn't find out. I've stuck a dozen on the dresser, three in with the fruit on the table (picking out two deceased lemons and a squashy tamarillo), which still leaves a bucket full. Some can go up to the cafe and be decorative up there. The rest need to be used, or they'll just turn to sludge in the larder and be thrown to the chooks sometime round the end of winter, which would be a waste.

.... ✥ ....

POMEGRANATE CORDIAL

The original grenadine, I think. And it's easy.

POMEGRANATES

CASTER SUGAR

Scoop out the seedy pomegranate centre; add an equal amount of caster sugar, leave in a jar for three weeks. By

then the sugar will have drawn out the red juice. Strain into a bowl, then bottle and keep in the fridge. Use a dessertspoonful to a glass of cold water or pour over a glass of crushed ice.

ROSE SYRUP

From the last of the roses, faded but still fragrant, so you can't bear to lose them. There are bowls full of petals on every table, and seven pots of this syrup in the larder.

ROSE PETALS (THE MORE PERFUMED
THE BETTER)

SUGAR

LEMON JUICE

JAMSETTA (OPTIONAL)

Take a pan of rose petals and just cover with water. Bring to the boil with the lid on, take off the heat at once and leave overnight. Mash the petals into a gruel with your fingers, then strain. Add an equal volume (not weight) of sugar to the water and a squeeze of lemon juice. Simmer till the mixture coats the back of a spoon. (If you want to cheat, add a packet of Jamsetta for every 3 cups of sugar.) Take off the heat, bottle and seal.

You can eat this with toast, but it's really a jam for scones or delicate pastries with cream.

✳ *May 25*

I once knew a murderer who sang about lemon trees. At
least the jury said he was a murderer. I never believed he
was. But that's another story (though the song was very
sweet). This is about lemon trees – and lemons – because
I'm writing this sitting lemonless in an airport. And I miss
them and wish for the hundredth time that I'd
remembered to bring one with me.

Lemons are maybe the most fragrant fruits. Lemon scents
are sweet, even if the fruit isn't. You can tell when the
lemons are ripe in our garden. The breeze grows tangy and
without knowing why, you dream of sorbets and fried fish.

Once upon a time Europe didn't have lemons and used
verjuice instead – the juice of slightly green grapes, which
is exquisite. The only sad things to say about lemons are
that their glory has eclipsed verjuice and that you can't
climb lemon trees; they're the wrong shape and too prickly
and the wood is brittle so you fall through the middle and
spike your bum on a bit of broken branch. Which is a pity
because I think I'd like life up a lemon tree.

The backyard lemon tree used to be where the males
relieved themselves after the third cup of tea following
Sunday roast mutton. The lemon trees grew all the better
because it's hard to overfeed a lemon – as long as the
libation's fresh.

Actually I did once know an overfed one. It was during
the drought and the world was bare and brown, except
around the lemon tree, which I mulched and watered. Our
chooks sat under the lemon tree from 1978 to 1982, and
when it rained again the tree was so surfeited with five

years of chook droppings (and the lemons consequently so thick skinned) that I haven't had to feed it since.

A lemon is the fruit I always intend to take when I travel and never do. If I'd brought a lemon with me the soup I was fed last night would have had a little savour (a dash of lemon adds piquancy to so-so soups) and the calamari I just ate for lunch (it's hard to believe it was ever alive and swimming gaily in the sea) would have tasted of sunlight and the scents of our garden, instead of washing-up liquid. And I could have slept last night with the lemon beside me on the bedside table, so I could pretend I smelled the orchard instead of the air-conditioning.

When I travel I wish I could also take the lemon tree – to be able to sniff the blossom (that's one of the glories of lemon trees: you get blossom and fruit at the same time); listen to the insistent peeps of baby birds (there are always nests in lemon trees) – or at least a branch of dark green glossy leaves and hard green fruit, to carry onto the plane like a talisman.

The flight's been called. An hour and half's flying, two hour's driving and I'll be home, among the scent of lemon trees.

VERJUICE VEAL

This is *incredible*.

4 VEAL SCALLOPS

OLIVE OIL *or* BUTTER FOR FRYING

1 ONION, FINELY CHOPPED

1 DESSERTSPOON FINELY CHOPPED
PARSLEY

1 CUP CREAM
1 CUP REAL GRAPE JUICE (*see note*)

Bash the veal scallops really thin. Fry fast till brown on each side. Remove from pan.

Take the onion and parsley and sauté till soft, then add the cream and grape juice. Boil till thick, then pour over the scallops.

Note: To make 1 cup of grape juice, take 3–4 cups green seedless grapes (or pluck out the seeds), whizz them in a blender and press out the juice.

LEMON CREAM

Sniff this before you eat it.

1 CUP CREAM
1 CUP FRESH LEMON JUICE (*see note*)
3 EGGS

Beat the ingredients together. Bake in small cups at 200°C for 20 minutes or till firm. Serve at once with almond biscuits and more cream if you're greedy.

(You can also bake it in pastry. Lemon-cream pie is excellent cold.)

Note: The lemons must be fresh. If they smell musty as many shop-bought ones do, avoid them.

❈ *May 26*

Home. Woke up to the cuckoo trilling at first light and the smell of water and shadowed rocks.

Pudge has dug under the gate. There are droppings all over the garden and fresh excavations above the parsnips or where the parsnips were. She didn't eat anything, except a few square inches of remaining parsnip; but the burrowing covered up all the sweet peas and the beetroot (wombats apparently don't like beetroot).

Bryan dug the hole even larger and inserted a very large rock, then tidied it all up.

It is very good to be home.

Garry Woods rang this morning, to say he'd burnt a chop. This was an achievement, given that he'd done it on a solar cooker. Usually it takes about two hours to turn sausage a pale shade of grey.

I'd mentioned to Garry that I'd like a solar cooker, when we were at lunch in Canberra (antipasto thick with olive oil – charred zucchini and soggy eggplant and grey olives and sun-dried tomatoes – a standard this-year's Canberra lunch, with bread that's not quite as good as it was ten years ago, before the factory started producing it in bulk).

I'd been pricing the commercial solar cookers – great aluminium dishes that you pointed at the sky – but they didn't seem very efficient.

Garry decided that there must be a way of doing it better. He had a two and a half metre dish, and a five and a half metre dish – I think it was the latter that burnt the chop. Bryan is going to borrow the smaller dish when he goes up next week with the four-wheel drive (Garry doesn't think the dish would fit on the roof-rack of his Peugeot), and we'll experiment down here.

WINTER

✳ June 1

Winter rain starts as mist, almost imperceptible at first, thickening till the white grains form drops and the air is transparent again. The fog rises above the mountains and trickles down into the gullies. The pattern changes every ten minutes. You can spend hours sitting at the kitchen window watching the fog, wandering when or if it'll turn into rain.

You get misty rain in summer too but summer fog usually comes after a storm, not before. The oppression lifts the hair on your neck and the air closes till you could almost slice it. Sounds stop. After the rain the thunder rolls across the valley and the lyrebirds sing (even in midsummer) and the fog descends for days.

Winter rain is softer. The drops coat your hair and dribble down your neck. You're wet before you realise it, cold only when you stop moving; wool is warm in winter rain but you smell like a sheep as soon as you come inside.

Winter rain is the time for visiting. Stoves are lit. People cook on rainy days; carrot cakes from frostbitten carrots and vegetable soup from the last of the celery and bread because it's a pity to waste the heat of the oven and kitchens are full of the smell of wet socks drying against the stove and the windows fog as the kettle boils.

Winter is a slower time.

You don't visit so much in summer rain. You're too impatient to be out, muttering at the unbroken grey and searching for a patch of sunlight. It's hard to take summer rain seriously. It isn't cold so you go out in it, get wet and not quite cold enough to make indoors essential and kids run out of dry trousers and you remember the umbrella broke a spike last downpour and you haven't yet replaced it.

You need a tin roof for rain. Tiles muffle it, make the rain just something that happens out of doors. You're part of the rain under a tin roof. You can't speak over the noise in a good downpour but who'd want to; you're at the window watching the water washing over the paving. The world is grey and what colour remains is changed – strange olive colours, almost-colours, faded under the cloth of rain.

When I was a child I walked in the rain. I still do when I'm by myself, when the rain is right for walking, steady rain, not the sheeting sort that blinds you, not the lightning sort.

Misty rain is lovely, a world of white around you, or the steady rain that seems to part before you, that drums around you, isolating you from the world more than a few metres away. You can believe that frogs come down in rain, like mushrooms or wireworms inching over the wet grass; that mud spontaneously generates, that trees turn silver and the light turns pale.

After the rain is as strange as the time before it – a clarity as great as the oppression earlier. The light is gold suddenly and the sky deep blue and you can see the green swelling even though you know it's impossible and the air smells like a child that has had its hair washed and you feel like dancing with the grass.

'Can I wear your gumboots?' asked Edward.

'Why?'

'Because mine filled up with rain.'

Which means they'll take a month to dry again, unless we put them by the stove, and they're almost too small for him already.

'Okay,' I said. All our boots are left outside the front and back doors (where the wombats occasionally chew a strap or shoelace). Mostly they're protected by the eaves, but an inch or two either way and they're sodden.

My boots fit Edward well. He's growing.

The pansies in the pot under the kitchen window were all scratched out this morning, limp and dying in the sunlight. The dirt had been scratched out too, all over the paving.

Lyrebird season has begun.

※ *June 3*

Warm days with high pale skies – there are still leaves drooping on the peach trees and Noel and Rod are counting hours of chilling – or rather, not counting them because we haven't had any yet.

Peaches need a certain number of cold hours to set fruit. Normally we'd have had plenty by now; but we haven't. You feel like tapping the year's back to say: 'Hey mate, it's winter.'

Pudge and friends have discovered the celery (I think it is just Pudge doing the depredations though).

I didn't think wombats liked celery – and they don't – just the roots. Which means what was once a patch of celery – not in the fenced-off garden, fortunately – is now a patch of chewed-up stalks and messy holes.

I cleaned it up, gave most to the chooks and kept the best remnants for us and have made them into soup, as a wombat-gnawed celery stalk isn't really much good for anything else.

MADAM POMPADOUR'S APHRODISIAC CELERY SOUP

Madame P made this for Louis XV, who drank it with presumably spectacular results, as she kept making it and he kept drinking it. No one told the poor bloke that celery is supposed to be *anti-*inflammatory.

2 ONIONS, FINELY CHOPPED

3 TABLESPOONS BUTTER

6 STICKS OF CELERY, FINELY CHOPPED

4 CUPS GOOD CHICKEN STOCK

Sauté the onions in the butter on a very low heat till transparent; add the celery and keep stirring till soft. Add the stock and simmer for 20 minutes.

Blend or just mash well – or strain the soup and serve it hot and clear.

KING LOUIS XV'S GINGER OMELETTE

Made by Madame du Barry this time.

Wombats don't like ginger, or at least Pudge hasn't discovered it yet.

1 TABLESPOON BUTTER

1 TEASPOON FRESH GINGER, PEELED AND CHOPPED FINELY

3 EGGS, BEATEN WITH A FORK

1 TABLESPOON ICING SUGAR

Heat the pan, add the butter and ginger and stir well for 2 minutes. Pour in the eggs and shake madly for another minute, then leave alone till the base is firm and the inside almost set. Sprinkle on the icing sugar. Fold in quarters (the inside will keep cooking for another minute or so) and serve at once.

❧

✳ June 4

The onion patch looked like someone had rotary-hoed it this morning. It's time to cover the gardens with bird netting and old bits of chook wire.

Each year I hope the lyrebirds might forget; but of course they don't. As soon as the ground gets winter dry – and probably as soon as they're nesting and want extra protein, either for egg laying or that peculiar male lyrebird cavorting that they do in the breeding season – our garden is ripped up. And if you think chooks can do damage, you should see lyrebirds.

Lyrebirds have big feet. Very big feet. And big tails too, but they are mostly drooping down in the dust instead of on display – and most are pretty ratty anyway. And they scratch and rip and the mess they leave is indescribable. The first time I saw an orchard torn thoroughly by lyrebirds I thought pigs had been there. But it was only the birds.

I raked the soil back again and replanted the onions that survived. Winter is a lovely time to get your hands in dirt – soil always seems to smell best in winter. But then I'm fond of dirt at any time.

One of my earliest garden memories is making mud pies. The little boy next door (his name was Raymond and he wore red sandals that I coveted) and I had been given our lunch under the mango tree. Unfortunately it was the wrong time of year for mangoes.

We ate our lunch and then tried shaking pepper on the tails of passing sparrows (my mother had told me if you put pepper on a sparrow's tail it won't fly away; I know some people prefer salt – maybe she didn't want her lawn salinated). But the sparrows were too fast so we made mud pies instead.

They were good mud pies. Gourmet mud pies. I mixed mine with raspberry cordial and he mixed his with … you know, I'd forgotten this till now … he was proud of his equipment though I was unimpressed. And then we mixed in salt and pepper as well and let them dry in the sun then turned them out.

I've had my fingers in the dirt ever since.

Dirt is lovely stuff. Good dirt smells like chocolate. Or maybe I just like chocolate as well as dirt so I think they smell the same. I get uneasy when I'm too far away from dirt: more than two storeys up for example or in air conditioning or anywhere that's smooth grey walls and carpet – you know the sort of place.

Down here in the valley there's nowhere you can look out the window and not see dirt or rock or cliffs. There's a bloody great mountain of it front and back. It's a secure feeling having all that dirt around.

Winter is a great time for dirt. The grass shrivels away from the hills so you can see their shapes, round and skull-like up on the Tableland above us, but beautiful skulls, and rocks like sheep and sheep like rocks.

You can see the dirt in the garden too – unlike in summer – when you pull something out of the garden a space stays there for a few months instead of filling up with weeds or parsnip or calendula seedlings. (There's a legend that your husband will always be faithful if you've got calendulas flowering ... and once you've had them flowering in your garden it's hard to get them to stop.) But for now we've got the dirt instead – even if it's accidental dirt, lyrebird inspired.

✳ *June 5*

Pudge was mooching round the jonquils this afternoon, just after the sun fell behind the ridge (which is about two and a half hours before dusk). She heard me picking lemons so trotted over, giving her *oof oof oof* noise, which means 'Please feed me'. (Each wombat I've known has had its own 'Here I am – now food' noise. Ricki used to give a shrill *geek!* and Fudge a sort of *yip*.)

So I poured her out a bowl of oats, and she snuffled in it happily, then fell asleep by the bowl. It's really the wrong time of day for a wombat to be out. But the winter sun shouldn't hurt her, not down here in the valley, so I left her asleep and counted the camellia buds.

I'll miss the wombats in summer. These pale winter afternoons are a perfect wombat time, with enough sun for warmth but not dangerous.

✳ *June 6*

Now that it's cooler Bryan is moving boulders down on the flat again.

They used to be mullock heaps, piled by the gold miners as they scurried after bright metal in the creek; then the thorn bushes grew among them and then the blackberries came ... Bryan is attacking them, one by one, hauling away the blackberry and the thorn bush they spread over, rearranging boulders and leaving gardens in their place ...

When I first came here a couple of decades ago, there were two obvious resources – blackberries and rock.

The larder is full of blackberry and apple jelly (Bryan doesn't like the pips in blackberry jam, so I have to strain the juice and make jelly instead), the garden is mulched with slashed blackberry and we're about to plant a new shrubbery (I love that word) on a patch of once dead ground reclaimed by years of blackberry roots foraging deep down and the resultant leaf litter. (There is also a fair amount of blackberry left for anyone else who wants to share this resource – we eradicate maybe half an acre a year.)

The rock is another matter. After all, there are rocks and rocks. Some of our rocks are lovely clean ones, shaped like a more interesting brick, washed down by each flood. Unfortunately one major and several minor droughts later, there are never quite enough floods to keep us in well-shaped rocks.

The other rocks come in two forms. The first are the rocks on the scree slope above the house. Whenever a band of rock on the hill above is exposed, it cracks and falls and forms a great slope of rock – lichen covered and thick with black snakes, and surprisingly stable, even though visitors sometimes assume we've built our house in the middle of a landslide. The lichen-covered rocks aren't much good for house building, however – the lichen continues to grow on the walls, and continues to breathe too, and a decade or three later the rocks pop out. (I once spent three days and seven scrubbing brushes trying to scrub off the lichen ... then gave up and used the rock from the creek.)

Then there are the mullock heaps. Our place is mostly either vertical or mullock heap ... or used to be, till Bryan met the mullock heaps.

Bryan's love affair with rock started in his cliff-climbing days. Not that he did anything with rock in those days – just admired it as he went up or down.

Then he met the mullock heaps.

First he redid the stone stairs I'd built up to the wood heap. My stairs sort of slid down the slope. Bryan's marched firmly upwards – and stayed there.

Then a rock retaining wall. And then another around a herb garden. Then a sort of pyramid-type garden. And then a stone fish pond with fountain for my birthday …

Bryan and the granite have bonded.

It's a close relationship. As I write this I can look out the window and see him, hands on his hips, regarding yet another pile of rocks. In the past six months he's made tiered gardens that face the morning sun (wonderful for druidical sacrifices or storing and reflecting heat on frost-prone plants), stone walls, rockeries – in fact everything you can do with a mullock heap he's done … I think. There are still a few mullock heaps to go and I'm not sure what he's planning with the next …

There's his new line in garden furniture too – a bit cold on the bum but very durable. The chairs look like Stonehenge remnants. The table is a massive two-tonne boulder, quite flat on top, which took six months of engineering to move from the creek to the barbecue. (I now have a theory that the pyramids were built by one mad Irishman and plenty of potatoes – shame about the chronology!)

It's not that I'm objecting, mind you. It's fascinating to mooch down every couple of hours and see what's been moved where and why. And the results are beautiful. Bryan's passion for rock and rolling is probably nine parts engineering to one part aesthetics – but good engineering can have some lovely results.

It's just that sometimes … sometimes … I look up at the granite cliffs above us, hundreds of feet of shining rock … and wonder what will happen when the mullock heaps are all transformed, and Bryan's love of granite is still undimmed.

What next? What next?

＊ *June 7*

Picked the Lady Williams apples this morning; a lovely firm late apple – it tastes of both sun and frost. You can bite into them fresh, or bake them, or keep them for six months and their skins shrivel and they are even sweeter, or stuff them and bake them, which I'll do for the next six weeks till Bryan and Edward get sick of them (I don't). Stuffed apples are so simple – thirty seconds' preparation and some cooking, and you have a dessert or an entrée.

SWEET STUFFED APPLES

APPLES

BROWN SUGAR

BUTTER

Preheat the oven to 200°C.

To prepare the apples: core them, slice around the outside through the peel a few times so they don't burst, and place in a buttered dish.

Fill with brown sugar and dot with butter and bake at 200°C for 30 minutes or so till soft and the juice and the brown sugar have melted together into syrup and the whole thing perfumes the kitchen with appley steam when you open the oven.

(The decadent stuff their apples with walnuts or dates. I don't.)

SAVOURY STUFFED APPLES

APPLES

CRAB MEAT *or* PRAWNS *or* LOBSTER
or YABBY FLESH

CREAM

Optional

A LITTLE ONION SEETHED IN
BUTTER TILL TRANSPARENT WITH
SOME VERY FINELY CHOPPED
PARSLEY *or* CORIANDER – A GOOD
ADDITION (IF YOU CAN BE
BOTHERED)

Preheat the oven to 200°C.

Prepare the apples as above.

Stuff with crab meat (and the seethed onion mixture, if you are using it); pour cream generously into each cavity. Bake as above till soft. The juice will be crablike and creamy.

⁂

❋ *June 8*

A lyrebird was dancing on the garden seat this morning, outside the kitchen window, warbling happily into the morning mist. I don't know if he was performing for the sheer joy of it or for a hidden audience in the pittosporums; or maybe as a warning dance to his reflection in the kitchen window; or maybe even to us, the triumphant dance of a bird who has just ripped up seven artichoke plants, leaving them in soft grey shreds …

I yelled at him and he went tail down and squawking off into the loquat tree; then reconsidered, glared at me and pranced back onto the chair. He was still there when I'd finished my porridge.

The sun isn't above the ridge till eleven minutes past nine (not that we're counting); and it's not midwinter yet.

✳ *June 11*

Suddenly the days have dark blue shadows with a chill around the edges and we've become fire worshippers. Only a few weeks ago a dusting of smoke on the horizon would mean anxious calls to the Bush Fire Brigade. Now the urge is atavistic – get the fire going and sit round it.

Visiting friends means a dive into their kitchens to press your bum against their wood-fired ovens. Conversations turn to the comparative virtues of yellow box (a good burn), wattle (the hottest wood around), red gum (the wonder wood) and casuarina (the stayer), with mutterings against the wood provider, be it spouse or commercial delivery – the pieces are always too long, too wide, too green and you look with envy at organised souls with neat wood stacks like ordered sentinels against winter. And the spiders leap off in terror as another log is jammed into the grate to boil the kettle.

Sitting by a fire or wood stove is one of humanity's ancestral joys. The warmth of wood is like no other, drier and more penetrating than gas and electricity that leave your skin dry and hot and your soul and bones chilled. Crouching by a kero heater or a central-heating duct just emphasises the blizzard outside. To sit by a fire is to be cherished.

Sometimes I wonder, wandering never quite dark city streets and watching the blue flickers in the front windows, if the modern affection for TV is just a substitute for something more primitive, the urge for a family to crouch together round a dancing light in the darkness.

Our fire is a slow combustion stove. It goes on combusting twenty-four hours a day through winter. When summer comes and the grass starts to crackle I miss it dreadfully.

The stove's the place that visitors head for as they burst out of the descending Major's Creek fog, opening the oven door for a blast of hot air as they unwrap; where kids dash for after a bath, leaving puddles and damp towels behind them. Why dry yourself? The fire will do it for you as you revolve your reddening body slowly till it's half cooked. I've known thin-skinned dogs and hibernating carpet snakes and a baby wombat to take up winter residence by the family stove and not move again till blossom time.

In the evening you can draw up a chair by the oven and toast your toes till bedtime on the oven racks; stick your wet head in for a fast hair dry; dry jeans overnight on the door and keep a genuine stockpot not quite simmering, so the kitchen smells of fresh wood and cooking throughout winter. It's amazing the amount of biscuits that are made and eaten when the oven is always hot, just waiting to be used.

I heard on a radio program somewhere where a farmer's wife bewailed the uselessness of her new microwave. She'd just stuck her gumboots in for a few minutes to dry them out …

You rarely come across genuine kitchen fires nowadays, deep smoky recesses in the kitchen walls and wide hearths.

I met one about a decade ago a few miles from here. Both its tenders have since died.

We'd called on an impulse, looking for an old chaff-cutter wheel to put on our cement mixer. The air outside had that still, dry winter clearness, but the kitchen was a warm brown fug, with steam from the kettle on the hob, the flames lapping just below it and the heavy caramel scent of crisping biscuits and drying socks on the line above the fireplace. Even in the daylight the fire glowed shadows on the sixty years of collected calendars on the walls.

It was four o'clock so we were invited to stay for a cuppa. I suspected the cuppa might be substantial when the table was set with dinner plates. It was.

There was homemade bread, at least the height of two normal loaves, cut breadboard-thick, with black tops and thick crusts and a close white texture that invited pulling, half a dozen sorts of jam (he later took me to see the trees they came from, quince and crab-apple, plum, cherry, mulberry and rows of currant bushes), two sorts of biscuits and fruit cake with slabs of cheese, all in plate-sized servings, and cold mutton with chutney and a cross between scones and pikelets that had just been cooked on the hearth – we scooped the cream like frozen silk from the top of the milk to eat with them.

Both our hosts looked at us mournfully whenever our plates were empty. They finally took matters in their own hands and just reloaded them without asking. The youngest son, who lived with them, just kept on eating. He was about two metres high and nearly as broad – all muscle – and needed a lot of fuelling.

Later she showed me how she made the bread, with flour she still had sent in sacks from Sydney, a habit she'd got into in 1910, though it came by truck now not bullock wagon. She mixed the dough in a plastic basin and it rose by the banked fire through the night (they kept casuarina wood for the purpose – a few logs at bedtime turned to thick ash with the embers still glowing underneath ten hours later).

In the morning they just tossed on some tinder and stuck the bread in the oven on one side of the hearth and went back to bed, to rise again with the kettle boiling and the smell of fresh breakfast bread.

She'd eaten homemade bread every breakfast of her life, except for the first day she was in hospital to have her veins done. She couldn't eat the tasteless stuff there, so her daughter had to bring in homemade supplies, and then all the other women in the ward wanted homemade bread too and eggs with deep yellow centres, and her daughter provided the lot.

That was the first time she'd been in hospital. She'd had the kids at home, suckled the last baby in one arm while she turned the handle of the shearing machine with the other. But after the War – World War One not World War Two, the man they'd hired to help said the work was too hard, and the shearing had gone electric.

We left with armfuls of loaves and pumpkins and a doorstop of fruit cake, as well as the wheel we'd been looking for, which he found in a rubbish heap next to the collapsing slab shed that housed his pride and joy – a purple and silver dune buggy that could do 100 kilometres an hour on the highway with a couple of sick sheep in the back.

(If you ever saw a gleeful octogenarian and two startled woolly faces dashing in a purple and silver buggy towards Braidwood, no, you weren't hallucinating.)

HEARTH CAKES

These can be made on a hot hearth by a fire. Alternatively use a thick frying pan.

1 CUP PLAIN FLOUR

HALF A CUP CURRANTS

A DASH OF VANILLA (REAL)

1 DESSERTSPOON SUGAR
(OPTIONAL)

A LOT OF BUTTER

Mix together the flour, currants, vanilla and sugar. Rub enough butter into the mixture to make it crumbly and stick together. Knead till it forms a ball of dough.

Roll out the dough till it is as thick as your finger. Cut it into rounds with a glass. Fry in butter till brown or cook slowly on a hot hearth.

Eat without butter or jam, hot or cold. They're not bad with a slab of cheese. They keep for months in a sealed tin.

❊ *June 12*

Three-and-a-half arrived at ten minutes past sun fall below the ridges, which at this time of year is about 3.20 in the afternoon. Her pouch is getting heavier daily.

I had a look at Pudge's pouch yesterday – still flat. Despite the fact she seemed to be on heat a while ago (she stank and so did everywhere she trod) there's no sign of any offspring … which reassures Edward, who was shocked that anyone who was still drinking from a bottle might think of sex.

The lyrebirds have ripped up the strawberries.

❉ June 13

Bryan cut firewood all this morning – some of the old wattle that fell last year, and the blue gum over by the shed that we had Charlie Heycox cut down (if either of us had tried it, it would have fallen on the shed). We spent this afternoon stacking it.

The wood smells wonderful – old sap and sawdust – and looks even better. A bulging woodshed, orderly as all Bryan's heaps always are, the driest wood at the corner closest to the house, the greenest furthest away.

There is something enormously reassuring about great piles of wood.

❉ June 14

Blue smoke sifting across the valley, a high blue sky, and a fluffy wombat sleeping stomach upward among the lavender …

This is the magic time, blue winter days and clear light and picking kiwi fruit. They are nothing like the fruit in shops, these brown fuzzy ovals that have ripened on the vine. When you pick them the fur sticks to your fingers, and most are just out of reach, even on a stepladder, even on a chair. So the bowerbirds get most of them.

I planted the kiwi fruit in the '82 drought, when the grass had crumbled into the hot earth and the creek was scummy puddles inhabited by ducks and desperate thirsty animals from the ridges.

It was a bad time to plant. But they'd been in pots for two years, waiting for a better season, which didn't seem to come. So I planted them along the pergola in front of the kitchen in baked ground that needed a crowbar to chip it, and fed them the less greasy washing-up water and duck-smelling dribbles from the hose.

I was pregnant. It was a waiting time, for the birth and for rain and for the thousand projects that might come from both. I spent most of those last few months sitting at the kitchen table by the window looking at the hot creek bed and the drooping trees and the kiwi fruit, surviving, but only just.

A photograph of that time shows the house as a bare stone rectangle, surrounded by dry ground, fresh posts and the small thin kiwi fruit with drooping leaves. That was when I brought Edward home from hospital. The wattle was blooming, a yellow carpet where the grass used to be, and in spite of the dust haze and the patches of dead trees creeping up the ridge I cried because it was beautiful, and I was glad to be home.

The trouble with photographs is that after a time you tend to remember them, little islands in the past, and not the events around them. They are more vivid than memory and distort the rest of your past with their colour.

The drought broke when Edward was six weeks old. A foot of water rolled down the hill, thick with years of wombat droppings, through the house, over ground too baked to absorb any moisture and rain too thick to see through. The flat below the house rolled and swam like an earthquake but it wasn't — just the tide of four years' litter, leaves and fallen bark, all flowing down to Moruya.

Like Edward, the vines began to grow. In the next photo he's bald and jumpered, so it must be winter, and the vines are bare. But there is lush clover and weeds below them. The trees in the distance are green. In the next one he's galloping on a feather duster under the vines and they're galloping too, reaching upwards to the wire. He's still bald, but they're leafy, have started the incredible luxuriance they have today.

The ground below them is paved in the next photos. The vines are only pencil thick, but there are roses planted too and herbs and people sit beneath them and drink tea and kids ride bicycles. Edward is growing hair, but still mostly naked, running below the leaves and blossom and drooping fruit, and there are birds sometimes in the background, blue wrens and yellow robins and the manic shrike-thrush who calls from the pergola every morning and bangs his beak against the glass.

I rarely take photos, so these are mostly relatives', a series taken after gaps of months. The vines grow thicker in each one, and Edward taller like the garden around him, both of them dating from the breaking of the drought.

By their third year, and Edward's, the kiwi fruit covered the pergola and were regularly hacked back, my excuse for pruning. The stems are as wide as my wrist now, twisted round on themselves and winding in patterns once bent by the wind and weight of fruit, now set forever, because I was preoccupied when they were young and didn't straighten them. But I don't regret it — their twists are individual. I've never wanted an ordered garden.

A few years ago an elderly Taiwanese woman visited with her daughter. Suddenly she exclaimed and pointed to the vines, but her daughter refused to translate. The elderly woman insisted, and finally her daughter (with great embarrassment) explained: it was the golden hairy goat's testicles, which she hadn't seen growing since she was a child in China; they used to grow wild outside her village.

Golden hairy goat's testicles seems a very satisfactory name for kiwi fruit. On the vine they're hairy. By the time you buy them in shops they're bald. (Bald goat's testicles really does sound rude.)

It's hard to believe the green leaves will come again this morning, looking at the bare twisted vines; that we'll sit under the dapples again drinking tea, watching the wasps hover over the blossom and the honeyeaters drink wisteria nectar and the shadows play among the casuarinas by the creek.

My first marriage broke up beneath the kiwi fruit. My second began there, though I didn't know it, drinking tea with friends in the still Christmas heat when a strange man walked up the steps under the wattle before a bushwalk up the creek. The kiwi fruit grow thicker and the garden round them taller, waiting for the next episode in the lives below.

✳ *June 15*

Most of the pruning is finished already down the valley, and I haven't even started here. Not that we do much, more hacking away a few branches that get in the way.

Noel Wisbey is carefully levelling what was once mullock heap, and carting in new soil; Rod is fencing, lovely straight fences that never dare to bend over. Both intend to plant more trees this year. They have to – the public gets sick of one variety and expects another, each yellower and firmer and with a redder skin that slips off like it was casting off a petticoat.

Some of the old trees here must be fifty years old; but the commercial peaches are lucky to make it to fifteen. Which means that most of the public are fools. The Wisbeys tore out their last orchard of Golden Queens this year – all except one tree for themselves – as no one buys them any more.

It was the same when Conrad down the valley grew traditional tomatoes – lovely fat things that oozed red juice. But hardly anyone bought them. Despite what people say, they don't really want an old-fashioned tomato. They want ones they can slice for sandwiches that won't wet the bread; or quarter for salads in neat obedient shapes. Old-fashioned tomatoes are soggy.

I don't think most people really taste things these days. If they did they'd never eat a packet cake again, or commercial biscuits or those cold fruit lumps mislabelled muffins or shiny, rattly packets that fraudulently claim to contain pasta marinara or carbonara, just add water and microwave …

RICOTTA CHEESECAKE WITH PINE NUTS AND PEACHES

6 DRIED PEACH HALVES

1 CUP WATER

2 CUPS RICOTTA

1 CUP SOUR CREAM

HALF A CUP CASTER SUGAR

2 TABLESPOONS PINE NUTS
(BROWNED IN THE OVEN IF YOU
CAN BE BOTHERED)

1 TEASPOON COINTREAU *or*
ALMOND LIQUEUR

4 EGGS, SEPARATED

Simmer peaches in water for 5 minutes. Cool in liquid. Drain. Mash.

Preheat the oven to 200°C. Mix everything except the egg whites. Then beat the egg whites until they are stiff, and stir in gently. Pour the mixture into a buttered tin; bake for about an hour, or until the top is lightly browned and feels set when you push it with your finger.

Eat hot or cold. Extra cream is decadent but good.

PEACH AND PARMESAN INDIVIDUAL SOUFFLÉS

The taste of peaches goes well with cheese, as anyone who's had that old English favourite – cheese and peach jam sandwiches – knows.

4 DRIED PEACH HALVES

1 CUP WATER

1 CUP CREAM

5 EGGS, SEPARATED

1 TABLESPOON FRESHLY GRATED
PARMESAN CHEESE

BLACK PEPPER

Simmer peaches in water for 5 minutes. Cool in liquid. Drain.

Preheat the oven to 200°C. Add flour to the cream, then add the egg yolks. Add this mixture to the peaches and stir over a gentle heat till it thickens. By now the peaches should be mush. Stir in cheese, take off the heat, add black pepper.

Whip egg whites till firm. Stir gently into the cream mixture. Spoon into four small buttered soufflé dishes, and place in the oven. Bake about 15 minutes. The tops should be dark brown.

Serve at once, with a slightly bitter salad.

.... ❧ ....

❋ *June 17*

Pudge has discovered the bathroom window. You can see through it from the hill outside behind the house – or hear, in Pudge's case. Which means that every time she hears us in the shower she tries to jump through the window. Luckily wombats don't jump very well and she just slides down the cliff.

It is disconcerting to be quietly contemplating on the loo and have a wombat shriek at you through the window. She has extraordinarily good hearing. What's discreet to a human ear reverberates to a wombat.

❈ *June 18*

Giles and Victoria and the kids came down last night, bearing chocolates and Giles's strawberry wine. I remember the wine bubbling beside the fuel stove last summer – it looks even redder now.

Strawberry wine tastes better than you might think; maybe because you expect it to be terrible (like the bottle of peach champagne I was given last year, which we drank at Christmas with the pud and which wasn't bad either).

But the chocolates were better.

The garden is alive with lyrebirds; six of them head down and dashing for cover when we come out the door, beeping alarm calls like apprentice road runners (which they greatly resemble – that road runner dash is obviously based on very close observation of some bird closely allied to lyrebirds).

❈ *June 19*

The navel oranges are perfect now. I know they're perfect because the bowerbirds are eating them, so you reach for a perfect fruit and find it's been hollowed out from the other side and only a bee left nuzzling at a shred of fruit …

Birds mostly like sour fruit, a couple of weeks greener than humans prefer it … except for bowerbirds and oranges. If you want to get the best fruit in the orchard wait for a bowerbird to begin to peck, then grab it from him and take it home to peel for yourself. Bowerbirds choose the ripest, deepest coloured, richest flavoured oranges there are.

We have oranges all year round but the navels are the best. Winter navels soft with cold, sweet from almost a full

year's sun (citrus are one of the few trees to fruit and blossom at the same time – generous trees). You do get a main flush of fruit but it's rare to find no fruit at all to pick on any citrus tree.

The one jam I never make nowadays is marmalade, simply because we have so much fruit (including the Seville oranges – great flat-topped bitter ones for making jam) that we give it away. And then we get marmalades in return. Some friends are better marmalade makers than others, which adds to the variety. But then Bryan is the only one who really likes marmalade. I just taste each batch, savour it and then go back to plum.

※ *June 20*

One of those evenings when you look back and realise you've done nothing but stare at the flames. Every now and then Bryan would say something … or I would. But mostly we just watch. The wombats are grunting at each other outside, with the odd shriek of rage when someone steps into someone's space, there is stew in the pot and three sorts of fresh biscuits in the four containers, and the chimney is yawning up the smoke – a restful sort of night.

❋ June 22

The longest night has gone ... and supposedly the worst of winter is over. But of course it's still to come. Winter is deceptive here. You gear yourself up for winter in June and the days are high and blue and golden; then you wait for the days to lengthen and the wind starts blowing off the mountains and the grass shrinks brown and dry, and you think oh shit, it really is another three months till decent warmth.

The sun peered though the window at 9.20 this morning and dropped over the ridge at 3.09 this afternoon.

❋ June 23

It's too cold to go outside before ten o'clock these mornings. You feel the early morning air is going to crack if you walk through it too fast. But by midmorning it's reasonably comfortable. Which suits Bryan well. Bryan dislikes hurrying his breakfast, especially in winter.

'Is there any more blackberry jelly?' he asks contentedly, one eye on the lyrebirds as they rip their talons through the parsley bed, the other on the piece of toast spread carefully with this year's lime and orange marmalade. 'No, there's no hurry ... just if you happen to be near the larder ...'

Bryan has blackberry jelly every morning on one half of his toast – except the year the blackberries failed and he had to have plum jam instead – and the toast is always a soft roll with sesame seeds on top, divided into two and lightly grilled.

The toast is preceded by a boiled egg – an Australorp egg, because Bryan is fond of Australorps. (He says they have more sense than Leghorns, at least three neurones whereas the Leghorns have only two and besides he likes the Australorps' fluffy knickers.) And before that there's porridge with cream and brown sugar, all taken in the high-backed wooden chair facing the large window to the orchard, where he can see the lyrebirds tearing up what used to be the onion patch and the bowerbirds slurping at the remains of the kiwi fruit.

It's taken Bryan eight years to perfect his breakfast. After all, he had forty-odd years of breakfasting to a schedule to overcome – the glance at the paper, the gulping of cereal all sandwiched into the half hour to spare before leaping into the car. Nowadays he doesn't leap anywhere. It's more of a mooch and there's no point galloping anywhere till the sun hauls itself over the ridgetop and drinks the last of the frost and, like most of us, the sun seems to have creaking joints in winter and it takes hours for it to stir itself.

There's coffee with the toast, the same mug every morning. Coffee drinking is the contemplative time, when you read out bits from last week's newspaper to your companion and ponder on their significance.

It's wonderful how many of the world's problems you can solve when you've got time for breakfast. The trouble is the rest of the world is still leaping into cars or buses without time even for a second cup of coffee, and doesn't have time to contemplate at all.

After the toast there's fruit, peeled slowly as the spinebills dip their beaks into the grevilleas and the lyrebirds rip up the last of what's in season and what the bowerbirds haven't eaten: kiwi fruit in winter (we snaffled a dozen boxes before the birds moved in) and apples (we're finishing off the Lord Derby now before we move on to Lady Williams) and oranges soft from the frost, the last of the brussels sprouts, the occasional mandarins, tangelo, tamarillo, feijoa or cherry guava. Then down to the chooks to check the eggs, or replace the artichoke seedlings the lyrebirds have gouged out, or pick grapefruit for tomorrow's breakfast and check again to count the eggs …

THE PERFECT EGG

The perfect egg is three days old, preferably gathered from the nest in the lavender bushes down in the backyard (chooks prefer lavender bushes to nesting boxes). We prefer Australorp eggs – softly tinted shells with golden yolks that make sponge cakes look like they've been dipped in yellow dye.

Anyone who can't taste the difference between the eggs of different breeds of chooks doesn't have a palate … or the eggs aren't from free-range chooks. Eggs taste of what the chook's been eating, and better foragers have better eggs. Battery eggs of course just taste of fear.

The perfect egg is not boiled. Boiling spoils the taste, making it more sulphurous and destroys the subtle undertones of last week's grasshoppers and watercress and the other goodies the chooks were sampling.

The perfect egg should be covered with water, brought to the boil, taken off the heat then left covered for three minutes. You can slide it into an eggcup or scoop out the innards onto buttered toast – the yellow will be still runny and the white gently coagulated. Dust with fresh black pepper.

On days when luxury is a necessity, cut off the top and spoon in sour cream and caviar or chopped smoked salmon, or peel it carefully, so the egg stays whole (you'll be surprised at the structural

integrity of a good soft-boiled egg) and lay it on a
dish of well-chopped silverbeet or spinach, steamed
and lightly buttered (or asparagus or artichoke
hearts if you can wait till spring) and cover with
cheese sauce and grill till the top just
bubbles brown.

Then thank the chooks and feed them any leftovers … and know that all those scraps of toast and
artichoke and silverbeet are helping to produce
another perfect egg.

❋ June 25

The frost seems to be sucking all the moisture out of the
ground – and the pots. Spent the morning watering and
moving hoses.

❋ June 27

Chocolate marched up while Pudge ate her breakfast,
growled twice and scared her off … almost. A minute later
she ran back, shrieked, then ran off again – and repeated
this at two-minute intervals till we'd finished breakfast and
so had Chocolate.

Meanwhile a currawong sat vulture like on the garden
chair above them, huffed up to double its size, stropping its
beak against the chair if any other bird even glanced at the
leftovers. It was a bit like a driver in a crowded car park
lurking behind a car about to pull out, glaring at anyone
who might even consider taking the space …

※ *July 1*

Jen and Nat to breakfast. Breakfast is a sociable sort of meal, friendlier than dinner. There are so often those people who *should* be invited to dinner; but breakfast is for the sort of friends whom you don't mind if they see you in your pyjamas if you've forgotten they're coming.

Marinated sliced orange in orange and Cointreau syrup. Also made omelettes.

※ *July 3*

Dry soil, dry air, dry leaves. Even in the cold the leaves are wilting.

※ *July 5*

No leaves on any of the deciduous trees now. Even the white cedars are bare. The gums on the hill look greyer too. The chooks are down to three eggs a day.

The bowerbirds ate the last of the kiwi fruit this morning.

※ *July 9*

The first of the peach blossom – tight pink buds that slowly open along the branches. Not spectacular – peach blossom rarely is unless it's en masse, and these trees have been pruned too severely to be stunning, except when you are at exactly the right angle looking down the rows or until a lot of the orchards are in bloom at once. As the peach blooming takes place over about two to three months this doesn't happen for too long – some of the orchards are in leaf when the others still have bursting flower buds.

It is beautiful even now though – partly because the world is slightly colourless, as though winter has put a plastic film over the world. It is mostly a factor of the light of course – or rather the lack of it.

If summer's light is so strong it takes the colour from the world; winter's light is not quite strong enough to show it. Winter is the sky-watching time – bright clouds and subtle colours in the sky. Only the highest hills, those closest to the sky, really have colour. Down here in the valley the world is too shadowed to be bright. (I've found myself lingering up on the Tableland to see the sunset – gold hills and glowing sky.)

CHILLI PEACH SOUP

4 CUPS CHICKEN STOCK

4 WHITE PEACHES (YELLOW WILL DO – *or* EVEN 8 DRIED PEACH HALVES)

4 RED DRIED CHILLIES

1 RED ONION, CHOPPED AND SAUTÉED IN A LITTLE OIL

1 TEASPOON FINELY CHOPPED FRESH CORIANDER

Simmer everything except *the coriander for 30 minutes. Strain. Add the coriander to the liquid and reheat, clear and sweet.*

DUCK STUFFED WITH DRIED PEACHES AND COUSCOUS, WITH BAKED PEACH GRAVY

I can't kill a duck, though I can kill chooks (who never realise what's happening) and geese (who battle, so you feel you deserve the fruit of victory when you finally get them to the chopping block). But ducks know what's happening. I killed one once and never will again. Which is why I make this with goose instead. But ducks are easier to get for those who rely on supermarkets, though I don't like eating what I'm not prepared to kill.

Take one duck. Make the stuffing from:

1 CUP CHOPPED DRIED PEACHES,
SOAKED OVERNIGHT IN HOT WATER,
THEN DRAINED

2 CUPS COUSCOUS, MADE
ACCORDING TO DIRECTIONS ON
THE PACKET, VERY BUTTERY

1 CHOPPED ONION

4 CLOVES GARLIC, FINELY CHOPPED

1 TEASPOON LEMON THYME

Mix. Stuff into duck – into the crop (the skin by the neck) as well as the cavity.

Roast the duck (the time will depend on the size of the duck – look at the back of the bag or wait till the leg wiggles when you push it). Add bottled peaches for the last 30 minutes. They'll still be firm enough to scoop out and serve with the meat.

The juice makes a wonderful sauce. Don't thicken it, but if you have any good red wine (cask stuff won't do) add about the same amount of wine as you have liquid in the pan (pour off the fat first) and bubble for 3 minutes.

.... ❧ ....

✳ *July 10*

'And how long have you lived here?' she asked.

'Twenty-something years,' I said, and she looked astonished, as after all I'm not that old − it's just that I've lived here almost all of my adult life.

It's a sad comment on the 1990s that when you tell people you've lived in a place for twenty years, they usually say (in a tone that combines condescension and mild amusement with pity): 'That's a long time.'

It isn't. It's an incredibly short time − just enough time to begin to speak the language of the land and animals around you.

I'm perpetually horrified at how short term most studies are − whether they're PhD studies on wombats or observation periods on genetically engineered plants or viruses. It only takes three years to do a PhD − of which maybe a year may be fieldwork − and most university or industry research projects want money-making results after three years.

Three years isn't enough to understand anything in a biological system − there are too many variables. Wombat behaviour varies according to the season and the generation of wombats. In fact you could almost say wombats have a sort of rudimentary culture, as do lyrebirds … but that's another topic altogether.

Just counting hoverfly numbers over the past twenty years I've noticed enormous variations – how some plants attract them in dry years; others when the temperature is over about twenty-six degrees Celsius; how they cluster over certain plants, like alyssum, when the bee numbers build up on other preferred foods (bees will oust hoverflies) – in fact the more I look at them the more I realise you can't just generalise and say 'such and such attracts hoverflies'. (On the other hand, if you plant masses of white alyssum you won't go far wrong either.)

Living in a place changes you – as you change it. I don't know if the land here has changed me more than I've changed the land – I reckon we're probably running neck and neck. But it isn't a short-term operation – or even something that takes place without a long-term commitment to each other.

Twenty years is nothing when you think of a lifetime spent watching and understanding – or many lifetimes, the heritage passed on from generation to generation.

But it's been a good twenty years.

❉ *July 11*

It's only when you have your hands deep in greasy washing-up that you realise how cold they were. It's a sort of seeping coldness, whispering into your bones so no matter how much toasting your skin gets by the fire you aren't really warm.

I'm just grouching because I want the sun again. The last four days have been cloudy – grey sky, grey air, grey creek, grey smoke just sitting above the house because there isn't enough wind to lift it from the chimney. Even the gum leaves look grey. Bryan has begun to worry about running out of power now the sun is no longer feeding the solar panels and thence the batteries; so we hesitate to put the light on till it's dark outside.

When I was a child I used to hate the dark. Now I love it – the scents of night, the colours – different colours, purples and rich greens – the softness of the air when the sun has sunk below the ridge. But I still hate it when it's grey.

I felt my wet hair freeze to my ears when I fed Pudge this morning. Pudge of course is well insulated – fat and fur.

THE PERFECT POTATO CAKE

These are Vladimir's mum's potato cakes, for very grey days when you need carbohydrate for lunch to cheer you up. (Blast it! If it has to be cloudy, why can't it rain?)

Vlad grew up in what was at one stage Yugoslavia. He spent his adolescence evading the Germans, taking parties of Jews and other refugees across the river, so he became an incredible swimmer. (When the water from the dam above his house was released in a flood last year and the water rose above the rooftops one night in a sudden terrifying rush, Vlad swam almost half a mile through the cold dark water with the town's inhabitants shining their car lights to show him the way and cheering as they saw him approach. He survived, though none of his possessions did.)

When he got back home as a youth, he said, his Mum gave him potato cakes to warm him up. He first made them for me about twelve years ago and I've been making them ever since; though mine haven't quite the rubberiness, the lovely garlicky meatiness, of Vlad's.

4 MEDIUM GRATED POTATOES

1 SMALL GRATED ONION

4 TABLESPOONS PLAIN FLOUR

2 EGGS

CHOPPED PARSLEY

CHOPPED CHIVES *or* GARLIC CHIVES

LOTS OF BLACK PEPPER

SALT (OPTIONAL)

OLIVE OIL FOR FRYING

Optional

GRATED CARROTS (UP TO 60 PER CENT)

CHOPPED HAM *or* BACON

CHOPPED SALMON *or* TUNA

CHUNKS OF YABBY *or* LOBSTER

LOTS OF GARLIC – FINELY CHOPPED, NOT CRUSHED

Combine all the ingredients (except the oil). Fry small spoonfuls in olive oil till brown on both sides. Serve hot.

Note: Each potato cake should be small and thin, or else the raw potato and onion won't cook properly.

❀

✳ July 13

Wind last night, moaning up the ridge at first (wind really does moan; or maybe the earth moans as the wind passes across it), then whispering down into the valley then suddenly shouting right against the house, so the roof shook and the doors chattered. We don't get much wind down here – it usually blows across the ridges – but when we do get a gust, it's a beauty.

But the wind has chased away the cloud. The sky seems to shiver, it's so clear, so the wind is probably still raging high above. The ground of course is even drier – cement dry – and the leaves are dropping as though to hide themselves from the wind.

Bad Bart was back this afternoon; I thought there'd been a lot of snarling in the night. I ignored him, so he tried to bite my ugh boot upon which I shrieked and ran inside and he looked hurt and startled as though to say: 'I was just saying hello.'

I thought he'd wandered off but he was back nineteen seconds after I'd poured out Three-and-a-half's afternoon snack (she arrives a few hours earlier than Chocolate).

Pudge now comes about 10 p.m. or just as we've gone to bed, so I have to traipse downstairs to get her tucker, otherwise she bashes up the garbage bin all night, which is not conducive to restful repose. She doesn't say thank you either, just pushes her face oatwards, so that half of the oats fall on her snout and she looks ridiculous – a snow-covered wombat.

I don't know what to do about Bad Bart. I doubt we can re-educate him. You don't educate wombats. Wombats are the most solipsistic creatures in the universe (apologies to all aliens who may be reading this). You can never teach a wombat to feel ashamed, or that it's done something wrong. Though of course you can make a wombat scared of you.

I don't want to frighten Bad Bart. I just want him to leave my knees alone. Neither works terribly well as it is …

'Don't feed him,' says Bryan.

To which I say: 'I don't – he eats the other wombats' food.'

'Don't feed *any* of them then till he gets the message and goes away.'

But I can't do that – the wombats have me programmed. When they yip or huff or bash the garbage bin, I grab the oats and carrots and obey.

LEMON, LIME, GRAPEFRUIT OR MANDARIN BUTTER

All these fruits are ripe now. I wonder why I planted quite so many lime trees – not that the cafe minds, because they can make lime tart – and eight grapefruit trees, when we really only need about a sixth of a grapefruit tree for our needs and our friends'. No one likes grapefruit much. I've suggested recipes to the cafe, but they weren't inspired. Even the bowerbirds eat the other citrus before they get stuck into them.

This recipe is more tart than most lemon butters – I like a tangy one.

125 GRAMS BUTTER *or* MARGARINE

JUICE OF 6 LEMONS *or* 10 LIMES *or*
5 GRAPEFRUIT *or* 3 LEMONS AND
3 MANDARINS

THE FINELY GRATED RIND OF
HOWEVER MANY CITRUS FRUITS
YOU CAN BE BOTHERED TO GRATE

200 GRAMS CASTER SUGAR

4 BEATEN EGGS *or* 2 BEATEN EGGS
AND 2 TEASPOONS CORNFLOUR IN A
LITTLE OF THE JUICE

*Combine in a saucepan and cook as slowly as you can,
stirring all the time till the mixture starts to thicken and
coats the spoon. Place in small clean jars, seal and keep
in a cool place till needed. Keeps two months or more in
the fridge but loses its best flavour quickly. If you keep it
in the fridge, let it warm to room temperature before you
eat it.*

*Serve in tarts, on toast, scones, pikelets or cakes – or
just eat it with a spoon.*

.... ✿ ....

* *July 15*

Finally a real frost, the sort where the grass snaps when you
tread on it. The top of the car was pimpled with ice this
morning, and the windscreen was frozen so I had to flap
upstairs in my ugh boots and get a saucepan of water (by
which time Edward had discovered that the hose wasn't
frozen, as I'd assumed, and had washed the ice off himself).

The long black stretches of soil where Noel intends to
plant new trees are white topped and the brown grass is
frozen solid. I don't know how the blossom is faring; last
season's late frosts destroyed all the lower fruit on several of
the orchards. You always get more frosts in dry years; and
this winter is certainly dry.

There've been about three glorious hours each day the
last week – from about noon, when the sun has finally
managed to warm the air, to three o'clock, when the sun is
so low that the trees on the horizon suck out its warmth.
That's when the wombats come out to sunbake, and lie in
the dust in the farm tracks or in special wombat sits they've
rolled bare themselves, fluffy stomachs exposed to the sky.

The chooks are laying again – in the lavender bushes, not in their boxes. I don't know why they're so fond of lavender. Maybe they think it hides that odour de chook from marauding foxes; maybe the lavender dust and detritus repel pests. On the other hand I like lavender too, and don't give any excuse for it.

It's a nuisance trying to find the eggs but very fragrant.

Friends to dinner last night; the sort of night when you need to have a hot drink waiting for them by the time they've stumbled up the stairs in the dark (we never remember to tell guests to bring torches), tripped over frozen wombat droppings and been attacked by Bad Bart. ('Isn't he sweet?' said one; so I didn't mention they were lucky to escape with their kneecaps.)

A CLASSIC BISHOP

Never boil your bishop. It spoils the taste. A bishop is a hot port drink – you'll find it in Dickens – very good, and not as potent as one might think. No, I'm not denigrating the power of the Church – I only mean that most of the alcohol evaporates with heating.

1 BOTTLE OF REASONABLE PORT

1 ORANGE WITH TWO CLOVES
STUCK IN IT

SUGAR TO TASTE (BUT YOU MAY
NOT NEED ANY)

Heat the cloved orange in the microwave for a few seconds or in the oven till it's hot. (A hundred years ago you would have toasted it by the fire.)

*Add the orange to the port, heat as slowly as possible
to just below simmering — use the lowest possible heat,
as the longer it takes to heat the better the flavour. Add
sugar to taste.*

Serve hot.

.... ❧ ....

LAMB'S WOOL

4 CUPS MILK

A LARGE GLOP OF BRANDY *or* WHISKY – BETTER, BUT NOT TRADITIONAL (*see note*)

4 CUPS STEWED APPLE, WHIPPED TO A FLUFFY PULP AND WELL SWEETENED WITH BROWN SUGAR

4 CUPS WHIPPED CREAM

NUTMEG TO TASTE

*Put milk, brandy and apple in a pan. Heat very
slowly till warm, whipping with a whisk (if possible)
or a wooden spoon all the time. Stir in whipped cream.
Take off heat.*

Serve hot, each cup dusted with nutmeg.

*Note: If you want to make a non-alcoholic lamb's
wool, omit the brandy and add a vanilla bean instead
(remove it before serving). You can of course add a dash of
vanilla instead of a bean, but vanilla essence has alcohol
added and it doesn't work as well anyway.*

.... ❧ ....

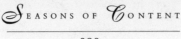

HOT PUNCH

As served to heroes in Restoration Romances.

1 CUP RUM

1 CUP BRANDY

3 CUPS SUGAR

3 SLICED LEMONS

3 SLICED ORANGES

A GOOD GRATE OF NUTMEG

BOILING WATER (*see note*)

Place all ingredients in a pan over very low heat or by a strong fire. Stir well till the sugar is dissolved. Serve hot and beware of hangovers.

Note: The traditional recipe uses 1 pint (0.6 litre) of boiling water – which makes a very strong drink. I add much more – but then I don't have my mind on seduction.

* *July 17*

Dug roots this morning and this afternoon, till the shadows rose as the sun dropped and I dashed indoors to warm my hands. It was hard work – the soil is baked dust, drier than concrete.

Winter is a great time for roots. We eat a lot of roots in winter – proper cultivated roots like spuds and beetroot and carrots and some wilder harvests like dandelions and dock and burdock and kangaroo berry and kurrajong and bracken (the latter are eaten just for fun). There are hundreds of wild edibles around here – but it's a hell of a lot easier to harvest the garden.

All roots are best in winter. The cold softens them and makes them sweeter. Beetroot always tastes insipid in summer. You need winter for real beetroot richness.

BEETROOT SALAD

I love winter salads of beetroot. I know it sounds disgusting. But even Bryan – who's definitely a spuds, gravy and vegies man with an absolute minimum of raw or rabbit food – eats it. And it's quick to make and always in the garden.

BEETROOTS, PEELED AND FINELY
GRATED (*see note*)

EQUAL AMOUNT OF GRATED
CARROT

EQUAL AMOUNT OF FINELY
CHOPPED PARSLEY

A GOOD, VERY MUSTARDY GARLIC
DRESSING

Optional

WALNUTS *or* TOASTED PINE NUTS *or*
A FEW SESAME SEEDS

HUNKS OF STEAMED NEW POTATOES
DRESSED WITH A LITTLE SESAME
OIL AND A FEW SESAME SEEDS

Mix together the beetroot, carrot and parsley and toss with the dressing. Add walnuts or potatoes if you wish.

Note: Peel them because beetroot peel can be bitter (so can carrot skin). There's no need to cook them, though you can if you like.

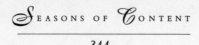

WILD ROOTS

Wild roots can be good. Not *very* good – if they were *very* good they'd have been domesticated. But not bad either and fun for kids. Kids love wild harvests. I used to set Edward and his mates to pulling up bracken roots to roast every time we had a barbecue. They're too sophisticated now …

The bracken roots didn't actually taste of much and were incredibly fibrous – but we did get rid of a lot of bracken.

Dock roots taste like they're good for you, just like dandelion roots. Dock and burdock roots are diuretic and laxative and supposed to clear the body of toxins – and a good deal else I suspect.

Dandelion root is used as a liver stimulant and prescribed for gout and eczema and pimples and gallstones and sometimes rheumatism. They're also laxative and diuretic. Don't eat them before you go to bed unless you have an ensuite or a bucket, but a meal or two of them won't give you diarrhoea.

Dock, burdock and dandelion roots taste best baked in cider with a dab of butter till tender – which is a waste of good cider and butter.

CELERY ROOT

I love celery root. It used to be used as a laxative (don't worry – not very), diuretic, digestive remedy and so on, but unlike the others it really tastes good – a sort of super celery taste. After digging it, clean it well (grit does not add to its healthful or culinary properties).

Sunflower roots can be used in the same recipe, though of course the taste is quite different. (And unless it was coincidence, they are also extraordinarily gas-producing.)

CELERY ROOT, WASHED AND PEELED
AND GRATED (*see note*)

CHICKEN STOCK *or* WATER

CREAM

1 EGG YOLK

A SPRINKLE OF NUTMEG

Simmer the grated root in stock or water till tender. Thicken with cream and the yolk of an egg too if the chooks are still laying. Serve hot in small dishes with a sprinkle of nutmeg.

Note: If you can't bear to dig up the root, you can make the dish with celery stalks – but it won't have the deep pungency and nuttiness of the root.

HOW TO BOIL A POTATO

Scrub your potatoes – don't peel them. The peel will rub off when they are cooked and keeping it on helps keep the potato firm. New potatoes should be plunged into boiling water. For old potatoes, just cover with cold water and bring to the boil *very* slowly. Add a little lemon juice or peel to old potatoes to keep them white.

When they are almost done (about 15 minutes of boiling) drain off the water and put the lid on. This way the potatoes finish cooking in steam, not water, and won't explode.

Spuds taste best in winter – dunno why. Maybe we just need all that carbohydrate to keep us warm. They're usually fresh in winter – autumn spuds start to break down in warmer weather.

.... 🖎 ....

ROOT BREAD

This is lighter and stores better than ordinary bread – it used to be a great favourite in colonial days.

1 TEASPOON DRIED YEAST

WARM WATER

4 CUPS PLAIN FLOUR – WHOLEMEAL
or WHITE (BUT WHOLEMEAL MAKES
THIS LOAF VERY HEAVY)

1 CUP *VERY* DRY MASHED SPUDS *or*
CARROTS *or* PUMPKIN (YES, I KNOW
IT ISN'T A ROOT) *or* EVEN PARSNIP,
WHICH TASTES SURPRISINGLY
EXCELLENT – DON'T ADD WATER *or*

BUTTER, AND DRAIN VERY WELL

1 TABLESPOON OLIVE OIL

Optional

HALF A CUP OF VERY FINELY
GRATED RAW PEELED BEETROOT, IF
YOU WANT A VERY FANCY LOAF
(THE EFFECT IS INTERESTING)

*Place the yeast in the warm water with a little flour.
Leave till it bubbles. Now combine the flour and mashed
spuds (and beetroot), add the yeast, oil and enough water
to make it bind. Knead for at least 20 minutes. Leave to
rise in a warm place – I cover it with a tea towel and
put it near the stove or on the windowsill.*

Punch it down, let it rise again to double its bulk.

*Bake in a hot oven till the top is brown and springs
back when you press it. The sides of the loaf will have
shrunk back.*

❉ *July 19*

'Remember when those were just sticks in the ground?'
asks Edward. On our way down to the bus this morning,
the car was rippled white with frost. The mild winter has
vanished under frozen grass and ice-dipped spider webs. 'I
was only three when those were planted, wasn't I?'

Now the trunks are thick, the main branches gnarled
and the peach blossom edging along each stem. In a year
or two they'll probably be bulldozed out to make way for
new varieties.

We pass the oldest orchards just breaking into pink bud,

and four-year-old orchards thick with flowers and then the new ground, razed level with tractor and bulldozer, where before there were only erosion gullies and mullock heaps, the sad reminders of last century's gold mining.

Further down are more new orchards, but these are replacing old ones. The Wisbeys' orchards of course never turn into wonderful old licheny tangles. They're too well managed, and are pulled out before the wood turns brittle and starts getting interesting hollows.

We've still got a few trees like that. They don't produce much – but their fruit is more beloved than the peaches from the tidy trees.

❋ *July 20*

They're one of the delights of winter – frozen spider webs between barbed wire. Usually barbed wire is hideous but now it's magic, silvered and dropletted and garlanded, even the casuarinas are dripping silver. Every day is different as we drive down to the bus; I don't think I could ever get sick of it.

Down in the valley the fog sits like a sleepy cat, too lazy to move till the day warms up. We're lucky up here – the cold drops into the heart of the valley, while the cold air on the Tableland above us sandwiches in the remaining warm air that's drifted up here, so we have a slice of warmth (relatively) amidst the cold.

❋ *July 23*

Left the sprinklers on the young grevilleas last night. (I can't remember when I last had to water like this in winter. Yes I can – the last bad drought.) And this morning the grevilleas were drowned in icicles – magic till they began to thaw and the poor things collapsed; so we hurriedly staked them up and I think they have survived.

The bowerbirds are eating the kumquats (I only noticed because they dropped a half-eaten one on the doormat and I trod on it this morning). So I've picked a bagful before they're gone … not that the bowerbirds will sweep through and devour them all. They've got the lemons, grapefruit, oranges, mandarins (which they like above everything else except maybe the navel oranges) and a few final kiwi fruit to eat too; so there's really plenty of time to pick the kumquats.

STEWED KUMQUATS

This is bitter, but it's an interesting bitterness, and doesn't taste like marmalade (I'm not fond of marmalade).

KUMQUATS

SUGAR

A LITTLE BRANDY *or* RUM *or* WATER

BUTTER FOR FRYING

THICK CREAM

Slice kumquats thinly. Cover well with sugar and a little brandy. Leave for 3 hours.

Heat some butter in a pan, drain the kumquats into a bowl and fry them till soft. Remove kumquats.

Pour the sugary liquid from the bowl into the pan and bubble till thick, add the kumquat slices again, then take off the flame at once.

Serve with very thick cream – like King Island double

cream – you'll need it to mitigate the bitterness. Forget about the calories for once.

.... 🪺 ....

❋ *July 24*

A grey day; mist seeping through the peach trees, and clouds higher up. It's not cold exactly, just a sort of dismalness that seeps into your bones.

I've been baking all day, which is the best way to cope with dismalness. The heat of the oven and the smell of food seeps through the house. (I suppose in all of us there's some deep racial fear of starving in the cold grey times.)

There are never enough of us to eat all I bake. Not that I really want more people here – just larger appetites.

Bryan likes biscuits (I think he'd pine if he had to eat bought ones), but Edward doesn't much, and neither do I; and when friends call in, they don't eat enough either ... damn it, it's a friend's *duty* to keep eating till the biscuit plate is empty.

I come from a long line of food-loving females. One of our great joys is stuffing sustenance into other people.

My great-great-grandmother – her maiden name had been Miss Quince, I don't know her Christian name – spent her afternoons on their property on the Southern Tablelands watching for any traveller she could lure inside to feed. Her kitchen was separate from the house, and so was the storeroom – a damp stone cave filled with barrels and the smell of rotting jam and always honeycomb suspended above a bucket and the steady slurp of sweetness. It was paradise in there, said Grandma.

Miss Quince's daughter Emily fed the birds as well as travellers. Emily set a special place for the birds at the ornate dining-room table set to the standard of her headmaster husband. She'd fallen in love with him when he was the local schoolmaster and she was fifteen with dark plaits down to her waist, and she peered at him through the window of the school.

It wasn't a happy marriage. He later wrote a book on letter etiquette (… and I remain Sir, Yours most sincerely …) while Emily fed the birds, her friends and her descendants.

Her daughter was my grandmother. Grandma's life revolved around food − buying it, preparing it, eating it and taking it on picnics.

'Chocolate isn't fattening, pet,' my grandmother told me many years ago. 'Nothing's fattening if it's a present from someone else.'

It was Grandma who taught me that two chocolate biscuit halves have fewer calories than one whole one; that no food is fattening if it's also eaten by someone thinner than yourself; and that it is your *duty* to eat as much as possible at Easter, Christmas, birthdays, afternoon teas and all Sunday dinners prepared by one's relations.

Grandma took entertaining seriously. There were always peanuts for the men, in silver dishes (with felt bottoms, so they wouldn't scratch the table) when I was young, but later in carved wooden dishes from Bali − Grandma liked to keep up with the times − and crisps and jubes for the children. And chocolates. Always a dish of chocolates.

Grandma ate chocolate for eighty-eight years, as well as

stuffed shoulder of lamb, apple teacake, Nice biscuits and ham sandwiches with yellow mustard. The sandwiches were wrapped in damp damask napkins and kept in reserve in the boot whenever Grandma drove further than the corner shops. Grandma grew up in the days when cars were infinitely unreliable. She grew nervous if she didn't have a bootful of provisions.

The stuffed shoulder of lamb was difficult. You can't buy shoulders for stuffing any more. They're boned and rolled and they shouldn't be lamb anyway, said Grandma. The best lamb is really hogget, the sheep equivalent of a teenager.

Grandma spent a decade or two trying to maintain her supply of unboned shoulders in a world where she had to increasingly depend on others to shop for her, and then turned to leg of lamb instead. But it wasn't the same.

Grandma's day started with buttered Saos and a cup of tea at 6.30, then continued into breakfast – stewed fruit for a first course, then porridge, followed by mutton chops with gravy and fried tomato, a toasted scone perhaps, left over from last night's supper, with marmalade or jam, and finally fresh fruit with yet another cup of tea – enough to last you, reckoned Grandma, till the apple teacake (fresh) at eleven after a morning shopping for provisions.

When I was a child, the apple teacake sustained Grandma and me until our picnic lunch – cold meat and tinned beetroot, grated carrot, shredded lettuce (always cut it with a silver knife, said Grandma, but she didn't tell me why) and sliced tomato all dressed with a mix of condensed milk, vinegar and dry yellow mustard, which isn't as bad as it sounds.

Grandma was suspicious of olive oil. Oils were strictly

medicinal. Overconsumption lead to appendicitis.

Grandma's days were crowded. Buying food (she bought fresh veg and fruit most days), cooking food, setting the table, washing-up, packing and unpacking the picnic basket. My boyfriends were startled to find that instead of necking in the doorway they were expected to come inside and dine on tomato sandwiches, fresh scones, pikelets with jam and butter …

(I still cover my scones with a tea towel as soon as they come out of the oven, just like Grandma showed me. It's the only way to get that lovely doughy richness; and, like Grandma, I feel uneasy with a naked cup of tea.)

Grandma spent the last years of her life in a nursing home. Other people took their relatives out to lunch. We went there to eat, hungry or not. Our children – her great-grandchildren – were ordered to eat at least two slices of lamington cake, and don't forget to take a scone when Great-Grandma offers you one.

The table would be set with the embroidered linen cloth hardly faded by sixty years of washing and ironing (I use it now). The special lemonade glasses (a sort of faded-beer colour, brown with yellow stripes, the same ones she'd had since I was young), sat next to the tea cups, the china plates, the dish of butter, the cake forks. It was our duty to eat, and we knew it. Bare plates – or, much worse, crumbless ones – were forbidden at Grandma's.

The gene for stuffing people with apple teacake missed my mother, who prefers reforming the world to mixing homemade biscuits. I learnt my cooking from Grandma.

Like most of my maternal forebears I feel naked without

food around me … nineteen bottles of blackberry and apple jelly in the larder, a few left of plum, eleven bottles of apricot, two bottles of strawberry, seven assorted chutneys, one green-walnut pickle, five bottles of varied herbal liqueurs, sun-dried tomatoes, apricots, capsicum and eggplant strips in oil, a fresh 'green' cheese dripping sludge in the shower recess … enough shelves of spaghetti, olive oil and canned salmon to last through a nuclear winter, and a vegetable garden sufficient to see us through the next two depressions …

When I was small I used to pretend to be the early NSW colony's quartermaster dealing out the stores, sitting in the sandpit doling out the flour and salt pork in my plastic bucket with the sea-shells on the rim. Later I dreamt of medieval sieges. My reaction to any news of strikes, nuclear catastrophe, nearby meteors or the imminent breakdown of civilisation is to go and buy another fifty-seven packets of seeds, a carton of dried pasta, a sack of flour or rice …

Sometimes I suspect I only live in the country as an excuse to feed the visitors with homemade biscuits and preferably a meal. After all, they've had a tiring journey, as Grandma would say as she filled the milk jug and rubbed butter into another batch of scones …

When a car pulls up on the flat below the house and the geese start honking 'guests' it's Grandma's voice that whispers: 'Don't forget the scones … wrap them in a napkin when you take them out so the steam will make them moist … remember, put out at least two sorts of jam …'

GRANDMA'S STUFFED SHOULDER OF LAMB

Find a butcher who sells half sides of lamb. Explain carefully that you don't want the shoulder boned. Take it home, find a long sharp knife and gently slit across the base of the shoulder on both sides, making a long deep pocket. (Yes, I know this sounds vague but once you get the knife in one hand and the meat in the other you'll see what I mean.)

1 CUP BREADCRUMBS (MADE FROM LAST WEEK'S WHITE BREAD BASHED MERCILESSLY WITH A ROLLING PIN IN A BROWN PAPER BAG; IF YOU DON'T HAVE EITHER ROLLING PIN *or* GOOD BREAD FROM LAST WEEK, COMMERCIAL BREADCRUMBS WILL HAVE TO DO)

1 ONION, FINELY CHOPPED

1 DESSERTSPOON *FRESH* THYME – REAL THYME, NOT LEMON THYME

A LITTLE GRATED LEMON PEEL – AS FINE AS YOU CAN MAKE IT, NO WHITE ATTACHED (NO, YOU DON'T GET THE TASTE OF BOTH LEMON AND THYME FROM LEMON THYME)

MELTED BUTTER (NO, I KNOW THIS ISN'T LOW CHOLESTEROL – NONE OF GRANDMA'S DIET WAS)

A BRANCH OF ROSEMARY

POTATOES

CARROTS

PUMPKIN

PEAS

For the stuffing, mix together the breadcrumbs, chopped onion, thyme, lemon peel and butter. Stuff the meat. It doesn't matter if it bulges out of its hole – the crisp edge of the stuffing is one of the delights of Grandma's lamb.

Place the meat in a baking dish with rosemary on top in a slow oven (150°C) to cook for at least 3 hours. Add dripping if you have it. (Nowadays I never do.)

Peel the spuds. Wash them, dry them, ditto carrots and pumpkin (you need both to make the gravy thick). Place peeled dried veg in with the meat as soon as there is enough hot fat at the bottom of the pan to coat them. (If the pan and dripping aren't hot, the veg will turn soft, not crispy.) Turn every hour or so.

Wait. The house will fill with the smell of roast dinner. This will linger for at least the next three weeks, but unlike the scent of say cabbage or old omelette the perfume of last Sunday's lamb just grows better as time goes by.

Boil the water for the peas.

When the meat is so tender it shreds rather than slices (the French would hate it – not a hint of pink) and the veg are black and caramelised at the sides (this is definitely how they should be) hoick the whole lot onto a plate to stay warm while you check the peas and make the gravy.

I'm not going to even try to explain how to make gravy – it's something you have to watch, the delicate browning of the flour and the cooking cooking cooking

*till you get something other than brown glue. The
water you add should come from cooking your peas (or
other veg) – this adds yet another layer of flavour and
the dissolved sugars from the vegetables helps colour
the gravy. (You can only make good gravy with long-
cooked meat – you need the flavours from the bits
stuck on the base of the roasting pan.) If you can't
make gravy already – and don't have a Grandma to
show you how – skim off the fat, add some good red
wine to the juices, boil severely for a few minutes, then
use that instead.*

*Finish with rhubarb and apple pie, custard, a box of
chocolates (if they are a gift they won't fatten) and a nice
strong cup of tea, and give a toast to Grandma.*

※ *July 28*

Cold sunlight, grey trees against blue sky and the fire
snickering in the kitchen as I came down this morning –
Bryan always comes down first and lights it, which I think
is one of the most wonderful things each day: to come
down to warm flames and the kettle boiling and Bryan just
finishing his porridge.

This was one of the perfect mornings: something by
Bach on the FM and the lyrebirds carolling in
counterpoint and the smell of good toast (Sue's bread, she
brought it down yesterday, she has another week at home
before she goes off shearing again), and everything seemed
to take on a particular pleasure: the bowerbirds eating the
grass seed and the feel of the bone knife-handle and the

smoothness of the mug in my hands and you realise that, even if these are simple pleasures, happiness doesn't come any deeper.

There is no point leading grey days, hour after hour, just for some special event – a holiday, an evening out, the two hours of the day you really enjoy – because by then you've probably forgotten how to really enjoy anyway, you're out of the habit.

And if days aren't filled with things you love, each second of them, from the sunlight shining through the blue glass on my right, the warmth of the stove on my back drying my hair, to the feel of the old wood under my hands as I type (my desk is an old one from a bank with that golden black splodginess of very used wood and I love it) ... and now I've lost the plot of the sentence except to say perhaps that life is very short and it is tragic to waste even a second on emptiness.

And here endeth the first lesson ...

❋ *July 29*

All warmth, all moisture sucked out of the air, and blown to who knows where ...

A soup day; we mostly seem to be eating soup for lunch now. Whatever is in the garden, peeled and sliced and seethed till soft in olive oil, which is the best way to bring out the flavour by caramelising the veg first – this doesn't just cook the veg, it changes their flavour and makes the soup much richer. After this initial cooking in oil or butter, just cook the veg enough to make them tender – too much cooking makes a bland soup.

I boil any old chicken carcasses when we've eaten the meat and keep the jellied stock in the fridge or freezer to add to soups. But these soups can be made without stock – the soups just aren't as meaty.

BASIC BOTTOM-OF-THE-GARDEN SOUP

Take whichever of the following the wombat has left you in the garden:

CARROTS

BEETROOT

PARSNIPS

CELERY

TOUGH WINTER LETTUCE

PARSLEY

PARSLEY ROOT, WELL SCRUBBED

OLIVE OIL *or* BUTTER

STOCK *or* WATER

Add them to a generous dash of olive oil or butter in a pan and cook slowly until they are tender and the scent fills the kitchen. This may take 30 minutes or 10 minutes – it depends on how many veg you have, how chewy they are and how big the pan is. Add just enough water or stock to cover, cook for a further 10 minutes, then mash or blend. Serve hot with buttery toast or hot bread.

CARROT SOUP

No, carrots haven't magically appeared among the
devastation that used to be the carrot patch. I've
been buying a few to keep us in carotene till next
summer and also because I hate to think what
carrot-deprived wombats might do to the doormat
and garbage bin, not to mention my pots.

2 CUPS CHOPPED CARROT

HALF A CUP CHOPPED ONION

4 TABLESPOONS BUTTER

CHICKEN STOCK (MUST BE
HOMEMADE)

A LITTLE CHOPPED PARSLEY *or*
CORIANDER

*Seethe the chopped carrot and onion in butter till tender.
Add just enough chicken stock to cover. Simmer 20
minutes. Add the parsley or coriander and serve hot.*
  This is my favourite soup.

.... 🐾 ....

✳ *August 1*

The creek is almost dry again, even in the cold weather.
Down by the bridge it's just thin channels seeping through
the sand, with thin green stripes to show where it once
flowed. Up here it's still slipping between the rocks, but
every day it's lower and the ground is harder and the trees
droop from dryness and the cold.

Chocolate wombat has decided it's time to be fed again. He stands with his nose to the door till we come out, looks at us suspiciously, sniffs the carrots even more suspiciously, then starts crunching. He is only really friendly with Edward. They rub noses sometimes. Maybe they recognise shared characteristics: they are both single-minded and dedicated to their food.

Every morning the frosts are deeper, ice patterns like spiders all over the car, the dam's frozen with cattle snoozing by the edges waiting for a drink. Then the sun slides down the valley, and you can see the ice melt as it passes and the grass steams for maybe ten minutes and the stalactites drip from the trees.

❋ *August 7*

The Wisbeys have lit the first of the frost fires – cut-off barrels of wood smouldering under each tree, lit to save the setting fruit from frost. Frost is worse when it's dry. The smoke sifts up here early in the morning. Down in the valley it is a choking cloud, sitting right above the trees and held there by a layer of cold air, like driving into a white world, then suddenly leaving it again as the road rose.

❋ *August 8*

I happened to be watching Three-and-a-half's rear end as she munched through her oats this afternoon when I saw a nose between her legs, a pink nose …

The nose inched out further, was followed by two eyes, an almost hairless face, just turning grey with fuzz and then a foot. And then it stopped, peering at the world between its mother's legs. Three-and-a-half realised something was wrong and promptly sat down thereby, I suppose, forcing Junior back into the pouch.

I gave her another carrot and she nested it between her paws, gnawing happily.

✳ August 9

Little Pink's nose poked out again today, peering down at the paving as though it wondered what it was. Bad Bart arrived. Three-and-a-half promptly bit his neck; when that didn't deter him, she backed into him, forcing him back with a muscular bum (there's nothing to bite on a wombat's bum; it's all bone and hair).

✳ August 10

Warm air mooching down from somewhere, you can just taste the first of spring. My fingers are twitching, wanting to plant seedlings but at least by now I know to restrain myself. Nothing will grow yet, the soil's still too cold, the seedlings would just sit there and sulk till December. And besides, it's crazy to plant much if there isn't going to be enough water.

I realised today it's been about twenty-five years to the day since I planted my first vegetable garden (in Queensland, where you can plant much earlier than here). The carrots didn't come up at all; the beans grew three inches then were eaten by beanfly. I tried tomatoes next. At least nothing ate them. They didn't grow much either. I didn't realise you had to feed your plants if you wanted them to feed you.

So I studied – everything I could get my hands on – gardening books and Department of Ag pamphlets and research reports. Then the avocado trees on the farm where we were staying began to die.

It was *phytophthera cinnamomi* – a root rot. All the avocados in the area were dying. It took six months of research to discover that what the Department of Ag had been saying was good for the orchard – feeding with sulphate of ammonia, overhead watering, ploughing and weeding – were exactly the right conditions to make the root rot thrive.

It was a good introduction to farming and gardening – to learn that what is officially 'good' isn't necessarily best. (Twenty years on, no Department of Ag would give the advice they gave me then – many of the 'radical' farming ideas of twenty years ago are commonplace now.)

By then I was hooked. I knew that growing things – and studying growing strategies – was what I wanted to do with my life.

That was only part of the dream.

The other part was mostly cliché – a hand-built house, a cow in the front paddock, an acre of vegetables and a couple of kids by the creek and a pantry full of jam and bottled apricots and a husband drying his gumboots by the wood stove. And we'd be self sufficient.

Well, that marriage failed (and gumboots stay outside). I've decided that cows are decorative but someone else can do the milking and the butter and cheese making. I've even given up bottling, mostly. Bryan and I are still finishing the house – and like most owner-builders will probably still be finishing it in another two decades – we seem to add a room every eighteen months.

We were self sufficient for a while, Edward and I – from poverty, not from choice. My income from the odd article covered rates and pre-school fees and that was about it. Actually we lived and ate quite well, but it was a strain I don't want to have to face again. There was always the worry about what would happen if I got sick – and then I did. And a bed of ripening corn and tomatoes aren't much use if you have pneumonia and don't feel up to harvesting them.

I've been lucky, I think, in the people I've spent the last twenty-five years with – like the elderly neighbour down the road. Jean was in her seventies when I was in my early twenties. She had the sort of classic cottage garden that's grown from seeds and cuttings, not from pots from a nursery. She'd learnt 'self sufficiency' back in the depression, except it wasn't called self sufficiency then; maybe thrift – it was what you did to survive.

I remember the first meal I had at Jean's – vegetable soup (from the garden) and roast Indian Game fowl, and boiled new potatoes and golden beetroot and three sorts of beans and fruit salad for dessert with cream from the cow on the hill, then sponge cake for supper, made with eggs from the ducks that ate the snails under the roses (the roses grew from her brother-in-law's prunings) and more cream and passionfruit and fresh raspberries – all grown by an elderly woman in a garden about the size of a normal suburban block.

Jean grew almost all her own food then – and illegally sold butter and cream and eggs and garden surplus – and she pressed cuttings and seeds on me that now form the basis of my garden, while she's moved to a tiny unit in town.

Jean taught me that it's easy to be almost self sufficient – all you have to do is plan and plant. It's the next jump that breaks your back – trying to grow it all.

I know that we could live on what we grow here – or even from the bush around us if we had to. I've gone through the stage of making our own rope from wonga-vine fibre, my own perfume from the garden, our own shampoo and dyes and paper. Sometimes we drink our own tea – or our own 'coffee' (of one sort or another). It's fun to do it sometimes. It gives you confidence to know you can if you have to. It makes life richer. But not when you've trapped yourself and can't afford anything else.

I think the other person who taught me most was Smudge, the first wombat I ever lived with.

I learnt to watch the bush with Smudge. I learnt to question gardening and farming lore. I began to wonder why the broom and blackberry invaded our orchards but stopped at the fenceline and didn't penetrate the bush; why a wild peach tree kept fruiting year after year, while the books said you needed to prune to get a crop; why an unfertilised wild apple tree fruited in half the time it took the cultivated ones in our orchard; how a hillside of helichrysums flourished without the soil being dug to receive their seed. I learnt to pattern the way I grew things – and to some extent the way I lived – on the bush around me, not on the standards that I'd been taught.

Smudge also taught me how to sit back and watch the bush and just enjoy the early morning sun.

Thoreau advised distrusting any enterprise that needs new clothes. I learnt to distrust anything I couldn't explain to a wombat. This isn't oversimplicity – *everything* can be reduced to its effect on people, animals and the world around. Sometimes reducing things to wombat terms makes you see them more clearly.

Dreams change. I'd hate to be stuck in the dreams I had twenty years ago. (In twenty years time I'll probably smile at the dreams I have now.) Not that the dreams have changed radically – they've just evolved.

What have I learnt? Perhaps just to look at things differently – as though the windows have been washed – and not to take for granted the images I grew up with, of the good life or the good garden or farm. I've learnt that things change – that humans are subject to the same laws as lizards and fruit-fly and ants, though the time scale is slower, that no matter what we do 'this too will pass'.

I've learnt to put my hands on the soil and feel the rhythm of the world – and if it's just my pulse that I'm feeling it doesn't matter.

I've learnt to rely on growing systems – biological ones not mechanical ones wherever possible. I no longer dream of having a tractor in a neat shed, or of getting bulldozers in to clear the blackberry. Things that grow will change – like dreams. Machines don't. If you buy a tractor you've trapped yourself into farming in the way that tractors make possible – if you buy a rotary hoe or mulcher you've trapped yourself again.

Growing things change with circumstances – they adapt. Machines don't. I suspect we'll all need to adapt and re-adapt and keep adapting in the next two, three, six decades.

What else? Keep planting. Plants are the best investment you can make. Banks give you – what? Twelve per cent interest? A young tree will double every year – and crop for a century and give you seedlings into the bargain.

I also learnt that you don't have to farm to make a living in the country – in fact farming the land may be a bad idea. Sheep and humans and cattle are the real weeds in Australia – too many of them and they destroy too much. It's better to cherish the land and enjoy what it is than try to change it. Just keep a small intensive patch to grow what you need – and harvest the rest like a wombat or Aborigine instead, giving as much as you take away. If you need to make your land productive, sell coppice firewood or a few fence posts, or farm emus or tourists. But don't feel that you have to farm to justify your land.

I learnt that growing your own doesn't have to be hard work. Our garden supplies most (not all) our fruit and veg – with about ten minutes work a week. Most of the work we do in our gardens is unnecessary. Weeding just makes bare space for more weeds, pruning just means we have to prune next year and add more fertiliser to make up for the growth we've taken; most of the fertiliser we give our plants disappears into the watertable (and does it no good at all). Most mowing, trimming and tidying are for the neighbour's benefit, not the gardens. Somehow our culture has decided that it's the job of humans to care for growing systems, rather than just let the gardens take care of us. It's the Adam and Eve fallacy – now we're out of the Garden of Eden we don't dare let ourselves back in.

And – don't try to be self sufficient. Self sufficiency was a nice dream. It led me to a good life, though not the one I expected. I learnt that I loved growing things – even if I didn't make my living selling them, even if I didn't grow everything I needed. I know that we can live by farming, if we have to – but experimenting and giving stuff away is much more fun. I always felt a bit like I was selling my kids whenever I got money in exchange for peaches or avocados – and as no money ever compensates for things you love, it seemed much simpler just to give them away.

Go as far along the self sufficiency road as you feel comfortable with. When it stops being fun, stop. That way you won't lose the joy of growing things.

Anyone who has ever watched a child's face as they fill a basket of oranges or as they disappear to spend an hour in the raspberry beds or who has let a child watch the progress of a seed as it becomes a vine and sprouts large melons – and who then lets the child pick it, all their own work – will know there is something very basic and very good about growing your own. This is, after all, what life's about – food and shelter, life and death and growing things. There is no better way to contact this than in a garden.

I, like all humans, am part of the earth. To work it, watch it, live within its rhythms – is, for me, the deepest satisfaction.

Happy birthday, garden.

❋ *August 14*

More frost fires, spheres of smoke in cold dry air. The men look half asleep on the motorbikes or on the ladders pruning the last of the trees. They have to get up when the alarm rings around 2 a.m. or, as Noel says, lie there awake anxiously wondering how low the temperature will go. Last year a lot of the early fruit was lost to late frost.

There's still the gauntlet of hail and drought to face this year, without the earliest loss of all to cold.

Little Pink sniffed the grass today, leaning out of his mother's pouch. For a moment I thought he might take a bite; but he didn't, just nuzzled back into the warmth.

If he gets too bold Three-and-a-half sits on him, which doesn't seem to hurt him, but it does stop him exploring.

Pudge attacked the garbage bin at 2 a.m. We ignored her. I am not feeding a fully grown wombat at 2 a.m. She has no sense of time.

※ *August 15*

Another clear cold day, so crisp it seems the air would shatter; the world has the pale clear colour it only gets at winter's end. There are perhaps fifty bowerbirds hopping round scavenging the last of the lawn's grass seed and threatening each other over the last of yesterday's lunch crumbs on the garden table, or pecking at the giant marrow wedged in the crutch of the crab-apple tree. They've been pecking there for months. When one marrow's finished we put out another. The currawongs guzzle it too and the smaller birds when there are no large ones to bully them away.

The hills are drying out. The trees on the ridges are paler now, only the ones in the moist gullies are still blue-green. The trees have thinned, too, so you can see vistas through them that I haven't seen since the last big drought, with flashes of hard orange soil underneath. On the dry slope the ground crackles like cornflakes, inches deep with flaking bark and brittle leaves and twigs and fallen branches, as the trees draw into themselves, casting off their surplus, waiting for rain.

I remember the last drought here, too clearly. Wombats driven mad by mange and thirst, stumbling down from the dry ridges, frantically digging in the damp sand in what once had been the creek; and one wombat that thrashed its head against a granite boulder time after time, insane with mange and drought, and pain, so the white bone showed under the blood.

There was no grass. Not even dead grass. Just a blank grey brown. And even tears seemed a waste of moisture, sacrificed to a dry blue sky.

It's too soon to have drought again. Not a bad one, please, not yet. The last year has been dry but not desperate. It's rained just enough for survival when we've needed it.

It's too soon since the last bad drought. Just too soon.

❋ *August 17*

Chocolate arrived at dusk – the first time he's been around for two months – so I fed him; and of course Bad Bart trotted down at the sound of the first mouthful of oats (he can hear a rolled oat fall 200 metres away); and then Three-and-a-half turned up with Little Pink; and Pudge emerged, still half asleep (she's more nocturnal than the others). So I fed them all, little heaps of oats and carrots on the paving, and left them munching while I went in to cook dinner.

Opened the last bottle of Golden Queens. You could almost taste the sunlight.

And then it rained.

We hadn't expected it. The weather bureau hadn't forecast it, and Roger the Ranger had claimed it'd be November – if we were lucky – before there'd be a decent storm (seventy-six per cent probability he'd said, over the froth of his cappuccino).

But it rained anyway. Good heavy rain so hard we couldn't hear the radio, the world was black and the frogs began to yell in an ecstasy of celebration.

About 2 a.m. Bryan got up to have a pee in the bucket on the verandah. The grind of the creek filled the room with the almost sickly sweetness of rotting debris.

'Leave the door open,' I muttered.

He brought his cold knees back into bed. 'The stars are out,' he whispered, as he went back to sleep.

I lay listening to the crash of rocks and the slow hoot of the powerful owl hunting possums in the gully and a shriek from a wet possum annoyed by the rain.

I fell asleep about dawn. I could almost smell the sunlight somewhere behind the ridge. Or maybe it was springtime and the peaches and the year to come.

Author's note

This book is a record of several years ago. Since then the valley has changed. Rod and Sandra Wisbey's has been sold, and Edward grown older. But there are still wombats on the doorstep, and peaches on the trees; and for the moment at any rate, the creek is flowing.

INDEX TO RECIPES